CONVERSATIONS WITH YOUR AUDIENCE

A Practical Guide for Preparing and Delivering Professional Presentations

FIRST EDITION

Lisa Kuchta
*and members of the Communication Department
at Southern Connecticut State University*

Edited by Lisa Kuchta, M. Sandra DiFrancesco,
and David John Petroski

Cartoons by Audrey Mora

cognella academic publishing

Bassim Hamadeh, CEO and Publisher
Michael Simpson, Vice President of Acquisitions
Jamie Giganti, Senior Managing Editor
Jess Busch, Senior Graphic Designer
John Remington, Senior Field Acquisitions Editor
Monika Dziamka, Project Editor
Brian Fahey, Licensing Specialist

First published in the United States of America in 2016 by Cognella, Inc.

Printed in the United States of America

ISBN: 978-1-62661-976-0 (pbk) / 978-1-62661-977-7 (br)

www.cognella.com   800-200-3908

Contents

UNIT 4

Designing and Using Visual Channels 205

UNIT 5

FINAL THOUGHTS

Acknowledgments

Thank you to all my fellow contributors who helped to author this book: Anthony Ahn, Mike Bay, Sandy DiFrancesco, Bonnie Farley-Lucas, Stephanie Kelly, Dave Petroski, Dyan Robinson, Linda Sampson, Meg Sargent, Frank Tavares, and Jos Ullian.

A second round of thanks to Dave Petroski for championing this crazy idea to write a textbook, and for stepping in to take on an editing role in my hour of need.

Thank you, thank you, thank you (and many more) to Sandy DiFrancesco for allowing me to drag her into this project against her will, and for her countless hours of writing, editing, and designing. Without her, I surely would have drowned in this project.

Thank you to Audrey Mora for all of her creative cartooning, for accommodating all of our many and varied visual-aid requests, and for enduring my constant, pestering emails.

Thank you to all of our patient, lovely, and cooperative models: Rheanna Behuniak, Connor Etter, Cesar Garcia, Libby Hess, Ashley Indrisek, Dan Jennings, Amy King, Sarah Lauture, Shedeen Neil, Mike Rabiej, Joe Rhivbs, and Ashley Steigler. Thank you to Isabel Chenoweth for her wonderful photography work. And thank you to my two last-minute models: Mike Howard and Zakiya Hamm.

Thank you to Roger Conway, Sr. for giving us your blessing to carry on the AIMC tradition.

Thank you to Dr. Karen P. Burke for her previous work that articulated the AIMC approach for SCSU students in her McGraw-Hill book *AIMC: A Communication Tool for Life*, co-written with Roger Conway, Sr. and Sandy DiFrancesco.

Thank you to Carol Culmo for all her help with scheduling, odds-and-ends requests, and general mental-health support.

Thank you to my Professional Presentations students, particularly those who have given me feedback on the preliminary edition of this book.

Thank you to my mother- and father-in-law for their babysitting services; without them, I don't know when I could have found the time to finish this project.

Thank you to my husband for his patience and lovingly feigned interest in presenting, writing, and editing.

For my daughter Carly, the most enthusiastic and confident presenter I know. May you never lose your voice, your nerve, or your self-assurance that what you have to say is important enough for everyone else to hear.
Lisa Kuchta

About This Book

This book is a compilation from a lot of people—some who have contributed their direct words to this book and others who have not.

When I first joined the Communication Department at Southern Connecticut State University, I was given a crash course on presenting the "Southern way." I was hired to teach a course called Fundamentals of Professional Presentations, and, in a two-hour information session, the course coordinator, Sandy DiFrancesco, drilled into my brain the core characteristic of the class: it is *not* public speaking.

Unfortunately for me, public speaking was my teaching and learning background. I was a student of rhetorical studies and had been an instructor of old-school public speaking. But that was not the realist approach my new department took toward teaching students how to speak effectively in front of others. The nature of the Professional Presentations course forced me to make a complete shift in the way I thought about—and certainly taught—speaking skills to students. I soon realized, though, that this new approach to oral communication was more beneficial for both the students' lifelong learning and for the goal of promoting effective communication.

The more I taught *presenting* to students, the less sense *public speaking* made to me. Presenting teaches students how to be effective oral communicators, not just decent speechwriters. Presenting promotes quick thinking, critical thinking, and appropriate behavior for the workplace, not just memorization and regurgitation. In short, presenting prepares students for life; public speaking, for most students, just fulfills an academic requirement.

And so, while most of the words in this book are mine, the thoughts and opinions expressed here do *not* represent the author alone; they represent the collective word of the Communication Department at Southern Connecticut State University—those still in the department and those who had come and gone and contributed to this presentations approach long before I ever arrived.

The ideas in this book have been taught in scores of presentation classes and have helped many generations of SCSU students learn to communicate successfully in their academic and professional lives. We have used a variety of texts and supplementary materials over the years to help accomplish this goal, but we had never found a modern, comprehensive book for students that advocated our real-world approach. Now, with this book, we hope to share these lessons with new generations of students in our classrooms and beyond.

We organized this book in the most logical format we could devise, but let me assure you that this is *not* the type of book to read from front to back as you move through a presentations course. In fact, it will likely make sense for you to jump around from chapter to chapter as you prepare different types of presentations.

Start with the Introduction and Unit 1, and make sure you understand the basics of AIMC (Audience, Intent, Message, Channel)—the planning approach for which we advocate. Then tackle the individual chapters as you need them. There are some chapters you may want for your first presentation experience, like **Chapter 9: Speaking in Outlines, Chapter 19: Being Nervous is Normal**, and **Chapter 23: "I. Am. Awesome!":** **Engaging in Effective Self-Reflections**. Likewise, there may be some chapters you won't need until you are ready to work on far more complicated and "high-stakes" presentations, like **Chapter 18: R-E-S-P-E-C-T, Find Out What It Means to—Them** and **Chapter 22: Vetting the Venue**. For each presentation you prepare, consider the skills you will need to successfully reach your presentation's intent. Then study the chapters that will help you learn or hone those needed skills.

We hope you find our approach to presenting helpful as you move through your academic career and prepare for your professional one. We realize that the skills we ask you to use in this book are often very different from what you might have learned in a public-speaking course. But we hope you soon agree with us that this method gives you a much greater opportunity to engage with your audience and create an impact with your presentation. We want you to learn to be a better *communicator*. This book can help you do that.

Lisa Kuchta

Introduction
I Hate Public Speaking and More
Initial Thoughts

After studying this chapter, you should be able to:
- *Identify the key differences between a* speech *and a* presentation.
- *Articulate the ways in which a* presentation *should mimic a conversation.*
- *Identify the rules for giving a* presentation.
- *Explain the benefits of a* presentations *approach, rather than a* public-speaking *one.*

Many of you are probably dreading this. I know. I get it. I hated the idea of talking in front of others when I first studied oral communication, too. After all, doesn't pop culture tell us that public speaking is humankind's greatest fear, even above death?

Talking in front of others may feel natural to you, or working on your presentations skills may feel like a terrifying roller coaster of a ride. But, regardless of your initial comfort level, the tools you will learn throughout this book will be invaluable to you as you move through your academic and professional life.

Presenting Is for Everyone

The primary goal of a presentations course is to teach effective communication. The fundamental communication skills you will learn in this book can help you in all aspects of your life, from your academic and professional career to social gatherings and everything in between. The ability to communicate information in a way that directly connects to your targeted audience is an important life skill that should not be overlooked.

It seems obvious to say that communication skills are vital for success in the working world, yet so many people seem to underestimate to what degree. Skim through a job-search site like Monster, Career Builder, or Hot Jobs, and you will see that a good number of the posted professional positions require "excellent oral and written communication skills." And those requirements aren't just "fluff" that employers throw in for good measure. In a study of recruiters, seventy-two percent said that communication skills were the *most important* skill for employees to have (Sharma, 2009).

That assessment should not be surprising. Communication competency in the workplace affects your ability to work in teams, conduct meetings, listen to others, resolve conflicts, engage in persuasion, develop working relationships, maintain positive connections, and behave ethically. In short, **good communication skills can help employees work more efficiently and effectively.**

Being a competent communicator takes more work than just opening your mouth and speaking. In fact, human-resource managers say that the most critical employee *deficiency* is the ability to communicate effectively ("News Briefs," 2008). This means that, in their estimation, most of us are not communicating well enough on the job.

Communication does not just matter in the process of obtaining a job, but it also affects how quickly or effectively you progress in your career. As management professor Todd Dewett of Wright State University notes, "Communication, including body language, becomes significantly more important when considering who's promotion material. As soon as you step into a supervisor role, it all comes down to communication skills" (Goudreau, 2012). Studies done on managers and the reasons for their promotions agree with this point (Shockley, Staley, and Morley, 1988): how well you communicate plays a huge role in how far your career can go.

Still, you may think, *you* won't have to be a public speaker in your chosen career path. This may very well be true, but **you will have to** *present* **in a professional career— whether it is on a large or small scale.** You may have to report on some financial numbers at a business meeting, sell products to clients, train new employees, or say a few impromptu words about a co-worker at a promotion or retirement party. At the very least, you will need to interview for a job, and that is, in essence, a sales presentation in which you are the product and the employer is the client. Knowing how to communicate well will aid you tremendously in all of these ventures, and learning these fundamental skills now will give you an advantage when you do enter the job market.

Presentations Are *NOT* Speeches

Speeches are petrifying, aren't they? Standing up behind a podium and trying to deliver a mostly memorized script of hardline facts intertwined with poetic language, all without making even the slightest error, is a distressing prospect. I wouldn't want to do that either. A choice few of you may have the fortune (or misfortune) of having jobs in which you will do just that—deliver pre-written speeches to throngs of observers. But for the rest of us, focusing on the skills of writing and delivering *speeches* is not particularly helpful. More realistically, we will be asked to give *presentations* throughout our careers, whether they are formal or informal, planned or impromptu.

Speeches … presentations … it may seem like I'm just parsing words, but I'm not. There is a significant difference.

Speeches: Grand Deliveries of Verbal Genius

Think of some of the greatest public-speaking triumphs of the modern American age: John F. Kennedy's Inaugural Address, Martin Luther King, Jr.'s "I Have a Dream," or Eleanor Roosevelt's "The Struggle for Human Rights." The speakers were passionate, eloquent, and poetic. In short, they were *perfect*. Of course, they were also speaking to enormous audiences on momentous occasions when it was essential that every last word be said correctly. If that was my model to follow, I'd be terrified, too.

Speeches are *grand deliveries* **to large audiences** with very little interaction between the speaker and his or her listeners. Because of the size of the crowd and the impersonal nature of the communication, speeches are often delivered in a memorized or manuscript (e.g., using a teleprompter, script, or index cards) style. Speakers are expected to be overly controlled in their body language and their vocal quality. Perfection seems to be the goal.

The transmission model of communication: I talk. You listen.

Perhaps the greatest shortcoming of the public-speaking approach is that it puts too much emphasis on the speaker and not enough on the audience. The rhetorical approach of yesteryear was based on the *transmission model* of communication. The presumption was that the speaker would send a message to the receiver, and the receiver would receive the message. The idea seems simple and logical enough, but the concept is faulty. The transmission model presumes that as long as the speaker plans the message well and says it artfully, the message will be received and accepted by the audience. As a teacher and as a parent, I can assure you that this is *not true*.

Audiences have input to give, and every audience member will understand and view your message differently. Your audience is not passive, and no matter how well you plan your message and how well you deliver it, you cannot be assured that your audience understands or agrees with it unless you ask or involve them. A *speech* doesn't allow for that interaction, but a *presentation* does.

Presentations: Conversations with Your Audience

Now, picture Martin Luther King, Jr. standing up behind a podium in front of a business meeting of twenty people, speaking in his reverberating, grandiose voice. Picture John F. Kennedy so poetically beseeching his clients to "Ask not what this company can do for you; ask what you can do for this company!" These scenes are absurd. Public speaking is undoubtedly an important skill, but for the vast majority of what you will do in the working world, it's impractical.

When employers say they want you to have "excellent oral communication skills," it is unlikely they are looking for someone who is a whiz at parroting memorized information back to an auditorium full of people. What they want is someone who can explain ideas clearly, persuade others when needed, be personable and likeable, and make dull information interesting. These are the skills of a good *presenter*.

Effective presenters make their presentations feel like conversations. They talk with individual audience members by asking them questions, eliciting their feedback, and encouraging them to interrupt and voice their concerns as needed. Effective presenters make direct eye contact with individuals in the audience one at a time, locking in as though it is just the two of them discussing the topic. Effective presenters talk with their audiences in comfortable, conversational tones. Effective presenters adjust their presentations to audience members' facial expressions, body language, and other signals that indicate whether or not they agree or understand. In short, effective presenters treat their audiences like a group of *individuals*, all of whom deserve a little one-to-one interaction.

To allow for these on-the-spot adjustments, presenters cannot memorize or read scripts; in fact, they don't even write them in the first place. Presenters are experts on their topics, and they *talk*—albeit in an organized and well-researched fashion—*with* their audiences. Good presenters speak through outlines, lists, and helpful language, but not *from* them. That is, good presenters don't need notes or the aid of a speechwriter; they know how to talk in an understandable way to their audiences without having to plot out every last word or turn of phrase.

Presenters, moreover, are not shut off from their audience members by podiums, distance, or impassive speaking styles. Presenters have a clear goal—to get their audience to take some specific action—and they converse and negotiate with their audiences to reach that goal. **Presenters are in the moment**, interacting with their audience members, adjusting their content to fit their audiences' needs, and walking around the room to show how confident they are in their ideas and how accessible they are to their listeners.

The Short List of Presenting Rules

What does this mean for you, a student of the art of presentations? While this entire book will give you much more in-depth advice on how to prepare and deliver effective presentations, we should start with the rules that underline the difference between a *presentation* and a *speech*:

- **It's all about the audience.** The primary purpose of presenting is to get your audience to do or feel something. They are the central goal, the driving force, of your whole presentation from brainstorming to execution. Every decision you make in the planning of the presentation and in its delivery should be focused on serving the audience effectively. We will revisit this idea of an **audience-centered approach** often throughout this book.
- **No podiums allowed.** Podiums are the mark of public *speakers*. You, as a *presenter*, should not need or want to hide yourself from the audience. You don't need a spot for a script (that's not allowed), you most likely wouldn't need the microphone attached to the podium (and if you do need amplification, most venues have portable microphones), and you shouldn't want to appear distant and detached from your audience (what are you hiding back there anyway?).

  A podium says, "Be quiet and listen to me." Stepping away from the lectern, walking around the room, and avoiding barriers between you and your audience says, "I'm here for you; let's talk and figure this out together." That's a far more inviting message.
- **No scripts allowed.** It is indeed tempting to write down what you want to say, but planning your every word and

Podiums cut you off from your audience. Poor Amy becomes just a "talking head."

attempting to commit it to memory will cause more nerves, unease, and distance from your audience than you want. You should certainly decide on the *ideas* you want to share with your audience, but you should not script the actual sentences and paragraphs you want to use.

- **No notes allowed.** Of all the introductory rules I share with my students, it is this one that they resist the most. They love their oh-so-handy 3x5 index cards, and having to part with them can cause severe separation anxiety.

So, let me tell you what I tell my students: your job is to be the *expert* and to talk to the audience about what you know. Plain and simple: experts don't need notes. Note cards, pieces of strategically placed paper, or slideshow presentations filled with words and bullet points hurt your credibility and keep you from interacting with your audience.

And, really, imagine how impressive you'll look—and feel—as a presenter without any aids or crutches. Scores of newbie presenters before you have spoken time and again without notes. Trust me: *you can do it, too.*

Speeches	Presentations
Talk about subjects. Aim to be perfect and make it into history books.	Present toward a clear intent or audience action
Hide behind a podium and hang onto the sides for dear life.	No podiums, desks, or other barriers between you and your audience.
Write a script or highly detailed outline that you read multiple times as practice.	Jot down topic you want to cover and practice by talking about your points.
Read from or reference a teleprompter, script, notes, or cue cards.	No scripts, notes or wordy PowerPoint slides.

The Upside to a New Approach

I realize that the above preliminary list of rules might have rattled your nerves even more than the general thought of talking in front of an audience. While it's true that it will take time and practice to get used to this new approach, there are direct benefits to doing so. As you learn to follow the aforementioned guidelines, keep the following pieces of advice in mind:

- **No one expects perfection, just information.** Remember, this is neither a course in public speaking nor in acting in which perfection is the goal. Presentations are delivered by humans, not robots, and with humans, mistakes are inevitable. If you have a momentary stutter, keep going. If you can't think of the right word, say so, and instead describe in simpler terms what you are trying to say. If you lose your place and can't seem to get yourself back on track, laugh and ask the audience, "Now, where was I?" In public speaking, students who make a mistake often freeze up like deer in headlights. In presentations, it truly is not a big deal. Focus on what you have to tell your audience, and keep moving forward as best you can.

- **No one knows what you were supposed to say.** Without notes and a pre-planned script, nerves may take hold of you and cause you to forget some of what you wanted to say. Maybe you forget an anecdote, perhaps you put your main points out of order, or maybe you even leave out a main point altogether. So long as what you *do* say is truthful and makes sense to the audience, it doesn't matter *that* much if something was skipped. Good presenters keep their audience members involved in the presentation. If you forgot to say something terribly important, an engaged audience member will undoubtedly ask you a question that will remind you of what you needed to say.
- **Presentations are conversations, not grand deliveries.** The more you keep your audience involved and talk *with* them rather than *at* them, the more you are likely to feel at ease. For most of us, one-to-one conversations are far easier than speaking to groups of people. Presentations, at their core, are really just conversations with your audience. You should ask for their input, try to appeal to them as individuals, and even make eye contact with them one at a time, as one individual after another. If you

Ashley's presentation feels like a conversation; her audience is engaged and involved.

remind yourself of this fact—that presentations are really just a series of conversations—you will feel much more at ease with the prospect of presenting to others.

The Goals of This Book

A book on presentations will naturally concentrate largely on presenting skills. But while helping you feel comfortable talking in front of others and learning to reduce the nervous tics you might have while presenting (saying "um," playing with your hair, kicking your feet, etc.) are certainly goals of this course, they are not the primary ones.

First and foremost, this book will focus on teaching you what to say and how to say it effectively in a business presentation. You could be incredibly charismatic and well spoken, but if you have nothing of value to say, you really should not start talking. A great deal of what you will learn, therefore, will focus on how to create and develop the content of an effective presentation. Moreover, you will be given helpful hints for the working world and for dealing with other professionals.

The true beauty of the presentations approach propounded in this book is that it is *not* public speaking. You will not be asked to write a lengthy script, commit it to memory, and deliver it flawlessly to your audience. Instead, this book advocates for a more audience-centered, real-world approach that teaches you the skills of a competent communicator.

At first, this approach may seem scary for those who find comfort in scripts and memorization, but I ask you to embrace the new strategies and techniques you learn. Competent communication skills take time to develop and hone, but they are learnable. Great presenters are *made*, not *born*.

Once you have gained comfort with this script-less and note-less technique, you will find yourself freer to talk about your ideas, share your knowledge, persuade your audience, and (gulp) have fun. The skills you learn in this book will help you meet the oh-so-important call for "excellent communication skills" so many employers are desperate to find. And after enough practice, maybe, just maybe, you can get to the point where you can compare speaking to something a little less dramatic than death.

Key Takeaways

- Communication is the foundation of a successful personal, academic, and professional life.
- Aim to learn the art of *presentations* rather than *public speaking*.
- Remember that presentations should be like conversations with your audience.
- Avoid writing and memorizing scripts, using notes and podiums, and engaging in other public-speaking habits that will prevent you from being in the moment with your audience.
- Rid yourself of the idea that you have to be perfect when presenting.

Questions and Activities:

1. **Reflection Question:** Think of a time when you were asked to give a *speech*. What was your experience—your nerves, your delivery, the process of memorization, etc.? Now reflect on the last time you explained a concept or idea to someone without having prepared a speech. How did those experiences differ? Which one did you prefer, and why?
2. **Learning Activity:** Relate the details of your day to an audience—your classmates, your friends, or your strategically placed stuffed animals—using three main points: your morning, your afternoon, and your night. You can think through what anecdotes you want to share, but *don't write anything down or try to commit anything to memory*.
3. **Learning Activity:** Reread this section. Now do another presentation to your audience in which you explain two or three concepts from the chapter. Again,

you can think through what you might say, but *don't write anything down or try to commit anything to memory*.

Credits

Introduction
The "Magic Key" to Presenting

By Mike Bay

After studying this chapter, you should be able to:
- *Identify how common personality traits can impact presentation style.*
- *Understand the differences between red and blue presentation styles.*
- *Assess your natural tendencies to devise a plan for improving your presentation skills.*

As my presentations class approached the end of the semester, I decided to give my class a lesson on "How to Get an 'A' on Your Final Presentation." In it, I laid out the expectations for the final team assignment and did my best to demonstrate the presentation techniques we had been working on throughout the semester.

After I was done, I was struck by the look on the face of one of my best students. She looked surprised and somewhat disappointed. I was surprised as well. I had just explained, in detail, all of the things they would need to do to get an "A" on the assignment. I expected to at least get an appreciative response, especially from one of my most motivated students. When I opened the floor to questions, the student raised her hand and asked sheepishly, "That's it? I just feel like there is so much more to learn about this." I was immediately stunned by her response. I realized that she had expected to learn *everything* about presenting in this class, and therefore thought that I was withholding vital information from her.

Although I certainly appreciate her desire to learn, I had to let her know the truth: **there is simply no "magic key" to presenting**. Audiences, locations, and objectives will vary, which means every presentation you give will be different. Most importantly, each presenter is unique, with different strengths and weaknesses that will be more fully revealed after years of experience.

Until then, it is essential that you learn the fundamental skills of professional presentations without over-coordinating your every move and thus stifling your performance. The basic skills you will learn about presenting, when practiced and reinforced throughout each presentation, will allow you to make a favorable impression on a wide variety of audiences in a wide variety of contexts. However, you should not lose your own unique, individual style. We are not asking you to resemble a robot, methodically moving from point to point. Nor should you impersonate an overemotional game show host trying to drum up enthusiasm from the audience. No one wants to see that. They want you to be yourself.

It's Good to Be Purple

Noted presentations guru Ron Hoff (1992) effectively uses the primary colors of *blue* and *red* (with variations in between) to categorize different presentation styles. If you are naturally low-key and analytical, you fall somewhere in the *blue* zone. If you are energetic and have a good rapport with the audience, you are *red*.

Blue zone presenters possess a calm, levelheaded, and analytical approach that radiates confidence and a profound command of the information. The audience is captivated by their intelligence, experience, and knowledge of their topics. Conversely, red zone presenters are naturally charismatic and engaging. Their presentations have a physical and visceral quality that attracts attention and connects with the audience on a more emotional level than those of blue presenters.

Realistically, very few presenters ever achieve a clearly defined blue or red designation. Blue presenters require significant professional experiences and accomplishments to

The ideal presenter is purplish—one part red, one part blue, with little to no gray.

establish credibility with the audience. Red-zone presenters spend years honing their performance skills until they can successfully adapt their style to different scenarios.

The goal of any presenter—newbie or veteran—is to avoid the gray zone. In a presentation, gray is an absence of red or blue. It can be characterized as a little analytical, a little emotional, a little effective, and entirely forgettable. Your presentations lack any of the identifiable characteristics found in the blue or red zones, and your audience will perceive you as mind-numbingly normal. If you finish a presentation and no one has any questions, your audience looks tired, and you receive no compliments or genuine smiles, you have found the *gray* zone. Unfortunately, most presenters are largely gray.

The color you want to strive for is *purple*. Purple is the blending of the best attributes of both the *blue* and *red* presentation styles and represents your best bet for leaving a memorable impression with your audience. A purple presentation style combines effective performance skills with well-researched and organized information. Initially, some of you will be more comfortable interacting with an audience (red), while others may be better at developing effective content (blue). Smart presenters play to their strengths without ignoring their weaknesses. It is fine for your presentation style to be magenta (reddish purple) or violet (bluish purple), but your approach must combine both style and substance for it to be effective. A unilaterally red, blue, or gray approach will fail to effectively persuade an audience.

Realistically, it can be daunting to try to address every aspect of a successful presentation all at once. After responding honestly to the questions below, you should be able to identify your natural tendencies. If you share similarities with a red zone presenter, be sure to focus particularly on your researching, organization, and message-preparation skills in this book. If you trend toward the blue zone, focus on improving your vocal quality, nonverbal communication, and audience-interaction skills. If you got a low or moderate score in both categories, beware: you are in the gray zone and need to get out.

Decide how much each statement represents you. Answer between 1 (not at all) and 5 (exactly like me).

1. I genuinely like to give presentations.
2. I notice a lot of smiling and nodding faces while I present.
3. I research thoroughly for my presentations and try to give as much proof for my main points as I can.
4. In presentations, I often see my audience visibly react to surprising statistics or facts I share.
5. I often incorporate audience interaction into my presentations.
6. I believe that logical proof is the most effective way to persuade an audience.
7. I believe that emotional appeals are the most effective way to persuade an audience.
8. When I tell a story, my listeners genuinely get drawn in.
9. I am a relatively calm presenter, even under stressful circumstances.
10. I enjoy sharing interesting knowledge or tidbits of information with others.

Add the totals for statements 1, 2, 5, 7, and 8. This is your red zone score.
Add the totals for statements 3, 4, 6, 9, and 10. This is your blue zone score.
A score of 21 to 30 indicates a high affinity for that zone.
A score of 11 to 20 indicates a moderate affinity for that zone.
A score of 0 to 10 indicates a low affinity zone.

What's in a Color?

Throughout this book, you will learn a number of skills—some blue, some red, and all designed to get you out of the gray. Here is a preview of the lessons you will learn:

Information – Blue Zone Skills

- **To analyze your audience.** The more you know about what your audience knows and feels, the more you will be able to tailor your presentation's message to them effectively.
- **To define your intent.** A clearly defined goal for your presentation will ensure that you include the right type of information to give your audience.
- **To improve your research.** If you are simply grabbing information from the first page of a Google search, I can assure you that your audience has already done the same thing.

- **To persuade with compelling arguments.** You need the right information and the right approach to lead your audience to your ultimate conclusion.
- **To use language appropriate to your audience.** Effective wording can help audiences understand otherwise-difficult concepts.
- **To communicate numbers effectively.** If you want to present the hard facts to your audience, you have to know how to package that information well.
- **To organize your materials effectively.** Break your presentation into three distinct parts: 1) an introduction that lays out the main points of your presentation; 2) a body that verifies your claims with facts and statistics from your research; and 3) a conclusion that reiterates your main points.

Performance Skills – Red Zone Skills

- **To make eye contact.** Make lasting eye contact to connect with people in every part of the room.
- **To abandon scripts and notes.** Your presentation should be a conversation with the audience, not a word-for-word reading or regurgitation of a script (like a speech).
- **To speak clearly and with conviction.** To be believed, you have to sound believable.
- **To move and gesture confidently.** If you want the entire audience to be engaged (and you do), you cannot stand in one place with your hands stiffly by your sides.
- **To engage your audience through story and interaction.** This is a conversation; stories and direct involvement are at the heart of a true conversational style.
- **To practice effectively.** Record your practice sessions to properly assess performance skills and increase your comfort level.
- **To use visually based visuals.** Visuals with minimal words allow you to be freer in your delivery and engage the audience more.

Find Your Own Set of Keys

In order to help illustrate the goals of this chapter, I would like to share a story I heard from a colleague about a student in her presentations class who was very *blue*. This student was a good researcher and adept at organizing his thoughts, but he was boring. During a skill-building exercise on storytelling, my colleague asked the student to tell a story he thought would amuse the audience or make them laugh. When he got his first laughs, he came to life and his nerves started to calm down. He still wasn't the loudest or the "cheerleading" type, but he started working in more stories and humorous side comments to keep his audience engaged and help him add more elements of *red* to his style. In his final self-reflection (done aloud as an impromptu presentation), he noted that this was one of the most important lessons he learned in the class: if he could get the audience to laugh, he could be much more engaging. Humor was one of his many keys to improving his presentation style—to moving from *blue-gray* to more *purplish*.

You likewise need to find your own keys to presentation success; there is no one magic formula. You will bring your own individual qualities to the equation. Once you ingrain the fundamental skills of professional presentations, how you refine your presentation style depends entirely on your willingness to assess your current communication skills. If you are prepared to try new tactics and embrace new ideas, then you will be able use the information provided in the following chapters to fine-tune your strengths and develop your weaker areas. Whether you are firmly blue, decidedly red, or lost somewhere in the gray zone, work hard to mix in the colors needed to get to a solidly purple state. After all, a splash of purple will invigorate any presentation.

Key Takeaways

- All presenters have their own styles, strengths, and weaknesses.
- Ideal presenters have a mix of red and blue presenting styles and are able to stay out of the gray zone.
- Discover which color best represents you, and improve on your weaknesses to achieve a more purple presentation style.

Questions and Activities:

1. **Reflection Question:** Reflect on your own presentation habits. Which presenting color best describes you—red, blue, gray (or some gradation in between)? What skills do you need to hone to make yourself a brighter red, a bluer blue, or a less monotonous gray? What is one specific goal you will set to add elements of a different color into your presentation?
2. **Learning Activity:** Tell the class what color you think suits you best (that is, which you hope to be), while exaggerating the qualities of that color. If you say you want to be red, be extra boisterous. If you say you're best suited for blue, throw in fun facts and work on making strong logical appeals.
3. **Presentation Preparation:** Write down—yes, I do mean actually write down— the one or two main skills you want to improve for your next presentation. Now write down the specific things *you will do* during your practice sessions. For example, if you have problems with eye contact, practice looking around the room until it becomes natural and comfortable for you to look at others. The main goal is not to try to work on *everything* at once.

Credits

1. Introduction: The "Magic Key" to Presenting Copyright © 2014 by Mike Bay. Reprinted with permission.
2. Magic Key Copyright © 2014 by Audrey Mora. Reprinted with permission.
3. Ideal Presenting Zone Copyright © 2015 by Audrey Mora. Reprinted with permission.

Unit 1

The First Steps in Planning Your Presentation

P resentations may be less rigid than formal, written speeches. That doesn't mean, though, that they take less preparation or careful planning. While there may be times when you are tasked with giving an impromptu presentation— one that you give without any time to plan—most presentations will come with a warning and at least a little prep time.

The sooner you begin the planning process, the more time you give yourself to collect all of the necessary data, create effective visuals, practice your presentation, and make the necessary adjustments. Trying to plan and practice a major presentation the night before "the big day" is likely to lead to an ineffective message with sloppy-looking visuals and a bundle of nerves for you (it's terrifying to talk to others when you're underprepared).

Take the time to work through each of the steps laid out in the forthcoming chapters before presuming your prep work is done. At first the process may seem time-intensive, but the more you plan presentations, the easier these steps will become. Besides, the payoff for your time will be a presentation that moves your audience and accomplishes its goals.

In this unit, you will read about AIMC (an acronym to help you plan your presentation, introduced in the next chapter) and about each of those steps. If you are currently working on a presentation, keep that assignment in mind so you can see how these chapters and suggestions will connect directly to what you have to do to prepare properly.

CHAPTER 1

AIMC
Easy as 1, 2, 3...4

After studying this chapter, you should be able to:
- *Identify and define the four components in the presentation-planning process: audience, intent, message, and channel.*
- *Articulate the importance of following AIMC in order while preparing a presentation.*

As I was thinking about how to begin this chapter, the "Do-Re-Mi" song from the *Sound of Music* popped into my head: "Let's start at the very beginning / A very good place to start / When you read you begin with A-B-C" (Hammerstein, 1965). Well, when you present, you begin with A-I-M-C.[1]

AIMC should be your guiding acronym when planning your presentations (Burke, Conway, & DiFrancesco, 2000). These four letters represent the four major elements that must be considered, *in the order in which you should consider them*, as you prepare a presentation: Audience, Intent, Message, Channel.

Let's talk about each of these levels in turn.

---

1   AIMC is a copyrighted approach, used with permission from Roger Conway, Sr., Associate Professor Emeritus of Southern Connecticut State University. This approach was first published in a workbook entitled *AIMC: A Communication Tool for Life*, written by Dr. Karen P. Burke, Roger Conway, Sr., and Sandra DiFrancesco.

A is for Audience

The most important—and thus the first—consideration of your presentation planning is your *audience*. As mentioned in the introductory chapter, presentations have specific goals: you are trying to get your audience to believe, feel, or do something. Your audience, then, is the most important piece to this presentation puzzle.

The mistake many presenters make is that they plan their presentations in a vacuum, with little consideration about who, specifically, will hear and consider the contents. If those canned presentations do not speak to the audiences' concerns, their interests, or their needs, the presenters will fail in exciting, informing, or persuading them. And if the presenters fail to affect their audiences, then what was the point of speaking at all?

For a presentation to be successful, every element of it must focus on what the audience wants and needs. This is called an **audience-centered approach**. What goal you set, what information you give, which visuals you show, how you dress, how you speak—all of these decisions depend on who will be sitting in your audience. A presentation to middle-school students will likely look and sound very different than a presentation to business professionals. The talk intended for students might seem too basic in content and too exuberant in delivery to business professionals (too *red*), and a presentation intended for business professionals might seem too advanced in content and too boring in delivery to middle-school students (too *blue*).

Even if the audiences you will present to are not as widely varied as seventh-graders and corporate representatives, *each audience is unique*. Let's say you are applying to two different jobs, both in the same field. Your cover letter and interviewing answers should be tailored specifically to each company. If you know one company's advertisement emphasized that they needed an applicant with creativity, you would do well to highlight your innovativeness. If the other company noted that they needed someone with excellent people skills, you might choose to discuss your work experiences that show your knack for customer service.

It cannot be stressed enough that being audience-centered is crucial to your presentation's success. At no point in any presentation should your audience have to wonder, "What does this have to do with me?" If the audience can't answer that question, your presentation is doomed to fail.

Moreover, if you've successfully tailored your presentation to your audience, they will be more motivated to listen to you; you will deliver information that matters to them in a way they can understand and believe. Trust me: presenting becomes much easier when you have a happy, attentive audience.

To tailor your presentation effectively, you must first learn about the people who will hear it. This process of researching your listeners is known as **audience analysis**, and it will be invaluable to you as you plan your presentation.

We will discuss audience analysis in more detail in the next chapter, but for now it is important to note that learning about your listeners is the *first* step to an effective presentation. It can be tempting to want to jump into researching or planning out what you want to say, but *the audience must come first*. Since the success or failure of your entire presentation is based solely on whether or not the audience is willing to buy what you're selling, you need to know who the audience is and what they want or need.

I is for Intent

After you have determined who your audience is, you need to decide on the specific goal for the presentation. **The intent is a one-sentence statement that describes what you hope your audience will know, think, or do by the end of the presentation.** Consider the following sample statements of intent:

- By the end of my presentation, my fellow classmates will understand the most common types of financial aid available to them.
- By the end of my presentation, the representatives of this business will agree to purchase their office supplies from my company.
- By the end of my presentation, my audience of potential investors will commit funds to my educational charity.

If you have a well-written statement of intent, planning your message and visuals will become remarkably easier. Your intent is your planning guide, your road map moving forward. For every element you want to add to your presentation, you must first ask yourself, "Does this help me meet my presentation's intent?" If the answer is "no" (or even "maybe," for those of you who tend to be more indecisive), then your fun fact, story, or visual does not belong in the presentation and should stay on the metaphorical cutting-room floor.

Whether you are given five minutes or five hours to present to your audience, your time is limited. With your well-crafted statement of intent in hand (or in mind) as you plan what to say and how to say it, you can be sure that you are using what presentation time you *do* have to its fullest.

M is for Message

Once your audience has been analyzed and your intent has been identified, it's time to get to the meat of the presentation: the *message*. **The message encompasses all you will actually say to your audience.** This, naturally, includes a number of different components, like the main benefits you choose to discuss, the research you find to support your points, and the level of vocabulary or specificity you will use in the presentation.

How to find and compile the different elements of the message will be discussed in more detail in Unit 2. For now, there are three important points about the message that ought to be emphasized:

1. **The message should not be written out.** Other chapters will give you tips on wording to use, research to share, and organizational elements to include, but the need to incorporate these components into your presentation is **not** an excuse to write a speech when you should be prepping a presentation. After enough practice, you will learn to use the right words, talk about research confidently, and keep your ideas organized without ever having to write a script.
2. **The message should be adjusted as needed during the presentation.** Engaging with your audience throughout the presentation will allow you to gauge how well your listeners understand your message and how well they are being persuaded by it. If the audience is not receiving the message as well as you had hoped they would, then you will need to adjust what you say to try to "right the ship's course."

3. **The message depends completely on your audience and your intent.** There is no effective one-size-fits-all presentation. Every element of your message—from the research you find to the words you use—must be the right choice for that specific audience and your specific intent. That's why the M for Message comes *after* the A for Audience and the I for Intent.

C is for Channel

Once you have figured out *what* you want to say, you need to decide *how* you want to say it. **The channel—our last letter of AIMC—is the means through which you present your message to your audience.** Most often in presenting, you will use three main channels to communicate: yourself, audience interaction, and visual aids.

- **You.** When presenting, *you* are the main channel—these are live presentations after all. The words you use are part of your *message,* but *how* you say these words is part of the channel. Do you sound humorous or serious? Are you loud or soft-spoken? Are you animated and using exaggerated hand gestures, or are you calm and relatively still? Are you dressed casually, or are you in your finest business suit? All of these elements—and many, many more—comprise the **you** part of the channel and will be discussed further in Unit 3.
- **Audience Interaction.** In a conversation-like presentation, audience interaction should be a relatively common occurrence. Audience interaction can range from asking your audience simple questions to engaging them in some activity to prove or exemplify your points. Involving your audience can enhance your message, show your listeners that they are important to you, and keep them awake and engaged; thus, the best presentations always include some element of audience participation. How to include your audience directly in your presentation will be discussed further in **Chapter 11: Involve Them and They Learn: The Power of Audience Participation.**
- **Visual Aids.** The last of our three channels is optional. You may choose to use visual aids—like charts, graphs, pictures, diagrams, and videos—to convey information, but you should only opt to do so when your visuals provide evidence or sentiments you cannot adequately express on your own. It is important that any visuals you use are understandable to your audience, aid in reaching your ultimate intent, and visually support your message. You should therefore choose your visuals carefully and select only those that meet these criteria. There will be much more information on selecting, creating, designing, and compiling visuals in Unit 4.

Put It All Together: AIMC!

Audience, Intent, Message, Channel—AIMC. Remember it. Love it. Cherish it. Let it haunt you in your dreams.

We will revisit AIMC throughout this book, and it will be our guiding motto as we begin to explore how to prepare and present presentations effectively. So, remember your order of preparation as we move forward: Audience, Intent, Message, Channel. AIMC.

Key Takeaways

- Start your preparation by analyzing your audience.
- Craft a clear statement of intent to help you plan what to include in your presentation.
- Develop a message that is suitable for your audience and intent without scripting it out or barring yourself from adjusting it on the spot.
- Consider the channels that will work best for your audience, intent, and message.

Questions and Activities:

1. **Reflection Question:** Write down the four to five points from this chapter that made you stop and think, "Interesting. I never thought about presentations this way." What are they? Why is AIMC a sound approach for making more effective, engaging presentations?

2. **Reflection Question:** What sort of preparation process did you do for the last presentation you had to give? How much prep time did you leave yourself? What were the results—that is, how successful was the presentation in influencing your audience?

3. **Learning Activity:** Pretend you are working for a sunscreen company, giving short sales presentations to potential clients. Determine how to approach the message and channel for each of the two audiences listed below. Then reflect on how those approaches differed, based on the audience.

Audience	Mothers of young children	Older women
Intent	To convince mothers to purchase this sunscreen for their young children.	To convince older women to purchase this sunscreen for themselves.
Message	?	?
Channel	?	?

4. **Learning Activity:** Pretend you are trying to convince others to vote for your favorite local or national candidate. How would your intent, message, and channel differ for each of the following audiences?
   - Working-class parents
   - Small-business owners
   - Doctors
   - Military personnel
   - College students

5. **Presentation Preparation:** Consider the next presentation you will give. Identify each of the four components of AIMC—Audience, Intent, Message, and Channel—as they relate to your own presentation.

Credit

1. AIMC Copyright © 2015 by Audrey Mora. Reprinted with permission.

CHAPTER 2

Getting to Know Them
Conducting Audience Analysis

After studying this chapter, you should be able to:
- *Define audience analysis.*
- *Explain the importance of analyzing your audience.*
- *Identify the three levels of audience analysis.*
- *Conduct various types of audience analysis.*

Often when planning presentations, presenters begin by asking themselves the question, "What do I want to say?" Already, they are setting themselves up for failure. Remember AIMC? The audience must be our *first* consideration. Thus, the first questions you should ask are "Who is my audience?" and "What do they want?" To get this information, you need to engage in an audience analysis, whether you do it

Demographics

Knowledge Level

Psychological Factors

The three levels of audience analysis.

formally (complete with reports and statistics) or informally (talking to people and finding out some basic background information).

There are three levels of audience information you should gather for a presentation: demographics, knowledge level, and psychological factors.

Demographics: What Are They Like?

Demographics are the kind of information you could find on a census: age, employment status, socioeconomic status, religion, race, gender, marital status, etc. It is likely that you will talk to audiences that are mixed in most (if not all) of these areas. If there are some commonalities, however, take note of them.

Who your audience is affects how you can approach your topic with them. Finding out important basic information about your individual audience members or about the client company they represent will aid you as plan your message.

You should not, however, use demographics to stereotype your audience. Presuming that an all-female audience only wants to talk about jewelry and shopping would be highly problematic for you (especially if I were one of those audience members). Instead, use demographic information to speak to topics that are relevant to your audience. A presentation on how to be successful at extreme couponing won't be as relevant to multimillionaires as it would be to those in the middle and lower classes. So the point here is this: **choose topics, sources, and approaches that are relevant to the people in your audience, but don't presume to know all the habits and attitudes of individuals based solely on their demographic characteristics.**

When presenting to representatives of a company, you would do well to find out basic demographic information on that organization. How old is the company? What does it make or sell? How are its profits? Who is in the company, and who makes the decisions on the issues you are presenting about? In many cases, your research might be as simple as reading through the company's website or talking to someone who works there.

Knowledge Level: What Do They Know?

The next step of your analysis is to determine how much your audience knows about your potential topic. The goal is not to bore your audience with information they already know, but also not to aim so high that they can no longer comprehend what you are telling them.

How do you find out just how much your audience knows?

Bored audience. They already know what you're telling them.

- If you have access to your audience beforehand, hand out surveys or quizzes to determine their base knowledge level.
- If you can't access the whole group, rely on select audience members to represent the group, and ask them pointed questions.
- If you don't have access to even a few audience members, ask the presentation organizers for their best guess as to the audience's knowledge level on your topic.

Confused audience. You're talking too far beyond their knowledge level.

Once you have an idea what your audience knows, you can determine what your presentation needs to cover and where it should start. If you gave out surveys to your audience and found that they knew very little about your topic, you now know that your presentation needs to cover the basics. If your surveys showed that your audience had some knowledge of the topic, then you would need to aim cognitively higher in your presentation. You would need to go into more depth on the topic and pepper your presentation with facts and information your audience is likely to find interesting and informative.

Remember: **your goal is to give your audience new knowledge, not just to repeat what they already know.** If you are giving your audience new information, they will be more motivated to listen to you. And, if your goal is persuasion, you want to ensure that your audience understands what they need to know to be able to see that your product or idea is the best choice.

Psychological Factors: What Do They Think?

In presentations, your audience's feelings and preferences are of paramount importance. A proper psychological analysis will additionally help you determine the audience's everlasting question: "What's in it for me?" (WIIFM). As many like to say, audience members are always tuned into the station WII-FM; that is, they really only care about how your ideas benefit *them*.

In short, you need to give your audience reasons to care about the information you present. How many times have you sat through a general-education requirement course and thought, "Why do I need to know this?" Your motivation for listening attentively in those courses was probably low.

Don't make your audience similarly wonder about the relevance of your presentation. Tell them outright why they should care: "Today I'm going to tell you about three important theories of persuasion *so that you can use these tactics in your own persuasive speaking.*" If your audience members are all tuned into WII-FM, make sure you're playing their song.

There are three types of psychological factors to consider when presenting: attitudes, beliefs, and values.

Attitudes

An attitude reflects whether or not someone likes a thing, person, or idea. If your clients are technology enthusiasts, selling the latest and greatest breakthrough to them will be easier than if they are more traditional, low-tech folk.

If you know your audience may have unfavorable attitudes toward your topic, be sure to address those dislikes openly: "I know that many of you dislike working in excessively high-tech environments, but our product is designed to mimic the working style of lower-tech methods … but with far greater efficiency." Help your audience overcome their

Remember your audience's primary concern: WIIFM (What's In It for Me). Find out what will make them care about what you have to say.

initial distaste for your ideas, your product, or even you by focusing them on the bigger picture and the ultimate goals.

Beliefs

A belief is a person's perception of what is true and what is false, whether or not those beliefs are factually correct. It is important to note here that *beliefs are often the underpinnings of attitudes*. For instance, in the previous example of the clients who disliked technology, it is likely that this aversion stems from an underlying belief that technology is not valuable in the workplace. If you were able to demonstrate its value, while showing that it is as easy (or nearly as easy) to use as their low-tech methods, your chance of making the sale would increase tenfold.

Values

Aristotle, the ancient Greek guru of rhetoric, said that there are three components to speaker credibility (what he called *ethos*): good sense, goodwill, and good values. To achieve *good sense* you must demonstrate that you are knowledgeable about your topic, and to achieve *goodwill* you need to show your audience that you care about them and are not just persuading them for your own selfish ends. Most relevant here, though, are *good values*. To achieve this aspect of credibility, you must show your audience that you share the same basic *values* that they do.

Let's say that you want to convince college officials to allow alcohol in a restaurant on campus. Members of the administration are against this idea, believing that it will promote partying and unsafe drinking behaviors on campus. Just saying to these administrators, "Hey, kids are going to drink anyway" will likely be ineffective. Students are also going to cheat on tests and get into fights. Should the administrators also hand out answer keys and set up boxing rings on campus?

So then, what's a different tactic to try? You might falsely think that this gem might work: "It would be so much easier for drunk college kids to get back to their dorms if the bar was on campus instead of a public bus ride away." Sure, and it would be much easier for administrators if they had personal masseuses and student servants feeding them grapes all day, but that's not going to happen either. The problem is that this persuasive approach is not focused on your audience.

Instead, you would be better served by speaking directly to the *administration's* values: "We know that you want students here to be safe and avoid heavy drinking. So do we. Putting alcohol in a public location on campus will reduce the amount of secret binge drinking in the dorms, which—as these studies here show—is the most dangerous kind of drinking for college students." That is an argument your audience of administrators would be much more likely to consider.

Remember, It's All about the Audience

As you move forward with planning your presentation, remember that the information you have gathered in your audience analysis is a vital piece of the puzzle. Ensure that every aspect of your presentation speaks to your audience specifically. Giving a generic presentation to differing audiences *will not work*. You must learn about your audience and tailor your presentation accordingly in order to sway them to your side.

Kenneth Burke (1969) calls this audience-focused persuasion *identification*. As he noted, "Here is perhaps the simplest case of persuasion. You persuade a man [or woman] only insofar as you can talk his [or her] language by speech, gesture, tonality, order, image, attitude, idea, *identifying* your way with his [or hers]" (55).

This doesn't mean that you need to pander to your audience by using fake accents or dressing identically to them. That usually will not end well and will likely result in eye rolling and head shaking. **Identification** *does* **mean that you should use the audience-analysis information you have gathered to speak to the wants, needs, and realities of that group of people.**

Here's the key point: **each presentation, each sales pitch, should be tailored precisely to the audience to whom you are speaking.** If you fail to do this, you will fail to respond directly to the needs and wants of your audience. And, if your listeners are left wondering how your presentation relates to them or how your product or ideas help them in any way, they will be confused and irritated … and your presentation will have been for naught.

Key Takeaways

- Audience analysis is essential to ensuring your presentation matches the needs of your audience.
- Demographic information will help you to ensure your topic, sources, and approach are fitting for your audience.
- Finding out how much your audience knows about your topic will help you ensure that you neither bore nor confuse your listeners.
- Identifying and demonstrating an understanding of your audience's attitudes, beliefs, and values will help you to persuade them effectively.
- Each presentation must be unique to the audience who will sit through it.

Questions and Answers:

1. **Reflection Question:** Based on your reading, why is audience analysis fundamental to the success of any message? Explain at least three ways that this chapter made you think differently about focusing on the audience.
2. **Reflection Question:** Consider your previous presentation experiences. Did you ever engage in any audience analysis—whether it was formal or informal? How did that affect the presentation you gave?

3. **Learning Activity:** With a partner, identify an instance in which you observed a speaker give a poor presentation due to failing to analyze the situation. What steps could the presenter have taken to more effectively analyze the situation?
4. **Presentation Preparation:** Research the audience for your next presentation to identify their demographic characteristics. Write up a short organizational or personal profile (can be bulleted).
5. **Presentation Preparation:** Research the audience for your next presentation to determine their organizational or personal mission statements and value sets. Compile a list of the values relevant to your idea or product.

Credits

CHAPTER 3

"Begin with the End in Mind"
Identifying a Clear Intent

After studying this chapter, you should be able to:
- *Articulate the importance of an accurate statement of intent when planning a presentation.*
- *Craft a statement of intent that is realistic, helpful, and audience-focused.*

In his best-selling book *The 7 Habits of Highly Effective People*, Stephen R. Covey (1989) asserted that successful people should "begin with the end in mind." While Covey applies this advice to the big picture—life goals and whatnot—he also notes that every task should be approached this way. This tactic, then, can also work for presentations.

The "end" to keep in mind for a presentation is what we call the *intent* (the I of AIMC). Creating a statement of intent is a relatively quick but important step in the AIMC process, and it should not be skipped over. **Having a clearly defined intent is paramount to your presentation's success.**

Let's start by learning a lesson from someone who seemed to lack a clear sense of intent in a presentation: the incomparable Clint Eastwood.

At the 2012 Republican National Convention (intended to rally the Republican troops around their soon-to-be-official presidential candidate, Mitt Romney), Eastwood was asked to be a guest speaker. Why, you may wonder, would an actor and director speak at a political convention? What was *he* supposed to offer the audience?

If you're unsure of that answer, take heart in the fact that Eastwood seemed to be equally confused. For more than eleven minutes (three times longer than his slated speaking time), Eastwood rambled on about his gripes with then-president Barack Obama, who was seeking reelection against Romney. But what made Eastwood's rant truly noteworthy was that he shared these criticisms by talking to an empty chair next to his podium, as though Obama were actually sitting in it. Eastwood cracked jokes and insinuated through his imaginary conversation that the invisible Obama was responding by telling Romney and Eastwood to "shut up" and "go f*ck themselves" (*New York Times*, 2012).

Sure, Eastwood's speech got a lot of laughs (and raised eyebrows) from the anti-Obama crowd, but did it really meet its intent? The purpose of the convention was to get Republicans (and perhaps

Eastwood and his empty chair: a cautionary tale.

some moderates) solidly behind Mitt Romney as their presidential candidate. Therefore, the goal of each presentation was to build up Romney's character, experience, leadership ability, and presidential potential.

Instead, Eastwood's spectacle served as a distraction. Little of the content actually had to do with Romney, except for some passing mentions and Eastwood's assertion that it might be time for a businessman (Romney) to run the country. In short, Eastwood's antics *pulled focus* from Romney. Clint Eastwood and his empty chair became the headline (and punchline) of the convention; *that* became its most memorable moment, rather than the uplifting words said about Romney or even Romney's acceptance of the nomination (which *really* should have been the highlight).

Eastwood, of course, caught quite a bit of flak for his unusual performance. During an appearance on *The Ellen DeGeneres Show*, he responded to criticism by saying, "It was an interesting reaction, actually. The Democrats who were watching thought I was going senile, and the Republicans *knew* I was ... but I was actually just trying to enjoy myself along the way" (*The Ellen DeGeneres Show*, 2012). An intention of just enjoying himself, though, was not in line with what he had been asked to do. His goal should have been to get everyone excited and talking about Mitt Romney for president, and, in that regard, he failed.

To avoid a similar gaffe, you need to ensure that the intent you choose clearly indicates what you aim to accomplish with your presentation. Then you need to make sure that every component of the message and channel you plan helps you to meet that intent.

Why Do I Need a Statement of Intent?

Designing the ideal statement of intent may seem like busy work to you, but I assure you that getting it just right will be a tremendous help moving forward.

Your statement of intent is your planning guideline, a central tenet for you as you move forward with your presentation preparations. It is just for you (and your team, if relevant); your audience will likely never see or hear it. Your intent should clearly represent what you can and need to accomplish by the end of the presentation. These clearly articulated goals will therefore help you to make decisions on what to include and what not to include in your presentation. The question you should ask when making every decision about the message you create and the channels you use (the M and C of AIMC) is, "Does this help me meet my intent?"

How to Craft Your Statement of Intent

Crafting the right intent will depend upon a number of factors, but good statements of intent should be or do all of the following:

1. **Be realistic for your audience.** Use your audience analysis to determine whether or not your goals are too lofty. Saying that you will convince each of your classmates to donate hundreds of dollars to a charity you support is probably not realistic. Conversely, your goals shouldn't be too easy. Giving a twenty-minute presentation on the ill effects of cancer with the goal only of convincing your audience to "like" a "Cancer Sucks" page on Facebook is overkill. (That presentation could be done in twenty seconds, with the same result.)

2. **Include the audience.** It is helpful to include the specific audience in the statement you create. Rather than saying, "My audience will be persuaded to buy raffle tickets for the Communication Club fundraiser," you would be better served by saying, "My audience of *college professors at this school* will be persuaded to buy raffle tickets for the Communication Club fundraiser." This helps to keep the focus on your specific audience as you move forward with creating the presentation.

3. **Focus on the audience.** The statement should identify what you want the audience to have gained or what you want them to commit to do by the end of the presentation. An intent of "I want to tell my audience of college students how to use the library" doesn't identify what you expect the audience to have gained. Are they just supposed to hear what you say, are they supposed to understand how the library works, or are they actually supposed to be able to conduct research within its brick-and-mortar walls? Here's a much clearer statement: "By the end of this presentation, my audience of college students will know how to use the basic search commands for databases and e-books."

4. **Be one sentence long.** A three-sentence statement of intent is likely indicative of a jumbled presentation. There should be one basic theme and one basic goal of your presentation (thus, it should all fit in just one sentence). If you have more than that, reconsider whether or not you are trying to cover too much in your presentation.

5. **Be neither too broad nor too specific.** If the statement is too broad, you will have difficulty deciding what evidence to include. As you research, too many varied support materials will seem relevant to your wide-reaching goal. That will leave your presentation unfocused and unruly. If the statement is too specific, you may miss the "bigger picture" of what you really need to accomplish for your job or assignment. If, as you progress to the message portion of AIMC, you find that you are struggling to identify materials that adequately support your statement of intent, revisit the scope of your goal to ensure it is—as Goldilocks would say—"just right."

   Too broad: "My audience will be in favor of my product."

   Too specific: "I will convince my audience of business investors to invest at least $5,000 toward the development of the U-Board because of its unique organizational functions that will attract a wide market of consumers."

   Just right: "I will convince my audience of business investors to invest money toward the development of the U-Board."

6. **Be realistic for the context.** In every presentation, you are constrained in some way by the context in which you give it.

The most obvious factor is time. Avoid the temptation to try to "say it all" in a limited amount of time; this is the pitfall that presentations expert Jerry Weissman (2009) calls a "data dump." Trying to cover too much ground in a short period of time will force you to gloss over your information too quickly, which means your audience is not likely to understand or retain much of it. You are better off narrowing your intent so that you can explain your ideas fully to your audience in the time allotted.

Beyond time, you also have other constraints: space, day, time of day, room configuration, etc. For instance, in a presentation on teamwork, you may be tempted to conduct physical team challenges with your audience to exemplify your points. If you are in a small room with unmovable furniture, though, that may not be possible (or safe). Be sure to consider all aspects of your context when developing your intent, so you can execute your presentation without major glitches.

A Well-Worded Statement

Now that you have the rules, let's put them into practice. Consider our old friend Clint Eastwood. What would his statement of intent have been, had he clearly articulated it? *By the end of this presentation, attendees at the Republican National Convention will be excited about the prospect of Mitt Romney as the next President of the United States.* This intent helps to meet all six of the previously mentioned steps. It is realistic for the audience and context, it includes the audience, and it is short without being too broad or too specific.

Had Mr. Eastwood had his intent in mind as he planned his presentation, he likely would have realized that the chair routine—no matter how *memorable*—probably wasn't the best use of his time.

Next Steps ... Preparing for the M of AIMC

So, you have crafted the ideal statement of intent. Now what? This one-sentence statement is your guide as you move forward in the presentation-planning process to the next step: crafting your message.

In every stage of the message-forming process, you must consider your audience and your statement of intent. What research to cite, which main ideas to use, which stories to tell, which vocabulary to include—these decisions should be made based on the presentation goals you have identified. If you find fascinating research, a mind-blowing visual, or a captivating story, use your intent as your measure to decide whether or not to include it. If it won't help you meet your intent, leave it out, no matter how riveting you think it would have been. Including information just because it is interesting is a waste of your audience's time, and it unnecessarily pulls focus from your main message.

Learn from Clint Eastwood's missteps: **your intent should be your guide.** Be sure that you can articulate it well and that you use it as your anchoring point for your presentation. It will help to keep your presentation focused and stay on the steady path toward informing and persuading your audience.

Key Takeaways

- A well-crafted statement of intent helps you to plan an organized and coherent presentation.
- Your intent must be appropriate to the audience and occasion.
- Crafting a statement of intent is an easy but crucial step in planning a presentation.
- Use your statement of intent to decide how to develop your message and use your channels.

Questions and Activities:

1. **Reflection Question:** Think back on previous presentations you've done or seen. Identify one that lacked a clear intent. How did that affect the quality of the presentation?
2. **Learning Activity:** Pair up with a partner. Together, develop a statement of intent for each of the following topics that would be realistic for a presentation to your classmates:
   - Volunteerism
   - Campus safety
   - Technology
   - Lifelong learning
3. **Presentation Preparation:** Write the statement of intent for your next major presentation. Be sure that it follows all of the above prescriptions. Conduct a brainstorming activity in which you try to think of all the possible points you could possibly make related to your intent. Once you've finished creating this list, see if you can find a meaningful pattern that helps you develop three main points for your message to come.

Credit

CHAPTER 4

Tell Them Something Good
Planning Your Message

After studying this chapter, you should be able to:
- *Distinguish between the* what *and the* how *of the message, and explain how to form each.*
- *Identify other considerations involved in planning an effective message.*

Once you have developed a statement of intent that defines your goals for the audience and presentation, you need to plan out the message that will help you achieve those goals. Unit 2 will discuss the message-planning phases in more detail, so here we will focus on an overview of the message.

In short, there are two main aspects to formulating your message: (1) deciding *what* you want to say, and (2) deciding *how* you want to say it.

The *What*

The first task of forming your message is becoming an expert on the topic. If you already have credibility in the area, great! This will be easy. If not, then be sure to research your topic to demonstrate to your audience that your arguments are sound and you are worthy of their trust.

Once you have done some research, you have the daunting task of weeding through the results to figure out just what you want to say to your audience. Consider the results of your audience analysis, and decide which main points or arguments will best fit the people who will hear them. If your goal is to inform, what facts or points might your audience find most interesting and relevant? If your goal is to persuade, what arguments are most likely to shift their opinions or decisions?

Make sure that any main points or arguments you consider not only appeal to your audience, but also help you reach your intent. You may think that your audience would find a certain fact fascinating and another statistic stunning, but if they are not related to your ultimate presentation goals, they merely serve to distract your audience.

Your goal should be to settle on three to five main points that are relevant to both your audience and intent, regardless of how long your presentation might be. Trying to cover too much information is a mistake; your audience will simply not be able to process a barrage of new information. At some point, they are likely to get tired and just mentally zone out from you. Moreover, if you try to cover a lot of information in a limited amount of time, you will be forced to skim over ideas quickly, without being able to explain them fully or ensure your audience grasps the concepts. You are better off explaining a few points in detail than you are brushing over a lot of points in general terms.

The *How*

After you have decided on the arguments or main points you want to make, you need to decide how you will support them. Here is a simple rule: **for every claim you make, you must include reputable support to prove it.** What form that proof takes, though, depends on the audience.

As will be discussed more thoroughly in **Chapter 15: Putting It All Together**, the ancient Greek philosopher Aristotle (2004) argued that all messages should include elements of ethos (speaker credibility), logos (logical arguments), and pathos (emotional appeals). Here are some types of claim support that could work for each of these approaches:

Ethos	Sharing your own experience
	Expert opinions and testimony
Logos	Statistics, facts, and figures
	Research study findings
Pathos	Personal stories

Try to use a variety of appeals in your claim support, but base your ultimate decision on how much attention to pay to each kind of appeal, based on your audience. If your audience analysis has revealed that your listeners appreciate facts and nothing but the facts, emphasize ethos and logos more than pathos. If your listeners have personal connections to your topic, work in some pathos to help them emotionally identify with your ideas, product, or plan.

You should avoid relying too heavily on just one kind of appeal. A presentation supported solely by your own ethos may start to sound obnoxious (even indisputable experts cite other people's research findings to support their claims). A presentation hinged completely on logos may become boring and/or overwhelming for your audience. A presentation based solely on pathos may have your audience rolling their eyes at your overly dramatic show. **Use all three appeals—to varying degrees, based on your audience—to have the best shot at persuasion.**

Other Considerations

Unit 2 will not only explore how to research your topic and how to use the different types of support listed above, but it will also explain other important aspects of the message. You will learn how to use language suitable for your audience and intent, effective means of persuading your audience, how to organize your presentation, strategies for adjusting your message while you present, and how to answer questions professionally.

Regardless of which aspect of your message you are planning, keep this simple idea in mind: it ain't over til it's over. If your presentation is like a conversation, then the message you plan needs to be flexible. If you write out your message as though it is a script you will read without interruption, you will struggle to reach and respond to your audience effectively. On the other hand, if you approach your message formation with the spirit of flexibility, you will find yourself to be far more effective.

Gaining knowledge on your topic and on speaking in outlines will work wonders for your ability to adapt to your audience. Work hard to understand the information surrounding your presentation topic. Research and become the kind of expert who can simply talk about the subject without having to script out what to say. Practice speaking in an organized fashion so you can share your ideas in an orderly manner without having to rely on notecards or teleprompters. Then, if you need to change tactics mid-presentation, or if audience questions or interruptions throw you off your planned course, you will still be able to talk coherently about the subject without appearing flustered or annoyed at just how awry your best-laid plan went.

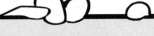

Key Takeaways

- Research your topic thoroughly to increase your own credibility and help you decide what arguments or main points your presentation should cover.
- Ensure that the claims you make are relevant to your audience and help you reach your presentation's intent.
- Use ethos, logos, and pathos to support your claims and arguments.
- Keep your message flexible; don't write it down or memorize it.

Questions and Activities:

1. **Reflection Question:** Of the three factors of credibility, which do you think is going to be hardest to establish with your peers during your next presentation? Why?

2. **Learning Activity:** Pair up with a partner. Together, develop a statement of intent for a presentation to your classmates on the topic of charitable giving. Then consider what points or arguments you might make that could reflect the three types of persuasive appeals: ethos, logos, and pathos.

3. **Presentation Preparation:** Brainstorm at least three steps you can take in your next presentation to make it clear to your audience that you are a credible speaker on your topic. In other words, what can you do to enhance your peers' perception of your credibility?

4. **Presentation Preparation:** Consider your next presentation. Brainstorm at least two claims you could make (or pieces of evidence you could use) to appeal to the audience's sense of logos, and two claims you could make (or pieces of evidence you could use) to appeal to the audience's sense of pathos.

CHAPTER 5

How to Spread the Good Word
C is for Channel

After studying this chapter, you should be able to:
- *Define channel and explain why it's an important consideration for your presentation.*
- *Identify the three main types of presentation channels and the basic components of each.*

If you've been following along on your AIMC map, you'll surely realize that we have now reached the last stop of your preparation path: the Channel. **The channel is the means by which you deliver your presentation.** In other words, now that you've planned the message you want to give, you have to figure out just how to deliver it with the greatest impact for your audience. In short, you have three main channel options: yourself, visual aids, and demonstrations/audience participation.

Channel = you, audience interaction, and visual aids.

Many presenters hardly think twice about the channel choices they make: they always use themselves (because that's what makes it a presentation) in a serious tone (because that makes it "professional," right?), and many are quick to throw in a PowerPoint presentation (because that just seems to be "what you do" in a presentation). But these decisions should involve more thought than that.

Remember that every consideration you make in your presentation preparation—including which channels to use—ought to start with your audience. If your audience needs to see your enthusiasm to be "hooked" on your ideas, then you need to present with some pizzazz. If the point you are trying to make would be easier for your audience to understand if they could see or do it for themselves, then include audience participation exercises and demonstrations. If your planned PowerPoint has nothing in it with real visual value to your audience, then throw it out, and let your own dynamism be enough.

The channel choices you make will ultimately affect how your audience receives your message. The most brilliant ideas and well-researched points will be lost on your audience if your presentation style is too jarring, or if you failed to provide the types of visuals or participation needed to prove your information. Let's now explore each of your channel options, one at a time.

Your Lovely Self: Verbal and Nonverbal Communication as a Channel

It seems obvious that you will use yourself as a channel in an oral presentation—it's just part of the presentation package. But how you color your communication is up to you. The most competent communicators match their communication styles to their audience, intent, message, context, and occasion. Serious audiences and serious purposes call for serious tones of voice, but *professional* does not have to mean *serious*.

In most cases, audiences want to see enthusiasm and a little pep in your step as you present. They want energy and passion; they want to be genuinely moved. Your tone of voice, your movements around the room, your hand gestures, and much more can help to communicate the appropriate emotions to your audience.

Presenters don't have to stick to just one emotion or presentation style for the whole presentation. Somber presentations can have moments of lightness (don't many eulogies include humorous anecdotes about the deceased?), and lighthearted presentations may need some moments of sober reality. A switch in style can be effective at grabbing your audience's attention, but don't do it too often. Emotional rollercoasters are exhausting for everyone, particularly your bewildered audience.

Unit 3 will explore in depth the various ways in which you can use your presentation style as a channel, and the chapters within that unit will offer multiple tips on how to improve your effectiveness. For now, let me note that controlling yourself while presenting is usually the most nerve-wracking task for newbies. It's daunting to attend to your vocal inflections, your volume, your rate, your body movements, your eye contact, and your posture while still trying to coherently deliver your message. But if you learn to focus less on all the ways you're sure you'll screw up and focus more on what the audience needs to hear and how they need to hear it, you will find presenting appropriately much easier to do. Visualize your success. Think positively, focus on the audience, and keep practicing; it will come eventually.

Visual Aids

Visual aids are a common occurrence in presentations, most often in the form of PowerPoint, but rarely are they done well. Unit 4 will give you many prescriptions for creating impactful visuals for your audience, from choosing the right type of visual to designing it effectively and professionally.

As a preview for the ideas to come, let me tell you this: visual aids are not always needed. Just because people expect presenters to use PowerPoint[1] or some other visual, that does not mean that you need to. Visual aids should be in your presentation for a reason. If you don't have a good reason to show a visual, then don't show one.

In particular, visual aids should do at least one of the following:

1. Help the audience understand or remember a concept.
2. Help persuade the audience.

---

1   When I say "PowerPoint," I mean any presentational slideshow software. PowerPoint just happens to be the most popular, and thus the fallback representative of its genre.

If the visual accomplishes neither of these goals, then it should *not* be in your presentation. Period.

If you use this yardstick to measure the slideshow presentations you have created in the past, my guess is you will find that many of your visuals had no real benefit for your audience. In particular, text-heavy slides fail to meet these visual-aid standards. Really, they are neither *visual*, nor do they *aid* the audience. I could go on forever about the reasons to avoid text in your projected visuals—and I will in Chapter 25. Just know now that if you plan to use visuals in your next presentation, you should read Unit 4 before proceeding to be sure that what you show your audience has purpose and persuasive power.

While multimedia slideshows are currently the most common presentation visuals, they are certainly not the only ones. Old-school visuals like whiteboards, chalkboards, flip charts, and overhead transparencies still find their way into meeting rooms worldwide. Another important visual aid discussed in Unit 4 is the leave-behind. This is, as its name suggests, a document you leave behind with your audience. It could be a handout, brochure, business card, pamphlet, or multi-page report, but all leave-behinds should be complementary to your presentation. They add extra information to what you said aloud, and they can be particularly useful in delivering concepts or calculations that would be too complex to explain in the course of the presentation itself.

Demonstrations and Audience Participation

Sometimes the best way of sharing your message is to show your audience how to do it, or—better yet—to let the audience do it themselves. The value of audience interaction is hardly news in the educational realm (Butler, 1992; Murray, 1991), yet so few presenters take advantage of it.

The problem is that presentations are often too "me-focused." Even if presenters consider their audience as they form their intent and plan their message, they are apt to lose that focus when they consider the channel. Don't let the channel be an afterthought. Think to yourself: "How will my audience best understand and be convinced by what I'm trying to say?" That will involve audience participation more often than you might now think.

Consider this: if you were a client being asked to invest in a new product, wouldn't you want to be able to see, hold, and try the product out yourself (just as investors often do on *Shark Tank*)? If you were being taught how to properly shake hands, wouldn't you want to try the method out on the spot? If you were being told how to handle difficult customers at work, wouldn't you want someone to hear your horror stories, learn from your success strategies, or help with the problems you just couldn't solve? Your audience wants those types of direct interaction, too.

Involving your audience beyond asking them to raise their hands silently in response to a question may seem scary, but you can learn how to use participation effectively (and you will in Chapter 12). Give your audience members a voice. Keep them engaged in the presentation, and enlist them to be active learners of what you're teaching and active accepters of what you're preaching. Moreover, making your audience a real part of the presentation will free you from the terrifying speech standard of "I talk; you listen." If presenting really is like a conversation, you have to let the audience actually be a part of it in a meaningful way. Audience participation can do that.

Choose Your Channel Wisely

After your audience has been analyzed, your intent identified, and your message made, your job is not done. Choose the channels that will work best for your presentation, and use them in a way that will work best for your audience. Don't let your channel selection be a matter of convenience or laziness; make the choices that will benefit your audience and, ultimately, facilitate your presentation's success.

Key Takeaways

- Choose the channels that will best suit your audience, intent, and message.
- Select a delivery style that will be appropriate and effective for your presentation.
- Only use visual aids when they benefit the audience's comprehension or they are effective for persuasion.
- Use demonstrations and audience interaction to help audiences see and try concepts for themselves.

Questions and Activities:

1. **Reflection Question:** Think of the last presentation you gave. How much thought did you put into which channels you would use and how you would use them? How could you have improved the presentation through different channel choices?
2. **Learning Activity:** In a small group, consider this presentation scenario: you are presenting with the goal of answering the question, "What is the most important quality for academic success?" You will present this to two different audiences: (1) college professors and (2) your peers. Which channels would you use for each audience? Be specific. For yourself, what presentation style would you use?
3. **Presentation Preparation:** Consider your next presentation, and decide which channels will work best for your audience, intent, and message. What delivery style will you use? What types of audience participation will you incorporate? Will you use visual aids? If so, which types?

Credit

1. Channel Copyright © 2015 by Audrey Mora. Reprinted with permission.

Unit 2
Making Your Message Meaningful and Memorable

Once you have completed the first two steps of AIMC—audience analysis and identifying your intent—it is time to move onto formulating the part of your presentation that your audience will hear: the message.

Deciding on what message you want to send to your audience is perhaps the most labor-intensive part of the planning process. You need to approach message creation in an orderly manner (single-file, please; no cutting), and be prepared to adjust and retune as needed. In presentations, there is no such thing as a "final version": you will be readjusting and retuning during the presentation itself to adapt to the audience and context. If you approach the message-planning process with the understanding that *you will need to be flexible*, you will find such on-the-spot alterations less jarring and less irritating.

Ready to fall in line? Let's look at the message-planning process:

- **Step 1: Revisit your audience analysis and your statement of intent.** What types of appeals and messages will move this audience? What do they not yet know (and thus need to be told by you)? What claims and proof will they accept, and what will offend them or cause them to shut down completely? What main points will help you reach your statement of intent? Keep coming back to these questions during *every single* step of the planning process and adjust your message accordingly.

    If you don't yet have a clear picture of your audience or your intent, go back to the first unit and clarify those points first.
- **Step 2: Do your research.** A good presentation requires good research. If your goal is to inform your audience, research will help to support the points you are trying to make (and make you look very well-read on the topic). If your goal is to persuade clients to choose your business or product, it is likely you'll need to research market trends, competing companies or products, and other factors to give a complete picture of why the client should choose you.
- **Step 3: Formulate arguments that relate to your audience and intent.** If you are aiming to inform your audience, choose the main points that will teach them something new and captivate their attention while still meeting your intent. If your job is to persuade, be sure you are focusing on benefits rather than features, and are making credible, logical, and emotional appeals.
- **Step 4: Organize Your Information.** For audiences to be able to digest all the information you try to share, you need to present the content in an organized fashion. Learn how to "speak in outlines" to ensure that your content is easy for your audience to follow.
- **Step 5: Work on Making It Engaging for the Audience.** Good information is important, but if your audience is barraged with too much of it, they won't remember most of it. Then what was the point? *It's better to cover less information in more depth than to skim over a lot of points.* Instead of a laundry list of facts, work in stories and audience engagement so the audience maintains focus for the duration of your time and can digest the information you are trying to share.
- **Step 6: Practice Saying It.** But don't memorize and recite it. Aim to use words your audience will be able to follow and that will have a lasting impact.

The message, the M of AIMC, may take some trial and error to get right. As you run through the material you plan to share with the audience, ask yourself (or others, if they are willing to be sounding boards), "Is this information my audience will understand and respect? Am I presenting it in a way that will keep their attention? Does this message fulfill my presentation's statement of intent?"

If any of your answers are "no," then head back to the drawing board. A presentation that fails on any of those three fronts will not be worth delivering to your audience. Find the message that works so you can find presentation success.

CHAPTER 6

More Reasons Not to Write a Speech
The Differences between Speaking and Writing

After studying this chapter, you should be able to:
- *Articulate why it is important that you do not write a script for your presentation.*
- *Identify the ways in which speaking differs from writing.*
- *Avoid the common presentational pitfalls that come from a scriptwriting approach.*

You might think that when I tell my students I never want them to write down their presentations, they would erupt in joy. After all, in other courses, when I ask students to write papers or journals or do anything that requires a keyboard, pen, or the written word, I am met with a chorus of grumbles and groans. Yet when it comes to presentations, students find something terrifying about the absence of a written plan: "No script? But how will I know what to say?"

They think that writing out a speech will make them feel better. We won't read it, they promise. We won't memorize it, they say. I, however, respond with this: reading a script to yourself over and over again as practice puts your brain into text mode. You are not doing a book reading or reciting the State of the Union from a teleprompter. You will have *no script* come speaking time. **You are a presenter who should be talking to your audience in normal speech, and a written script won't help you do that.**

I've taught many college writing courses, and I know how many times I have had to tell my writing students, "You can't write like you talk." Well, the flip side is also true: *you can't talk like you write.* There are distinct differences between speech and text, between talking and writing. Recognizing these differences will hopefully not only convince you to step away from the word processor when planning your next presentation, but it will also point out the necessity to translate the information you get from your sources into spoken English for your audience.

Walter Ong and the Principles of Orality

In his seminal text *Orality and Literacy: The Technologizing of the Word*, Walter Ong (1988) sought to explain the ways in which our culture and minds were transformed in the movement from an oral culture (before the written word, when communication was spoken) to a written culture (when ideas could be disseminated through text). While not all of Ong's findings are relevant to our discussion here, many of them are.

In short, Ong identified that there are important differences between how we speak and how we write. How we approach each of these tasks should, therefore, be very different. What follows are a few of the more relevant lessons we can glean from Ong's observations: speaking should be redundant, concrete, situational, participatory, and agonistically toned.

Say It Again … and Again … and Again: Speaking Should Be More Redundant than Writing

In a novel, the author can introduce a character ("In came John's brother James, a sallow sad sack of a man wallowing in his own misfortunes and missteps"). That character could disappear from the next hundred pages of the book. When he reemerges, the author only needs to write "James." If the reader can't remember who he is or what his character was like, she can flip back in the book to remind herself.

In presentations, your audience doesn't have that luxury. They can't pause and rewind live presentations to help them figure out your message (there are, as of yet, no DVRs for real life). Instead, you need to remind them of important facts and main points.

Even in the structure of presenting, redundancy should be built in. If you follow the rules for organization that will be discussed in **Chapter 10: Speaking in Outlines**, you should be telling the audience your main points *at least* three times:

- **Preview** – Tell them what you will tell them.
- **Main Points** – Tell them.
- **Review** – Tell them what you just told them.

In addition to repeating your main points, each point you make should be concluded by giving a summary of what you just said, and transitions between points reiterate the main points to come. So, basically, you'll say your main ideas *a lot*. If you were to write this all down as a script, it would seem repetitive and a bit ridiculous, but these reiterations are necessary when speaking out loud for audiences to understand and remember your points.

"Wait, What Did You Just Say?": Speaking Should Be More Concrete than Writing

Text is a wonderful avenue for expounding lofty ideas and complex workings of the mind. If you have had to reread the same paragraph multiple times to figure out what it was saying, you know what I mean.

Your audience doesn't get those opportunities for rereads in a presentation. They have only that moment the information is reverberating in their eardrums to figure it out, judge it, and categorize it. Help a brother (or sister) out, and **make your words simple and easy for your audience to understand.**

- **Put away the thesaurus.** Here in print, I can really flex my vocabulary muscles and give my trusty thesaurus a workout. I could tell you to use *epizeuxis* to add emotion and emphasis in your language, or I could give you tips to overcome your *glossophobia*. Not sure what I just said? Go look those words up. Go ahead; you've got time.

When talking aloud, though, *you need to stay simple.* Using overly complicated words won't make you seem brilliant; it will make you seem pretentious. If you avoid writing down your speech and practicing off the paper, you will be more likely to talk to your audience with words and phrases they will be able to understand quickly; then they can focus on your ideas, not on decoding your language.

- **Be specific.** While simplicity is important when speaking, it should not come at the cost of precision. Don't say "good" when you mean "acceptable." Don't say "fun" when you mean "exhilarating." Presenting offers you the ability to draw your audience into your story while they sit in front of you. Do this by using colorful language that allows your audience to visualize what you say. For more tips on language use, read **Chapter 11: Say Whaaaat?**
- **Translate your research.** I should note that difficult words often worm their way into presentations, not because presenters write down the words in a script, but rather because they read them in their research and, not fully understanding them, decided to just regurgitate them to their audience. This is even more obvious when presenters mispronounce the words: "Writers use on … uh … on-om-oh-to-poh-ee-ay." Yikes. Did you mean *onomatopoeia*?

  Remember this idea of translating your sources for your audience as you proceed to **Chapter 7: The More You Know.** You must show your audience that you have some expertise on your topic—even if you had to gain that expertise the week before through careful research. Tripping over pronunciations or using unnecessary jargon because you don't realize there is a much simpler word available damages your credibility. Know your topic and ideas well, and demonstrate your command of that information by explaining it in your own, much simpler words.
- **Give specific source citations.** Specificity should also apply to the supporting materials you reference. In writing, you can make vague references to studies you've read, and if your audience has a question about the studies' validity or methodology, they can flip to your sources list and look up the original works. In oral presentations, you need to be more specific when discussing your sources and your ideas. When presenting an idea, precede or follow up that information with the citation the audience needs in order to evaluate the source quickly. This should *not* sound like an aloud APA reference: "Smith, 2010, pages 125 through 126." Instead, say something like, "Joan Smith is a dermatologist for the National Skin Care Institute and is a leading expert on skin care. She says that you should enjoy some sunscreen-free time outdoors, too."

YOPO (You Only Present Once): Speaking Must Be Situational

One of the true testaments of good literature is that it is read by people from all walks of life, transcending time and space. That is *not* the case for presentations. Presentations happen right here, right now, to the specific people in front of you at this moment. To be effective, presentations must be *situational;* that is, they must reflect where you are, what day it is, what time it is, and who is in the room with you. Ignoring these factors makes you seem out of touch or too "canned."

Chapter 14: Calling an Audible will give more detail on how to adjust to your audience, but for now, let me give you an example: I've taught my presentations course for many years, and some of the "talks" I give my students are fairly routinized for me at this point. Nonetheless, I never say them the same way twice, not only because I've never written them out, but also because they *have* to change to accommodate the contextual factors of class that day. Maybe my students are overtired and not focusing well. Maybe they lack the background knowledge needed to understand the concepts at hand. Or maybe their apprehension about an upcoming presentation is making it hard to hear over all the very scary voices in their heads. Whatever the circumstances, I have to adjust to my audience. Just bowling forward with a preplanned lecture when my students are unwilling or unable to pay attention would be a major teaching fail. Audiences want presenters who acknowledge them as they are.

You can practice your presentation until you can think and dream of nothing else, but what you say and how you say it should—in large part—depend upon the situational factors of your presentation time, place, and audience. A script will lock you down and make it hard to accommodate these factors when presenting. Never having written a script will keep you free to adjust as needed.

Sarah invites her audience to participate.

Yakety-Yak ... Please Talk Back: Speaking Should Be Participatory

Actually, speaking *is* participatory, whether or not you want it to be. The audience is an integral part of the presentation process, and for you, they are the most important part.

In text, the audience has no way to immediately respond. Sure, they can add comments to an online message board or write adoring or inflammatory letters to the author, but they cannot *interrupt* the text; they cannot change what will happen on the next page. In presentations, the audience has that power. They can interrupt, ask questions, lob criticisms, rise to standing ovations, or hurl rotten tomatoes at your head (but let's hope they don't). Or they can show you nonverbally that they approve or disapprove of what you are saying. All of these actions can interrupt the presentation and potentially change its course. You will have to adjust accordingly.

As a presenter, you should recognize this and work to bring it out more fully. Respond to their nonverbal cues. Ask your audience if they have questions, comments, or criticisms. Make them a more direct part of the process to show them that their feedback matters to you. After all, they are the ones you need to convince, right?

And beyond simple conversation, you can take advantage of presentations' participatory nature by including activities, demonstrations, exercises, and other types of audience interaction, all of which are discussed in **Chapter 13: Involve Them and They Learn**.

You Wanna Fight about It?: Speaking Is More Agonistically Toned

If you've been on the wrong end of a question-and-answer firing squad, I don't need to tell you that presentations can get heated. **Because they happen in the here and now, and because the words come directly from people's mouths, presentations feel more personal.**

If you say something offensive, your audience will respond—either verbally or nonverbally—to let you know you screwed up. If your information is unreliable, you'll get questioned on it. If your ideas are ridiculous, you'll be told so. If your presentation had some content issues, the question-and-answer session may feel like a debate forum. All of these examples represent the agonistic nature of oral communication.

As a presenter, don't shy away from it; embrace it (easier said than done, I know). Know your information well and be sure that it is sound. Revel in the spirit of debate, but make *collaboration* your ultimate goal. Remember that every question raised is a sign of audience interest. Use the immediateness and personal nature of presentations to call your audience to action—to inspire, to motivate, and to convince them of your ideas. And, if the idea of responding to audience members' concerns still freaks you out, skip forward to **Chapter 15: Question, Question, Who's Got a Question?**

Say a Presentation. Write a Paper.

The major takeaway from this section should be that speaking and writing do not go hand in hand. Writing puts you in "writing mode," in which you pen longer sentences, use bigger words, rely on more abstractions, and write in a vacuum devoid of immediate criticism.

In presentations, you need to *talk,* not orate. This should be easy; you talk far more than you write anyway. Learn your material well and trust that you can communicate it clearly in an extemporaneous fashion.

If you know your stuff—if you are the expert you claim to be—you shouldn't need a script (and, based on what you just read, you shouldn't *want* a script anyway). I know you may think you'll find safety in a script, but it won't do you any favors with your audience. It's time to learn a better way, more audience-friendly way that avoids writing and focuses on presenting.

Scripts? Pffft. You don't need no stinkin' scripts!

Key Takeaways

- Writing out a presentation is a bad idea, because speaking is fundamentally different than writing.
- Repeat your main points multiple times to make sure your audience remembers them.
- Be specific in your language and your evidence to aid audience understanding and increase your own credibility.
- Tailor your presentation to the context in which you give it.
- Include audience interaction, and be prepared to adjust as needed to deal with negative feedback.

Questions and Activities:

1. **Reflection Question:** Reflect on the process of formulating a presentation and writing a paper. Which one do you find easier? Why?
2. **Learning Activity:** Choose a paper you have written for a different class. Give a short presentation on that paper, adapting what you have written to the above guidelines for effective speaking. Don't write out what you want to say ahead of time. Just *talk* about it.
3. **Presentation Preparation:** With a partner, friend, or particularly helpful stuffed animal, talk through the main points you want to cover in your message. Hold a conversation about what you know and what you want to say so you can become comfortable talking freely about the content, rather than feeling like you will need to write a script.

Credit

CHAPTER 7

The More You Know
Finding and Using Research to Build Credibility

By Linda Sampson

After studying this chapter, you should be able to:
- *Explain why research is an essential part of every good presentation.*
- *Identify the types of information you might need and where to find it.*
- *Evaluate the sources you identify.*
- *Properly cite the sources you use in your presentation.*

In "The Magic Key" chapter earlier in this book, you learned the importance of being "purple"—of not only having a palpable dynamism (being "red"), but also supporting your presentation with interesting and valuable facts and information (being "blue"). Research is the first step in becoming more "blue": it helps you find the information that will speak directly to your audience, and it allows you to build up your own knowledge and speaker credibility.

But just as Kermit the Frog tells you that "It's not that easy being green," becoming "blue" in your presentations will also not be a cakewalk. Good research is much more involved than typing a search term into Google and using the first three entries that pop up. This chapter is aimed at helping you effectively conduct the researching process and find information that is credible, valuable, and relevant.

Feeling and Sounding Smart: The Importance of Research in a Presentation

Let's face it: research takes time and energy, and it's much easier on you just to speak "from the gut." Unfortunately, audiences rarely care about what your gut, stomach, or other digestive organs have to say. To create logical arguments (Aristotle's call for *logos*) and build trust with your audience (*ethos*), you need to research your topic. Even those people widely proclaimed as experts in their fields research the work of others. Why? To put it simply, locating and using reliable sources of information about your topic can help build your confidence, create a stronger and more interesting message, and establish your credibility as a presenter. Let's take a closer look at each of these points.

First, you want to feel confident when you talk to your audience. Research is the most direct way for you to learn more about your topic. If you do it well, you will know more about the subject than most of those sitting in your audience. During your research, you are also likely to find new information that you are eager to share with your audience. After all, you'll know something they don't. And when you share new knowledge with your audience, they will start to look at you as the expert—as the person in charge—and that vote of confidence in your knowledge and ability will most certainly give you a large boost of confidence.

Knowing a lot about your topic also helps to dispel some of the fears surrounding questions from your audience. Those most afraid of what the audience may ask are generally those who have the fewest answers to give. If you have "done your homework" on your topic and learned more than just the bare minimum needed to "fake it" through the main presentation, you will feel far more prepared and self-assured when you present.

Second, the content of your presentation matters. If you've ever sat through a boring presentation, you know this is true. Giving your audience information they already know is uninspiring and dull; your presentation needs to include information that is interesting enough to grab and hold your audience's attention. If the content of your presentation is based solely on your personal knowledge and experience, you are likely to repeat common information or well-known facts. "Boring! We already know this!"

On the other hand, solid research allows you to do things like quote a well-known expert, provide a startling statistic, or give an example from current events. These types of supporting evidence show your audience you have much more to offer them than just your own opinion. Research helps you find those key pieces of information that make your presentation both meaningful and worthwhile for your audience. As a side benefit, research also helps you organize and focus your message so that you stay on topic.

Finally, research builds your credibility as a speaker. Being credible means you demonstrate that you are a trustworthy presenter and that the content of your message is reliable. It is the *ethos* in Aristotle's three-pronged approach to persuasion. Your increased knowledge of the topic and the research findings you share will help your audience to see you as an expert. When you refer to specific resources you've found, you assure your audience that you took time to do your homework, and you demonstrate that the information you are presenting can be backed up by outside sources.

This builds your credibility as a speaker, which is essential if you want them to listen (and believe!) what you have to say.

Let's Get Started: How to Begin the Researching Process

Research should be the first step in planning your message. If you do some reading and research *before* your ideas are completely formed, you'll be able to integrate your outside sources into your content as it develops. Keep in mind that every main idea you offer needs supporting evidence. That establishes the credibility of your message. It makes sense to consider what information you have available as you determine what those main talking points will be. That saves you the hassle of scrambling to find sources to back up the things you're saying. If your ideas come directly from a source, you already have some of the support you need.

In addition to your topic ideas, you need two key pieces of information before you choose potential resources: your audience analysis and your statement of intent.

It's All About That Audience Again

When you begin to look for resources, your audience analysis will play an important role in finding the sources that are right for your audience—and thus are right for your presentation.

First, it is important to think about your audience's knowledge level—what they already know about your topic. Your audience analysis should identify this for you. **Knowing what your audience knows (or doesn't know) will determine the type of information sources you need to locate.** For example, if you're planning to speak to an audience about careers in medicine, you'd want to know whether they are incoming college students with little practical knowledge of the field, or if they are pre-med college juniors with more medical training and education. The entering college students need more general information, such as which science classes they should be taking and how to find a pre-med advisor. The more advanced students probably want information about various medical specialties and how to choose a graduate-level medical school. You would look for completely different types of resources for these two presentations, even though the general topic is the same.

Another consideration is identifying how technical or advanced your information sources need to be. This depends on the knowledge level of your audience as well. If they know a lot about a subject, they'll probably understand complex concepts better. If they know very little, a lot of jargon or complicated explanations will be confusing.

The audience knowledge level also helps to identify the type of sources they consider credible. It might be appropriate to quote *Time* magazine's latest medical report on advances in chemotherapy treatments if you are speaking to a group of college students. But it's probably inappropriate to use a popular magazine as a source when speaking to oncologists (medical doctors who specialize in cancer treatments). The sources that physicians would find credible would be scientific research journals that report medical findings to those in the health field, like *The New England Journal of Medicine*.

Finally, your audience's values and beliefs will also give you clues as to which sources to pursue. If you are speaking to a room full of hard-right Republicans about environmental issues, quoting or relying on research from Al Gore's[1] environmental work will hardly sway hearts and minds. Likewise, when speaking to a room full of hard-left Democrats, citing Fox News[2] as a source will not work to increase the credibility of you or your arguments. Instead, **you have to find the kinds of sources that your audience will respect—the ones that are either unbiased and beyond reproach or the ones that are well respected by your specific listeners.**

Keep Your Presentation Intent in Mind

Remind yourself what your goal is for your presentation. In order to keep your audience interested and engaged, they need to be learning something new. One of the frequent challenges during the research process is **information overload**, which occurs when you become overwhelmed by too many sources and too much information. When that happens, it becomes difficult to determine what information is appropriate for your presentation and what is not. This is where a clear statement of intent can help keep you focused.

Here's a helpful tip: **write or type your statement of intent on a note card or piece of paper, and keep it in front of you while you do research.** Whenever you feel yourself getting lost in the details or overwhelmed with too much information, refer back to your statement of intent. If the research does not directly support your presentation's intent, move on to the next source.

The Quest for Reliable Sources: Where to Look for Your Research

After you've carefully considered your audience and your intent, you need to begin your quest for appropriate types of sources. Your search will most likely include the campus library (either physically or electronically) and the Internet. Let's consider both of these avenues:

Loving the Library: In Person and Online

When you think of the library, you probably think of books. If you need a comprehensive source on your topic or a clear explanation of a difficult concept, a book might be helpful. Use indexes or the search function for an electronic book to locate the specific information you need.

For some topics, though, books might not be the best resources for your presentation. If you need ones that are more current, you can often find the best up-to-date sources through the electronic databases that your campus or local library provides. To see what online sources are available, go to your library homepage and look for tabs or links that say something like "search for articles," "article databases," or "electronic databases." These databases provide searchable indexes that will help you locate specific

---

1 Al Gore is the former Democratic Vice President of the United States under Bill Clinton. He also ran against—and lost to—George W. Bush in the 2000 presidential election.

2 Fox News is a 24-hour news channel known to have Republican leanings.

articles related to your topic in publications like newspapers, magazines, and academic journals.

The best general or multidisciplinary database to use to find articles from a wide range of resources is *Academic Search Premier* (EBSCO). Two other exceptional electronic resources that deal with current issues, and usually provide balanced coverage as well as facts and statistics, are *CQ Researcher* and *Opposing Viewpoints*. Many libraries have these databases available to you free of charge, and there are often detailed research guides or tutorials posted by the librarians to help you figure out how to use them.

Trouble navigating databases, Connor? Just ask a librarian for help!

If the prospect of navigating a library website or journal database is overwhelming for you, you should simply stop by the library reference desk and ask for help. Be sure that you bring with you specific information about the presentation you are planning, as well as any guidelines given to you by your instructor or supervisor. Most databases are relatively easy to use once you become familiar with the platform.

Using the Internet: Beyond Just Googling It

When you look on the Internet for sources, you most likely start with Google, Yahoo, or some other popular search engine out of habit. These search engines comb through websites, blogs, social media postings, and other information outlets to return the most relevant and most popular results. Relevance and popularity, though, do not make the sources *credible*. Much of what you find on the Internet is opinion—information that is unverified, exaggerated, or outright wrong. Just using Google as your guide will likely lead you astray. **You need to employ critical thinking in your research and approach Internet searches more systematically to find sources worth your audience's while.**

As a case in point, let's consider Wikipedia, the popular online encyclopedia generated by expert and non-expert users. Wikipedia is often a good place to *start* but it is *not* appropriate to use as one of your references. Wikipedia is an encyclopedia (when was the last time a teacher actually let you use an encyclopedia to write a paper?) that is written and edited by the general public, so it is *not* a credible source to claim as a reference. It should be used only for background reading and getting ideas for your topic, and all the information you read should be considered tentative until you confirm it through more verified sources. Sometimes, if you carefully examine the list of sources or further reading at the end of the entry, there might be links to primary sources that would be appropriate for your presentation or to further your research.

A better way to search the Internet for suitable articles is to use a specialized search engine like Google Scholar (scholar.google.com). This searches the Internet, but it specifically targets information on educational websites (generally posted by professors and librarians), so it will generally locate a higher quality of information than the results of a regular Google search. Google Scholar will at times fail to provide you with full articles (rather, many search results will just include citation information and an abstract), but if you look through enough of the findings, you will likely be able to find some useful sources.

If you truly need up-to-the-minute information on current events, Google also offers a news database (news.google.com). This specifically searches through news-agency websites, which are generally updated continually throughout the day. Moreover, Google will tell you when the article was posted to the news site (one hour ago, two days ago, etc.) so you can verify just how recent the information is. Just remember that not all news sources are created equal. Opt for articles from news agencies that are more likely to vet and corroborate their information, and avoid opinion or editorial pieces when looking for unbiased factual information.

Another idea is to use a search engine that looks only at a particular type of Internet source, like www.usa.gov, which delivers search results taken only from government agency websites. Presuming you are not a conspiracy theorist, the research and studies commissioned by the government are likely to be far more credible than the opinion of the random blogger.

One more resource of note is a website called "Noodle Tools" (http://www.noodle-tools.com/debbie/literacies/information/5locate/adviceengine.html). Although this site is primarily set up for grade-school research, the advice/links are quite useful. It lists kinds of information needs and provides links to Web resources that may be able to offer sources. While it isn't exhaustive, it can help get you started if you're drawing a blank.

When All Else Fails, Go Straight to the Source

In some cases, you might need to get more creative with your research. If you want to research how a local store trains its employees, you could spend a long amount of time seeking written or Internet sources and still come up empty handed. For all research questions, ask yourself where you should start looking. For a case like the local store, it would be best to go to the location and ask to speak to the manager.

In researching (and when you are citing), these types of sources are called *personal interviews*. Whether this is a formal sit-down with preplanned questions or just an informal chat where you took note of what the other person said, the classification is still the same. Be sure to note the person's name (first and last) and when the conversation took place. You'll need these facts to contextualize the information for your audience when presenting, and you'll need them to appropriately cite your source on your references list.

Evaluating Your Sources: Sorting through CRAAP

Whenever you find a source—whether it is in print or online—you should use your critical-thinking skills to evaluate its credibility. The commonplace joke of "I read it on the Internet; it must be true" pokes fun at just how blindly many people accept what they read. Just because someone wrote it and posted or published it, that does not make it

Table – Types of Sources

	Printed Materials	Library Databases	Web	Personal Interview
Examples of Sources	• Textbooks • Books • Journals	• Academic Search Premier • CQ Researcher	• Google Scholar • INFOMINE	• Experts in the field • Professionals
Strengths	• Detailed information • Print sources may be more credible than web sources	• Easy Searches • Save results • May have easy electronic access to full text documents	• Easy access • Can be very current (up to the minute)	• Draws on expert testimony • Can generate more leads/ information sources
Weaknesses	• Textbooks are not considered "scholarly" • Information may be out of date • Books and journals may be too technical • Dependent upon library collection	• Depends on library collection/ Website • May need some training for some databases	• Information may not be reliable • Careful evaluation of information is necessary	• Time consuming • Need to find the "right contact" • Often difficult to take notes

accurate, reliable, or true. If you in turn quote or cite sources that have little credibility, it is likely that at least someone in your audience will pick up on that, which will cast doubt on all the points you make and your own credibility as a presenter.

What follows are suggestions to help you gain or refine your **information literacy**—the ability to read and evaluate the credibility of information.

Know Your Source

While library databases and the Internet will produce dozens of potential sources, it is essential that you make sure to pay attention to those who are considered experts on your topic. Just choosing anyone who has something to say on the topic is an invitation for trouble. Lots of people use the Internet, and even some print sources, to share opinions on topics they don't know enough about. **To increase your own credibility, you need to cite people or organizations who are undisputed experts in that field of study.**

If you are new to your topic and don't know who reigns as current experts, ask your reference librarian for help. The expert can be an individual scholar or person with extensive experience, or it could be a nonprofit organization or government agency that acts as a repository for important current information on the issue.

For example, if you are presenting on the latest birth-control techniques, you should know that a very reliable source on reproductive health is Planned Parenthood. If you are talking about product safety recalls or the evaluation of consumer products, *Consumer Reports* is considered a reputable source. Specific nonprofit orga-

Joe, Shedeen, and Rheanna know to carefully evaluate their Internet sources before using them in a presentation.

nizations like the American Cancer Society can be the right place to start if you are doing general research about cancer. Government agencies like the National Institutes for Health (NIH) and the Centers for Disease Control (CDC) are the undisputed sources for official information on almost any health-related topic. Often the web sites for sources like these are a good starting place because they provide valuable background information as well as current news, events, and relevant statistics, all of which will be helpful to your presentation.

Be Choosy: Find the Sources that Are Just Right

Just finding any source is not good enough. You need to use your critical-thinking skills to make sure that what you find is a source that will not only add to your credibility, but will also make your presentation more interesting. If you just use the first two or three sources you locate with Google, your audience can usually tell, which can detract from your credibility.

One of the best ways to evaluate resources is to collect more than you need. If you are required to use two or three sources, collect more like five or six. When you sit down and compare and contrast these resources, it will be easier to determine which ones are the best for your main points, your overall intent, and your audience. Taking a few minutes to carefully select your sources will make the difference between resources that enhance your credibility and audience's interest level and those that merely serve as "filler."

The CRAAP Test

So, how do you find the sources that are just right? Miriam Library at California State University, Chico developed a list of questions to help you do just that. The test helps you evaluate your sources through five different criteria: Currency, Relevance, Authority, Accuracy, and Purpose (see table below). The test's acronym (CRAAP) is fitting for its purpose—to help you weed through the crap you are likely to find in Internet searches and other popularized sources to find the sources worth using. While the test's first two criteria of Currency and Relevance apply to *all* types of resources you consider, *the criteria of Authority, Accuracy, and Purpose are especially crucial when you evaluate Internet resources.*

Table – Evaluating Resources – The CRAAP Test

Criteria	Evaluation Question	Tips
Currency *Timeliness of information*	When was the information published or posted?	• Most sources should be dated within the last year or two. • Your topic may require more recent sources (e.g., technology information might be out of date in 6 months).
	Has the information been revised or updated?	
	Does your topic require current information, or will older sources work as well?	
	Web sources—Are the links functional?	
Relevance *Importance of information for your needs*	Does the information relate to your topic or answer your question?	• Watch for sources that seem related but really aren't. Example: Students researched providing meals to local residents who did not have enough to eat. Their resources were related to homelessness in our *state*. The state-wide statistics were not an accurate representation of the local area.
	Who is the intended audience?	
	Is the information at an appropriate level (i.e., not too elementary or advanced for your needs)?	
	Have you looked at a variety of sources before determining this is one you will use?	
	Would you be comfortable citing this source in your research paper?	
Authority *Source of the information*	Who is the author/publisher/source/sponsor?	• If you do not know if an author is an expert, look for information about the author's qualifications (education, employment, etc.) or try Googling the person or agency who published your source. • URL addresses ending in .edu or .gov are generally more reliable than .com.
	What are the author's credentials or organizational affiliations?	
	Is the author qualified to write on the topic?	
	Is there contact information, such as a publisher or email address?	
	Web Sources—Does the URL reveal anything about the author or source? Examples: .com, .edu, .gov, .org, .net	

Criteria	Evaluation Question	Tips
Accuracy *Reliability, truthfulness, and correctness of content*	Where does the information come from?	• This is the most difficult criterion to evaluate, especially if you are unfamiliar with your topic. Try looking for other unrelated sources on the same topic and see if they provide information that verifies what you have found.
	Is the information supported by evidence?	
	Has the information been reviewed or refereed?	
	Can you verify any of the information in another source or from personal knowledge?	
	Does the language or tone seem unbiased and free of emotion?	
	Are there spelling, grammar, or typographical errors?	
Purpose *Reason the information exists*	What is the purpose of the information? Is it to inform, teach, sell, entertain, or persuade?	• This criterion relates to the source's objectivity or bias. This is especially important for Internet sites. On websites you can often locate a mission statement or other helpful information about the organization's purpose on "about us" or "contact us" pages.
	Do the authors/sponsors make their intentions or purpose clear?	
	Is the information fact, opinion, or propaganda?	
	Does the point of view appear objective and impartial?	
	Are there political, ideological, cultural, religious, institutional, or personal biases?	

Source: https://www.csuchico.edu/lins/handouts/eval_websites.pdf

Give Credit Where Credit Is Due

Like in all other academic or professional ventures, you must give credit to your sources in a presentation. There are two primary reasons why citations are important. First, citing information from carefully chosen sources increases your credibility as a speaker. If you rattle off a list of facts or ideas without attribution to anyone significant, your audience might presume that everything you said was merely your own opinion or assumptions. Citing sources—particularly credible and expert sources—gives a needed veracity to your information so your audience knows to believe it. Moreover, citing expert sources makes you appear well read—that you know where to look and who the experts are. For example, if your presentation is about the Ebola virus and what we should do to prepare for a potential outbreak, you can find sources related to this topic almost anywhere. If you know enough to cite information provided by the Centers for Disease Control and Prevention (CDC), which is the national government agency responsible for managing such national health concerns, you would sound much better informed and knowledgeable than if you quoted a regional newspaper or a local doctor who appeared on the news.

The second important reason you must carefully cite your sources is that if you fail to give credit where credit is due, it is considered **plagiarism**. In the United States, we are extremely careful to preserve the intellectual property of others, and we have patents, trademarks, and copyrights to provide legal protection to those who publish their thoughts and ideas. Just like you have learned to ask before you borrow your room-mate's belongings, one of the most essential parts of being a responsible college student is learning how to properly "borrow" ideas and information from published sources so that you can use it correctly in papers, outlines, and presentations. If you fail to borrow information responsibly, it can be considered plagiarism, and the results can include a failing grade on your assignment, a failing grade in the class, or even academic dismissal from your school, depending on the seriousness of your offense.

It is not enough just to list your sources for your instructor on a sheet of paper. It is required that you clearly indicate *within* your presentation what specific information was borrowed from which source. When you do not specify an outside source, the implication is that the information or idea belongs to you.

There are several important types of citations your presentation will require:

- **Provide an oral citation of specific sources during your presentation**. A verbal citation requires that you state out loud where your information came from during your presentation. There are some obvious places where you should *always* stop and verbally state your source, such as when you use a quotation or when you report any numbers or statistics. If you're in doubt about whether to provide an oral citation, it is better to be safe and do so.

  Aloud citations do not need to mimic a written APA citation in which you list the author, year, and page number. Since your audience won't be able to look up your sources on the spot, it is more important that you give them the information they need to quickly evaluate the credibility of your source. For example: "According to an article in the *New York Times* last Sunday, New York City Mayor Bill deBlasio reported that seventeen city schools have missed more than twelve days of school during February due to the snow." The author of the article and the page number on which it appeared was unimportant for the audience to decide whether or not the information was trustworthy. What *was* important was who provided the information (New York City Mayor Bill deBlasio), where it was published (*New York Times*), and when it was published (last Sunday).

  For some academic articles—particularly those involving the hard sciences—multiple people may be listed as authors (sometimes more than ten people). You do not need to commit those names to memory for your presentation; that's a waste of your brain space. If one or more of the authors is a well-known name in the field, then, by all means, mention them. But if the names would ring no bells for your audience, use the credibility of the journal itself to highlight the article's veracity: "A 2014 study published in the *Journal of Applied Behavior Analysis* found that . . ."

- **Cite sources for all images and graphics on your visuals**. Give a brief citation on, next to, or under all pictures you have borrowed for your presentation. If you have or know the name of the photographer or graphic designer, use that. If it is a picture you got from the Internet without a specific caption that gives the source credit, cite the main website or the organization that posted the picture. For example: "Image from Hartford Chamber of Commerce website."

- **Provide written citations of sources for all written statistics and direct quotations on your visuals.** Particularly when you provide a specific fact, statistic, or direct quotation, you should clearly provide the source and the date in parentheses directly after the information appears in print, like this: (Microsoft Annual Report, 2014). Because the source and date of any statistic is an essential part of its authority, reliability, and currency, this type of citation helps demonstrate to your audience that this specific information is from a credible and carefully chosen source.
- **Compile all full-source citations in a separate reference list.** Just as you need to provide a full references list of all your sources at the end of a paper, you need to have a full citations list for your presentations. The citations should *not* be the last slide of your PowerPoint (no one will have time to look up those sources in the few seconds you leave it on the screen). Rather, the citations list should be on a separate sheet of paper or created as a separate document to be submitted to your instructor. If you were giving a presentation to a professional audience, you should likewise have a list of all your sources, just in case one or more audience members wanted to verify the information for themselves. Your citations list should not only include the sources you used for your information, but it should also include any citations for visual aids that need appropriate attribution.

Learning to Cite the Academic Way

Following a proper citation style may seem like a lesson in tedium, but proper citation style ensures that others can look up your sources to evaluate them for themselves. Moreover, the citation process often helps to alert you, in your research, to problematic sources: if you can't find an author, sponsoring organization, or date to complete the citation, those are major clues that the source is not credible enough to use.

You may already be somewhat familiar with a specific documentation format for listing your citations and references. Since you likely learned this in English class, you have probably been taught the Modern Language Association (MLA) documentation style. In the field of Communication, many professors prefer American Psychological Association (APA) style. Ask your instructor or check your syllabus to see which format you should follow.

Once you know which citation style to use, you can seek help for the basic formatting requirements in many different places. One possible source is your school's library website. Often the librarians will post guide sheets or helpful links to websites that give examples of documentation styles. Another excellent resource is the Online Writing Lab (OWL) from Purdue University (https://owl.english.purdue.edu). Most campus writing centers also have tutors to help you if you have not yet learned to cite sources correctly.

If you use online academic sources (like your library's database), your citation job might be even easier. Often electronic resources that are frequently used by students will provide a link that shows you how to correctly cite the source using APA or MLA. For example, if you use the electronic database *CQ Researcher*, you can click on a link they provide called *CiteNow!*, and it will display the correct citation format for the article you are viewing. Take a few minutes to examine your electronic sources carefully—some will make it very easy to cite correctly and quickly.

Research Skills Are Life Skills

While it may not seem like it at the moment, good research skills are a critical addition to the skills you'll need to make a successful career. We've been discussing research in an academic context, with a particular focus on how it applies to classroom presentations. But let's take that a step further. What happens when you have a job and your boss asks you to help make an important decision? Will you just rattle off the first thing that comes off the top of your head? Probably not. If an employer asks for your input, it's not just about your opinions. It's about the ideas and information that help you form an opinion or recommendation. What will you say if your boss asks, "Why do you think that?"

Research helps you to prepare well-reasoned responses to questions. They don't always have to be based on data and hard facts, but, more often than not, that's what professionals are looking for. We often overlook that the previously mentioned reasons for conducting research—to increase your confidence as a speaker, to offer valuable information, and to establish your credibility with your audience—are all a big part of establishing success in the workplace. If you can speak confidently about a topic that matters to your employer, as the "resident expert" you will be far more valuable as an employee. Research is the key in helping you gain that needed knowledge.

Research is a fundamentally important process in the message-planning phase of your presentation development. It grounds your presentation in credible and interesting information, it gives you a well-deserved aura of credibility, and that in turn increases your confidence as an expert. When it comes to presenting, the more you know, the more confident you'll be—and then you'll be a presenter worthy of your audience's rapt attention.

Key Takeaways

- Research allows you to provide relevant and interesting information to your audience, increase your sense of speaker credibility, and improve your own confidence.
- Use your audience analysis and statement of intent to guide your research process.
- Use the library for credible and reliable sources of information.
- Be careful and critical when searching for Internet sources. Apply the CRAAP method to ensure the value of the sources you find.
- To increase credibility and avoid plagiarism, cite sources appropriately: aloud, on visuals, and on a references list.

Questions and Activities

1. **Reflection Question:** Based on the information in this chapter, clarify why it is important to use support for every claim made by you in your presentation.
2. **Reflection Question:** Think of the presentations you've seen—whether they were given by your fellow students or given in the public sphere. What role did research play in the speakers' credibility? That is, did you find those who offered more research and verifiable information to be more credible than those who did not? Give specific examples to support your claims.
3. **Learning Activity:** Talk to people who present regularly (e.g., teachers and professionals), and find out the role of research in their field. Why is research important when trying to sell an idea, proposal, budget request, product, etc. to an audience or client?
4. **Learning Activity:** Choose a topic that interests you—any topic that interests you—and put that search term into Google. Look at the first website entry that comes up. Evaluate that source using the CRAAP test. Which, if any, of the five areas of the test did the website "pass"? Which, if any, of the five areas of the test did the website fail? Explain your responses.
5. **Presentation Preparation:** Look at the presentation you are currently preparing. What types of support are you using? Could you enhance the credibility of your presentation by using other types of support? If so, what types of support do you think you are lacking?
6. **Presentation Preparation:** Find three credible and reliable sources for your next presentation. Ensure that all three of your sources—whether they are electronic or in print—pass the CRAAP test.

Credits

CHAPTER 8

What Infomercials Do Right
Selling Benefits Instead of Features

After studying this chapter, you should be able to:
- *Explain the difference between benefits and features.*
- *Identify the key components in a basic presentational outline.*
- *Plan an effective introduction, body, and conclusion for your audience and intent.*
- *Practice "speaking in outlines" without scripting the words you will say.*
- *Map your movement effectively in your next presentation.*

You might be wondering if the title above is a joke. It is not; infomercials actually have some wisdom to offer.

Despite the perception that most of what is sold on television is useless junk, many infomercial-based products have achieved great success: the Snuggie, ShamWow, Bowflex home gym, Thigh Master, OxyClean, and Proactiv Acne Solution are just a few of many. Even the most ridiculous products seem to find some paying customers (go to YouTube and search for these infomercial gems: UroClub, Potty Putter, Tiddy Bear, ASpray, and Poo Trap). Why? Are Americans just mindless buying machines? Maybe. But another factor is the selling technique many infomercials follow, one that adheres to an important persuasive guideline you should also use: talk about *benefits*, not about *features*.

The feature of a product is a description of what it is and what it can do. It's the product's "specs," if you will. If you were selling the Pajama Jeans (a popular as-seen-on-TV product), the features would include the following facts:

- They are mock jeans.
- They are made from a cotton–spandex–denim blend.
- They come in a variety of sizes.
- They are $39.95, plus shipping and handling. (ThePajamaJeans, 2011)

The problem with just focusing on features is that doing so ignores the audience (which you, of course, know never to do). **A benefit shows the audience how a feature relates to them and their needs.** It includes the audience's desire to hear the sounds of that infamous radio station WII-FM ("What's in it for me?").

Benefits in Action: The Pajama Jeans

Consider the beginning of the Pajama Jeans television ad:

> Do you love stylish, sexy jeans? Do you love soft, comfy pajama bottoms? Now get the best of both worlds with Pajama Jeans, the hot, new fashion sensation that fits every figure perfectly. Pajama Jeans look like designer denim jeans: mock fly, front and back contrast pocket stitching, brass rivets, and smooth, butt-lifting design. (ThePajamaJeans)

Already, the commercial has focused in on *benefits* and spoken directly to the audience's needs and wants—they want jeans, and they want comfort. Bam! The Pajama Jeans can deliver both desires in one product.

When describing the look, the ad did not just offer a mere description; it said up front that these pants "look like designer jeans" (the crème de la crème) and that the design is "butt-lifting" (because no one wants a saggy rear end). Even the ad's description of the fabric does more selling than telling: "The secret is the cotton-spandex-denim blend that stretches to fit every figure perfectly like a sexy second skin."

Focusing on benefits should be your goal, too. Instead of only talking about a product's feature (like the fabrics used), tell the audience how that feature benefits them (like that the fabric gives the fit of "a sexy second skin").

Even the aspects of a product that might seem negative can often be sold as benefits. A forty-dollar price tag for stretch pants may seem high to the audience, but that didn't stop the ad from trying to sell the heck out of it: "A good pair of jeans could cost you eighty dollars or more, but now through this special TV offer, you'll get the designer-jean fit with Pajama Jeans for just $39.95!" (ThePajamaJeans). Comparing the price of their jeans to that of their "competitors" makes it seem as though the lovely people at Pajama Jeans are giving you quite the bargain.

For every aspect of the product or plan you pitch to your audience, you have to tell them why they should care. So what if the Pajama Jeans have a fuzzy lining? Well, that makes them as comfortable as your favorite pajama bottoms! Who cares if they have a boot-cut leg? That makes them sexy and stylish! The audience doesn't ever have to guess what this product can do for them; from beginning to end, the commercial is focused on benefits, and thus on the audience's wants and needs.

The Slobstopper: A Cautionary Tale

Of course, infomercials don't have all the answers, and there is plenty from the as-seen-on-TV world that you should *not* emulate. The most important infomercial tactic to avoid is exaggerating the audience's need. If there is no need for a product or plan, your audience will see through that, regardless of how well you think you've crafted the benefits. For a benefit to have some persuasive bite with your audience, the premise of your pitch has to be legitimate.

Take the sad case of the SlobStopper (yup, that's a real product name). The SlobStopper is a glorified adult bib intended for adult drivers to wear when eating or drinking in the car to protect their clothes from coffee or food stains. The commercial starts with a young man in a nice button-down shirt who's about to drink coffee in his stopped car. The lid to his coffee cup comes off as he tilts the cup toward him, and all its contents pour onto his chest and into his lap. To make matters worse, this all happens just as a pretty lady is walking by his car. Horror of horrors! She sees his unfortunate spill, and her previously come-hither smile turns quickly to a look of shock and disgust. As this whole tragedy unfolds, the ominous voiceover says, "Has this ever happened to you?" Most people would probably (hopefully!) respond, "Uhhh ... no."

Nonetheless, the commercial continues by now showing the same scenario, only this time with the huge SlobStopper bib securely fastened around the man's neck. He smiles at the woman walking by and again attempts to drink his coffee. But, once again, he can't quite seem to get the cup to his

Spilled coffee? Oh, well. At least he has his giant man bib!

mouth successfully and spills coffee on himself. This time, though, both man and woman smile, because everything is okay; he didn't spill on his clothes ... he only spilled on his giant man bib.

Of course, the presumption—the need upon which this whole product pitch was predicated—was that adults are incapable of drinking coffee or eating food without spilling on themselves in a toddler-like fashion. The ad, while comical to watch, didn't actually resonate with the adults for whom it was intended. Most of the ad's viewers probably wondered, "Who actually needs this?" And if the audience can't see themselves in the story being told, the pitch will fail. Audiences have real problems, real goals, and real values; speak to those rather than inventing or inflating issues in the false hopes that they will sway your audience.

What If You're Selling Ideas, Not Products?[1]

The persuasive pitch works the same for ideas as it does for products. There may be occasions when you're trying to convince someone to do something or think about an issue. Even though it's not getting them to purchase a product, you still have to "sell" the idea. You might try to convince your classmates to take a certain action, or you might try to persuade investors to fund the development of your product. Even in a job interview, you need to convince the interviewer that you are the best choice for the position. In all of these examples, regardless of the context, you're still in the position of "selling" the idea to people.

While the "product" is different in an idea pitch, the basic approach is still the same: you should focus on the benefits of the idea, rather than on its features. You probably already do this in your everyday life without even noticing. Let's say you and a group of friends are trying to make a decision about what to do for lunch. You could fix something at home, order take-out, or go out to a restaurant. If you were in favor of going out to eat, you might point out that there are lots of food options at restaurants, you wouldn't have to cook yourself, and you could go shopping right afterwards because you're already out. That quick list shows the benefits of going out to eat. And, if you sell those benefits well, you won't be stuck having grilled cheese sandwiches at home—again.

Tailor the Benefits to Your Audience

As you plan your persuasive presentation, start the message phase of AIMC by considering what realistic *benefits* your product has to offer. **This should be the basis for your persuasive presentation: selling benefits to your audience.**

Infomercials—unlike most presenters—sell their products to an incredibly vast and varied market. If you've done your audience analysis well, you will have the benefit of knowing your much smaller and more specific audience better. Therefore, you can ensure that the benefits you include in your presentation speak *directly* to your audience's needs. If there are features you find fascinating that aren't relevant to your audience, leave them out.

For instance, if you're selling a ShamWow (an absorbent cloth) to a group of sports-car fanatics at a car show, focus on how the cloth can be used for streak-free car cleaning. If you're talking to parents of young children, concentrate the pitch on how effectively the ShamWow can clean up juice spills and other kid-related messes. **Keep the pitch relevant to the audience.**

Remember that any persuasive pitch will come with a time limit. Make sure that you are using that limited time wisely to sell your plan or product effectively to the audience in front of you. You don't need to cover every feature to be persuasive; much of it would be boring and irrelevant to your audience. Instead, **focus on your audience's needs and on giving them valid reasons to buy your product or implement your ideas.** Sell the real *benefits* for your audience—don't just rattle off features—and you will find persuasive success to be far more attainable.

Key Takeaways

- Focus on *features* rather than *benefits* when attempting to persuade audiences to do or buy something.
- A concentration on benefits helps audiences answer the question, "What's in it for me?"
- Make sure you don't invent or exaggerate the need for your plan or product; speak to the real needs of your audience.

Questions and Activities:

1. **Reflection Question:** Search YouTube for a thirty- or sixty-second infomercial (beyond the Pajama Jeans and Slobstopper ads). Watch the commercial a couple of times. Then critique its approach, using the following questions as guides:

   - Whom do you think is the target audience for this commercial?
   - What benefits did the commercial claim the product has?
   - Did the benefits speak to the target audience's needs?
   - Was the premise/problem of the commercial believable?
   - What did you find particularly effective about this commercial? Explain.
   - What was least effective about this commercial? Explain.

2. **Reflection Question:** Think about a time when someone tried to sell you something in a person-to-person contact (whether over the phone, online, or in person). What was the product or idea being sold to you? How well did the sales pitch focus on benefits rather than features? Did the benefits speak directly to your wants and needs as the potential customer? Did the pitch convince you? Why or why not?

3. **Learning Activity:** In class, choose a product to sell and a target audience. Focusing on benefits only, pitch your product to your target audience in a short, one- to two-minute presentation.

4. **Presentation Preparation:** Use your audience analysis research to decide how best to pitch to your audience. Make a list of the possible *benefits* of your plan or product. Then narrow down that list to the best three to five. Make sure that the benefits you choose are realistic (don't overinflate their impact) and that they speak directly to the audience's needs and wants.

Credit

1. Spilled Coffee? Copyright © 2015 by Audrey Mora. Reprinted with permission.

CHAPTER 9

Speaking in Outlines
How to Organize Your Presentation

After studying this chapter, you should be able to:
- *Explain the importance of using a clear organizational structure when presenting.*
- *Identify the key components in a basic presentational outline.*
- *Plan an effective introduction, body, and conclusion for your audience and intent.*
- *Practice "speaking in outlines" without scripting the words you will say.*
- *Map your movement effectively in your next presentation.*

I have heard a number of presentations that probably seemed brilliant to passersby: the speaker was eloquent, the stories were engaging, and the facts were interesting. The organization, though, was confusing and convoluted. What results from such scenarios is that audience members each remember different fragments—that funny story or that little-known fact—but they lose the bigger picture. The audience is entertained, but they are not led to the conclusion the presenter had wanted. The problem, in a nutshell: the presentation's intent is not met.

A common presentational pitfall occurs when presenters feel compelled to tell their audience *everything* they know or found in their research about their topic. This pitfall is quite fittingly known as the **data dump** (Weissman, 2009). **Remember that audiences don't need to know** *everything* **there is to know about your topic;** too much information will overload and overwhelm them, and they will therefore retain very little of it. Start by ensuring that your statement of intent is focused on an achievable goal, and then diligently adhere to that focus by only including the information that your audience needs to hear and that will help you meet your intent.

To ensure your audience understands the basic ideas of your presentation and can follow you to your conclusion, you need to definitively organize your ideas. Clear structure is at the heart of a successful presentation. Your audience will not be able to remember long lists of unorganized facts and stories, but if you chunk your information into clearly organized main points, listeners will have a much higher retention rate (Lindley, 1966).

Good organization won't just help your audience's memory; it will help yours as well. One of the great fears of presenters—especially of those without scripts, notes, and wordy PowerPoint slides—is that they will forget something. Think about it: if you tried to remember a long list of facts to share with investors in your presentation about a product you designed, you might find the task difficult. If, however, you grouped your facts into three main points—the product's wide potential market, its profitability, and its uniqueness among competing products—you will be much more likely to remember them. And even if you forgot a fact or two along the way, you still would have shared the three overarching reasons why your product is a smart bet for investors. Those are the most important points for your audience to remember.

The key to good organization is to **map your movement** throughout the presentation. In other words, you want to keep your audience informed of where the presentation has already been, where it is currently, and where it is headed so your listeners can easily follow along. This is not a thriller movie; there is no need for unexpected twists and turns. Being overt in your organization will help your audience see the most important points you make. To do this, you need to follow a clear structure and include organizational cues throughout your presentation.

Basic Structure: Introduce, Prove, and Conclude

While the specific flow of your ideas will differ from presentation to presentation, most times you should follow the same basic structure. This basic structure is commonly used in speaking, and is most similar to the organization you would use for a research paper; this means your audience will know it and be able to follow it easily:

1. Introduction – introduce your audience to the basic point of the presentation.
2. Body – make and prove your main points.
3. Conclusion – summarize and remind your audience what you covered.

Let's look at each of these sections in more detail by considering a potential presentation with the intent of warning college students about the dangers of unintentionally or purposefully pirating music online.

Introduce: Orienting the Audience to the Ideas to Come

Just like in writing, the introduction's goal is to grab the audience's attention and orient them to the main topic. A solid beginning will include four steps: an attention-getter, a self-introduction, a thesis statement, and a preview.

1. **Grab attention:** A good introduction starts with a strong opening line. First impressions happen right away, so you want the first words out of your mouth to be something more substantial and captivating than, "So, um, hi. My name is Jane, and I'm here to discuss piracy laws." Instead, an interesting question, factoid, or anecdote could better set the scene:

   In October of 2007, Jammie Thomas-Rasset was found guilty of sharing twenty-four songs on Kazaa, which was a music-sharing program similar to Limewire. In March of 2013, the Supreme Court refused to hear her appeals case, essentially upholding the guilty verdict. Her punishment for sharing only these twenty-four songs? *222,000 dollars* (Haskell, 2013). Online piracy is a *big deal*.

Deliver clear, numbered previews to let your audience know what to expect.

2. **Introduce yourself:** *After* you have captured the audience's attention, you can give a self-introduction (first and last name). It also helps to tell the audience your credibility on the topic. If you have studied piracy laws or have run into your own legal troubles with file sharing, then share that connection with your listeners.

   When your self-introduction is complete, you can discuss any necessary background or introductory information your audience might need to understand the rest of the presentation. If there's nothing more that needs to be said, then you can just skip to the next step

3. **State thesis:** The thesis is an upfront statement telling the audience the point of your presentation. It is similar to the statement of intent you have already crafted, but the thesis should be worded for the audience: "My goal here is to help you understand piracy laws and how they relate to sharing music files, which many of you do." Be sure that you additionally share why the audience should care about this topic: "By understanding these laws, you can hopefully avoid being in the same boat as Ms. Thomas-Rasset."

4. **Preview main points:** The preview is essentially the agenda for the body of your presentation. You should list all of the main points you will cover in the order in which you will cover them: "We will explore three important points: first, we'll look at some copyright laws that relate to music sharing; [pause] second, we'll pinpoint what these laws mean you can and can't do; [pause] and, third, I'd like to hear from you about what you pirate so we can discuss what specific consequences you could face if you got caught."

   The preview may seem like unnecessary filler, but I assure you it is not. Audiences like to know what's coming up before it happens. It helps to set the stage for what is to come, the same way a meeting agenda or wedding program would. As an added bonus, if you forget mid-presentation which main point should come next, you can simply ask the audience: "What did I say I would talk about second? Oh, yes: what these laws mean for you. Thank you!"

Prove: Filling the Body with Substance

The body is the part of the presentation in which you discuss each of your main points. It is generally preferable that you choose between three and five main points, depending on time restraints, since audience members will not be able to remember much more than that.

Remember that it is better to go into more depth on a few main points than it is to brush over many. Be realistic in terms of what you can cover well in the time restraints you are given. You do *not* need to cover every facet of your topic, product, or plan; you only need to highlight what is most relevant and important for your audience to know. If they have questions beyond what you choose to share, they'll ask, and you can provide that information then.

Once you have decided on your main ideas, how you arrange them is up to you. For some main points, there may only be one logical order. For others, though, the order may not matter as much. If that's the case, put your strongest points first and last; your audience is most apt to remember what is said at the beginning and what is said at the end, so be sure to anchor the ends of your presentation with the "good stuff."

The internal organization of each main point will vary, but there is a basic guideline you should follow for all your points: **for every claim, there must be adequate support.** You do this by following five basic steps: make a claim, explain it, prove it, summarize, and transition.

1. **Make a claim:** This is your main point, said in a clear statement: "The laws on copyright are clear that sharing copyrighted music files is illegal."

2. **Explain it:** Give more detail on your claim in one or two sentences: "Songs are protected pieces of intellectual property. Just like the shirt on your back is property you own, the music Justin Timberlake records is *his* property."

3. **Prove it:** For your audience to accept and believe it, you need to provide specific proof to support it. Proof can come in many forms: statistics, research findings, stories, demonstrations, and audience activities are just a few types. The point here is to give your audience some tangible evidence that what you say is true. By the end of your main point, your audience should be able to say confidently that they believe what you told them.

   In our sample piracy presentation, your proof could perhaps be an explanation—in simple terms—of what the Copyright Act of 1790 says about intellectual property. Then you could mention a more recent update to copyright law by explaining the No Electronic Theft (NET) Act of 1997's stance on online piracy. Including the support of what these laws actually say gives more intellectual weight to your arguments (and makes you seem more credible) than if you had merely stopped after the Timberlake analogy.

   This step of providing specific proof is essential to building your case, yet so many presenters skip over it. **The proof is needed to make your arguments valid and logical.** Otherwise it may just seem like your unsubstantiated opinion. That means that if you want to make a claim but can't prove it, then *don't make that claim*. It would be unethical to make unsubstantiated claims to your audience just to try to sway their opinions.

4. **Summarize:** At the end of each main point, summarize what you have just said: "So, the Copyright Act of 1790 and the NET Act of 1997 make it clear that we do *not* have the legal right to share music files just because it's easy to do it." The summary serves two functions: (1) it helps to reiterate the takeaway message of that main point, and (2) it signals to the audience that you are about to move on.

5. **Transition:** While the summary is the signal that you are about to move on, the transition is when you actually move on. This is a sentence you include to move into the next main point or the next section of your presentation: "Now, let's look at how these laws dictate what you can and can't do with music online." Include transitions between the introduction and body, between each of the main points, and between the body and the conclusion.

A Note to Job Hunters

The first four steps described here also work wonders when answering questions in a job interview (which is, in essence, a sales presentation in which you are the product). DiSanza and Legge (2012) call it the **four-step process**: answer briefly (i.e., make a claim), explain your answer in a couple of sentences, provide concrete testimony (i.e., specific support), and reconnect your answer to the original question (i.e., summarize). Imagine that a job interviewer asked you this: "We are looking for someone who can lead a team effectively. Do you have any leadership experience?" Now, picture your four-step answer:

1. **Make a claim:** *Yes, I do have quite a bit of leadership experience.*
2. **Explain it:** *I have served as president of my university's community-service organization and as a resident advisor on my floor. Even in my schoolwork, I tend to end up in leadership roles in group projects.*
3. **Provide specific support:** *For instance, in the last team presentation I did for my presentations course in college, we had a lot of tasks to accomplish in a short amount of time. The professor suggested we elect a team leader, and my teammates chose me because I have a level head, and I am good at keeping timetables. I set up a schedule and we all chose the tasks we would be best at accomplishing. Even though we were all pretty different people, I kept us focused on the goal, and we ended up getting an A.*
4. **Summarize:** *So as a leader, I'm able to keep the peace and keep my team focused to get the job done.*

That answer not only sells your skills, but also *proves* that you have leadership experience by explaining exactly what you did.

Conclude: Ending Your Presentation with Impact

Once you have made your claims and proven them, you can wrap up your presentation. The conclusion is the shortest part of the presentation, and only includes three quick steps: review, restate the thesis, and end with a clincher.

1. **Review:** This is the ending equivalent of the preview. Simply restate the main points you made in the order you made them; no extra explanation is needed: "So, we discussed what online piracy laws are, how they relate to online music sharing, and the lawsuits that have resulted."
2. **Restate thesis:** Reiterate what the purpose of this whole presentation was: "Hopefully today you have learned about online piracy laws and how they could affect you."
3. **End with clincher:** A clincher is a definitive ending that drives home the final point (the "take-home" message for your listeners) and signals to your audience that the presentation is done, and that they can now begin their thunderous round of applause. Consider this ending: "So the next time you want to hear a new song, resist the temptation to get it illegally. Give iTunes your money; saving a dollar isn't worth the potential costs of a lawsuit." Isn't that so much better than the awkward, "And, um, yeah … So, that's it!" that ends far too many presentations?

No Scripts or Pseudo-Scripts Allowed: How to Use an Outline Effectively

It is crucial to note that while I have given you a clear outline to follow, you should not use this as an excuse to write out detailed plans of what will go in each section. Resist the urge to write a pseudo-script.

Planning out all of your words will make you sound too formal and over-rehearsed. Presentations should sound like *talking*, not like *reading* or *reciting*. If you write out a list of facts and commit them to memory, you will sound too robotic when you give the presentation. You are supposed to have some expertise on your topic (even if that expertise comes from recent research you've conducted); delivering a prewritten speech hurts the audience's perception of your credibility.

Moreover, planning your presentation in excruciating detail will bar you from being able to adapt effectively to your audience. Your presentation should not be a one-way transmission in which you unilaterally send a message to your audience. This is supposed to be a two-way street—a *conversation* between you and your audience. You have to leave a lot of wiggle room in your presentation plan to account for that audience interaction.

So, how do you plan out the presentation if you can't write it all down? Jot down *really short* phrases on a basic presentation outline to remind yourself of the points you want to make. Only put notes where you need them; don't add anything extra (like your name next to self-introduction) or you will start to head down the dangerous path of scriptwriting and memorization. The actual content of

---

Basic Presentation Outline

I. Introduction
    • Grab attention
    • Introduce yourself
    • State thesis
    • Preview main points

Transition into Main Point #1

II. Main Point #1 piracy laws
    • Make a claim
    • Explain it   Copyright Act of 1970
    • Prove it   NET Act
    • Summarize

Transition into Main Point #2

III. Main Point #2   Court cases
    • Make a claim
    • Explain it   P2P sites
    • Prove it   CDs
    • Summarize   Individual Use

Transition into Main Point #2

IV. Main Point #3   Ask audience
    • Make a claim   about pirating
    • Explain it   Legal consequences
    • Prove it
    • Summarize

Transition into Conclusion

IV. Main Point #3
    • Review
    • Restate thesis
    • End with clincher

---

your sentences shouldn't need to be on the outline. You're the expert; it should be in your head.

Take a look at the outline pictured to the right. This illustration represents the amount of notes you should need to help you organize and prepare your presentation. (Please note: you will *NOT* use this outline to present. It is for *preparation and the first stages of practice only!*)

This very basic outline can serve as your blueprint to make sure your presentational flow works well. Talk through the presentation a few times while looking at this bare-bones outline. You will undoubtedly say your message differently each time, but this is a good sign: it means you are able to just *talk* about the topic rather than recite a lecture on it.

Get It in Your Head: Learning to Talk in Outlines

In addition to practicing the specific content of your next presentation, you should also practice speaking about *any* topic in an organized way. Here's a fun activity (well, at least I think it sounds fun): give yourself a nonsense topic to talk about in an impromptu presentation. *Without preparing what you will say*, look at the outline above (ignoring the blue notes), and talk your way through each step. The goal is not to come up with brilliant content, but rather to follow all of the organizational steps and clearly map your movement throughout. It's the organization cues that matter in this exercise.

Let's say your topic is the alphabet, and your main points are A, B, and C. Use the outline in Figure 2.2 and try to get through an entire presentation following the steps. Start with your attention-getter: "A-B-C. It's easy as 1-2-3. As simple as Do-Re-Mi, A-B-C, 1-2-3, baby, you and me, girl" (Gordy, Perren, Mizell, & Richards, 1970) and move through each remaining step of the outline. Here is a sample of what you could say after your musical first line through the first main point:

- Self-introduction – *My name is Jane Doe...*
- Thesis – *... and today we are going to explore the first three letters of the alphabet.*
- Preview – *We'll start first with A, [pause] then move onto B, [pause] and finally end with C.*
- Transition – *But first, let's start at the beginning with A.*
- Make a claim – *A is a vowel that can make two different sounds.*
- Explain it – *It can make a long sound—AY—or it can make a short sound—AH.*
- Proof – *There are many words that start with the long A: ape, angry, and age are just a few. There are also many words that start with the short A, like apple, alligator, and astronaut.*
- Summarize – *These two sounds and all of the words they start make the letter A a great first letter.*
- Transition – *Now that we have discussed the amazing letter A, let's bounce our way over to the beautiful letter B.*

You'll notice that this is not the most eloquent or cleverly worded example, but that's okay; impromptu presentations rarely are. The point of this exercise is to drill the *organization* into your head, not to get you to talk poetically. The more you practice talking in an organized manner, the more it will become second nature to you.

Learning to "talk in outlines" will be a tremendous benefit to you as a communicator. If someone asks you a two-part question, you will be quick to answer with, "I hear this as a two-part question. Let me start with your first concern about the cost, and then I'll address the availability" (a heck of a preview!) or after you finish the answer, you'll say, "Now that I've addressed cost and availability, does anyone else have any questions about any other facet of our product?" (a stellar transition!).

Good presenters are able to speak in an organized manner, whether or not they've had time to prepare their content. They nonchalantly talk in lists, include transitions, and provide frequent summaries; organization just seems to come to them naturally. Well, it probably doesn't come naturally; it comes from lots of practice.

I know the idea of practicing how to "speak in outlines" may seem silly, but this is an incredibly valuable skill to have. If you want to be understood easily when you present—or even just talk—learning to speak in a highly organized fashion will be a large leap in that direction.

Organizational Cues: Tips for Mapping Your Movement

Throughout the entire organizational structure, there are other tips you can follow to help map your movement for your audience:

- **Use extra summaries.** It's helpful to end each main point with a summary, as was already mentioned, but it's also helpful to include summaries whenever you have finished a long explanation. Let's say it took you three or four sentences to explain the legalese surrounding the Copyright Act of 1790. Sum up the main takeaway for your audience before moving on: "So, basically the Copyright Act protects intellectual property for fourteen years." This will ensure your listeners understood the "moral of the story" before you move on.
- **Use extra transitions.** Major transitions are worked into the basic organizational structure already described, but transitions between minor points are also helpful. So after discussing the Copyright Act of 1790, you might say, "Now, let's fast-forward all the way to the Internet Age to look at the No Electronic Theft Law, also known as the NET Act."
- **Use signposts.** If the organization of your presentation is your metaphorical road map, then signposts are the street signs along the way. Words like *first, second, third* or *then* and *next* help the audience know the relationship between the sentences and ideas in your presentation. Use clear signposts, rather than relying on the words "and also."
- **Use lists.** When you can, chunk information into lists, and then number off each point for your audience. Lists not only help to organize information neatly and succinctly for your audience, but they also help to alert them that something important is coming.
- **Pause appropriately.** Sometimes even all the right verbal cues get lost on an audience when the presenter races through the presentation at warp speed. To make previews, reviews, transitions, lists, and signposts really effective, you have to pause a little before or after them so they stand out to your audience.

Organize with Your Audience in Mind

As with every aspect of your presentation, your audience should be in the forefront of your mind when planning your organization. When you've successfully figured out your organizational structure, talk through each section of your outline and critically think to yourself, "Does my audience need to know this? Does this appeal to them? Will they care?" If the answer is "no" to any of these questions, adjust your content or approach and try again.

Not only should you include the type of content that will appeal most to your listeners, but you should also ensure that your organizational structure allows room for you to engage directly with the audience. Don't cram so much into the outline that you have no time for talkback and interaction. If you don't readily converse with your audience when presenting, then consider more carefully how you can work it in. When can you ask them questions, get their feedback, have them participate, or get them otherwise involved? Jot it down on the organizational structure and plan for it in your time.

The key takeaway of this chapter is that **organization is important—to you and to your audience.** When you are asked not to write a script, it is tempting just to talk freely and abandon organizational conventions. When your presentation's structure is lacking, though, so will your audience's understanding. Keep practicing aloud with the organizational structure provided so that previews, summaries, transitions, and reviews will come easily to you as you speak. Being able to talk clearly in a well-ordered fashion will serve you well in presentations and in all areas of your communication moving forward.

Key Takeaways

- Clear organization is essential to a successful presentation and successful communication.
- Use previews, summaries, transitions, reviews, signposts, lists, and pauses to clearly map your movement.
- Only write down short phrases on your outline to plan your content.
- Practice using the bare-bones organizational structure to prepare for your presentation.
- Once you've put together your content, think of how you will *engage* the audience!

Questions and Activities:

1. **Reflection Question:** Use your laptop, tablet, or cell phone to record yourself answering one of the following questions. Don't plan out the answer ahead of time. Answer this immediately after reading it:

A. What are your two best qualities as a presenter?

B. What two areas of your presentation style need the most improvement?

C. What are two things you love about your favorite television show?

D. If a genie could grant you any three wishes, what would your first two be (no wishing for more wishes)?

Review the recording of your answer and listen for your natural organization. Did you use a preview? How about transitions? Now try to answer it again, this time clearly **mapping your movement** through the answer. Watch your second attempt. How did it compare to the first try? If you were an audience member, would this be easier to follow than the first version?

2. **Learning Activity:** In the section on learning to talk in outlines, there is an example of an impromptu presentation on the first three letters of the alphabet. Choose a nonsense topic below (or make up one on your own) and do your own impromptu presentation. Remember, the point of the exercise is to speak in a highly organized manner. The content you give doesn't need to be particularly brilliant or insightful.

3. **Presentation Preparation:** Use the outline from earlier in this chapter to practice talking through the points of your next presentation. If you are still in the early planning stages, do a rough talk-through, using the outline, to see what information is needed, what is extraneous, and if your main points make sense for the intent of the presentation.

> **"Nonsense" Topics:**
> Numbers: 1, 2, 3
> Primary colors: red, yellow, blue
> Coins: penny, nickel, dime
> Basic driving gears: forward, neutral, reverse
> Disney characters: Mickey, Minnie, Pluto
> Summer months: June, July, August
> *Harry Potter* characters: Harry, Ron, Hermione

Credit

1. Deliver Clear, Numbered Previews Copyright © 2015 by Audrey Mora. Reprinted with permission.

CHAPTER 10

Say Whaaaat?
Using Easy-to-Understand Language

After studying this chapter, you should be able to:
- *Explain the importance of using easy-to-understand language when presenting.*
- *Identify the ways in which you can make your language easier for your audience to follow.*
- *Use terms, sentences, and metaphors that will increase audience understanding.*

In almost every presentation you give, your goal will be to provide new information to your audience. Whether you are there to clarify a difficult concept, explain your brilliant new plan, or convince them to invest in your cutting-edge invention, your audience needs to gain new information. And guess what, kid? They're lookin' at you.

It seems like explaining a new idea to someone (or, in the case of presenting, to a group of people) would be an easy task. Many presenters, though, miss the mark on this point, mostly because of their own expertise on the topic.

What seems obvious to you in your level of expertise may be completely foreign to someone else. Let's say, for instance, you are trying to explain how to use Microsoft Word to someone who has an extreme technological deficiency:

As with all presentation preparations, you must start with the audience. Use your audience analysis, particularly the findings on the audience's knowledge level, to find out just how simplistically you need to communicate your information. **Put yourself in your**

audience's seats and try to imagine what they already know and in what areas they could most benefit from your brilliant explanations.

Beyond the scope or depth of information you choose to share with your audience, you should also consider what type of language you will use. Whether your audience knows quite a bit about your topic or knows nothing at all, you should aim to speak simply and clearly. Doing so will allow for maximum clarity. After all, you want your audience to be able to focus in on your *ideas*, not spend large chunks of the presentation tapping each other on the arm and asking, "*What* is she saying?"

Here are six tips to help you keep your language easy for others to follow:

1. Use Simple Terms

When you have been in a field of study or in a job for a while, you will probably begin to use the jargon of that discipline. If you are talking to an audience who may not know those terms, then opt for simpler explanations. In teaching communication to non-communication majors, for instance, I try to avoid using terms like *self-reflected appraisal*, *cognitive dissonance*, or *epistemology* when simpler terms or explanations will suffice. If you must use an industry-standard term your audience won't know, make sure you define it clearly and frequently.

Beyond jargon, it is also important to avoid big words for the sake of big words. Don't say *conflagration* when you can just say *great fire*. Avoid *lackadaisical* when *lazy* will do. Ditch *propitious* and instead use *favorable*. Spouting off the terms from your word-a-day calendar will only make your listeners' job that much more difficult. Make it easy on them, and use the words you would normally include in an everyday conversation.

2. Use Shorter and Simpler Sentences

When you write, your sentences can be long and poetic. In speaking, though, that wordiness can be difficult for your audience to follow. Read the following sentence aloud: "While it is obvious from looking at this chart that your collective knowledge level of RAM (Random Access Memory) is lacking, it is essential that we delve into the topic so that you can gain enough insight to be able to successfully purchase a new computer." Yuck. That is unnecessarily complicated for your listeners. Using shorter sentences is easier for your audience to comprehend, even if you end up turning one long sentence into two or three shorter ones. Consider this reworked version of the above sentence: "This chart shows that many of you don't know much about Random Access Memory. So, let's learn more about it so you can be confident when you buy your next new computer." Wasn't that much easier to follow?

Beyond making your sentences short, make sure that the sentence structure is simple. Don't overcomplicate statements by using difficult sentence structures or phrases. One of the more common examples is the phrase "being that": "Being that this is the first product of its kind, you should really want to invest in it." Instead, try, "This is the first product of its kind. For that reason alone, you should want to invest in it."

3. Be Descriptive and Specific

While it is important not to use overly complicated words when speaking, it is equally important not to use overly vague ones either. If you want to guide your audience's minds toward your information and conclusions, you'll need to avoid giving them reasons to mentally veer off course. If you were telling a story about your new computer as an example of why learning about processors is helpful, you should avoid a sentence like, "So, I loaded some stuff onto my computer and started playing with some programs." The audience might be left to wonder: "What *stuff* did you load? Which programs did you use?" And while they play the mental guessing game of what you meant to say, they will find it difficult to continue to listen to you completely. **Be more descriptive and specific in your speaking to make your ideas easier to understand:** "So, I loaded an Excel spreadsheet and two Word documents to my desktop, and then I started playing alternately with iTunes and Minesweeper."

Be sure, too, that the nouns and adjectives that you use adequately define what you intend to communicate. Words like *things*, *stuff*, *good*, and *bad* are not particularly descriptive. If you say something is "good," do you mean it is *acceptable* or *exceptional*? Or perhaps you meant it was *well-behaved*, *reliable*, or *bona fide*? Choosing the right word will make that intention clear.

4. Use Metaphors

When attempting to introduce new concepts to non-expert audiences, it can often be helpful to relate the new idea to a concept your listeners already know and understand. For instance, if you were discussing what the central processing unit (CPU) of a computer is to a nontechnical audience, you may have difficulty explaining its functions in a way your audience can understand. Technical explanation after technical explanation will keep whizzing right over your listeners' heads.

If, however, you used a metaphor to describe the CPU, you could harken back to something the audience already understands, like the human brain: "The CPU is the brain of the computer. If I gave you a math problem, your brain would do the calculation. The same is true for the CPU."

You could even continue the metaphor throughout other points in the presentation: "Just like some of our brains work more quickly than others, some CPUs are better and faster than others. You want to make sure your CPU is capable of handling the workload you give it. You wouldn't expect the brain of a kindergartner to be able to calculate advanced physics problems, so you shouldn't expect a basic-level processor to be able to handle complex computer programs."

5. Translate Numbers

Numbers can also prove tricky for audiences to grasp quickly, particularly those numbers that are excessively large or excessively small. **Whenever you have numbers to share that don't belong in a chart or graph, consider how you can make them easier for your audience to understand.** One step you can take is to round off complicated numbers.

Unless it is essential that the audience know that profits were exactly $198,352, then instead say that they were just short of $200,000.

The other option is to translate those numbers for your audience into something they will comprehend. Yes, your audience can understand that twenty-five tons is a lot of weight, or that a nanometer (one billionth of a meter) is very small. But translating those numbers for your audience will give them a *better* understanding of just how big or small they are. For instance, you could note that twenty-five tons is about

25 tons = 3 full-grown, male African elephants. That's a lot of weight!

the weight of three full-grown male African elephants. You could also point out that a nanometer is a thousand times smaller than the width of a single strand of hair. "Wow," your audience might think, "that really *is* small!"

6. Use Repetition

Repetition is an important part of any presentation. Professional presentation audiences rarely take notes on all of the speaker's points; repeating yourself will help some of the more important ideas to stay in the audience's minds.

As discussed in previous chapters, repetition is part of the very structure of speaking itself: the preview, review, summaries, and transitions all help to reiterate the main points of your presentation.

In addition to organized repetition, you can repeat words, phrases, or sentences for emphasis. Let's say you wanted to impress upon your audience the importance of not posting anything incriminating on Facebook or other social media sites. As evidence, you tell the unfortunate story of twenty-four-year-old Ashley Payne, who was forced to resign from her job as a high-school English teacher after a parent complained about a Facebook post showing her holding alcohol (Moriarty, 2011): "She was forced to resign because she was *holding alcohol* in a picture on her private Facebook page. She wasn't actively drinking it. She didn't look drunk. She was just *holding alcohol*. She even sued to try to get her job back, and she lost that suit. Why? Because she was *holding alcohol*." Through the repetition of the phrase *holding alcohol*, you can hopefully impress upon your audience just how cautious they need to be on social media.

Check Audience Understanding

Despite all of the brilliant advice given above, your audience may still have questions or be confused about your topic. To find out if this is the case, it never hurts to just ask them directly: "Do you all understand how data mining works before I move on to discuss how you can protect your information from it?"

Yes, questions in the middle of your presentation may take you slightly off course, but audience understanding is essential for presentation success. If a detour will help you reach the ultimate goal, then the "scenic route" is worth taking.

Simple Language, Happy Audience

Following the guidelines for easy-to-understand language will help your audience decipher your message clearly and accurately. When you are preparing difficult content to share in a presentation, think through how you might incorporate these suggestions:

- What does your audience need explained?
- What words should you define?
- What is a metaphor you can use?
- How can you translate your numbers?
- What is the best descriptor for this product?
- When should you pause to ask for questions?

Thinking through these matters will make a big difference in the comprehension rate of your audience. And if you want them to follow through on your presentation's intent, you need them to understand what's going on.

Key Takeaways

- Use language your audience will be able to understand easily so they can focus on your message.
- Use simpler terms and sentences, specific language, metaphors for ideas and numbers, and repetition to make your language easy to understand.
- Check in with your audience frequently to be sure they understand what you are saying.
- Think through your message from the audience's perspective to see where you can improve the language you use.

Questions and Answers:

1. **Reflection Question:** Think of the presentations you have given or the ones you have seen. Identify a presentation in which the speaker violated one or more of the rules for language given in this chapter. Identify the rule, and explain how it was violated. What was the result? How could the presenter have better presented that portion?
2. **Learning Activity:** Translate the following measurements into easy-to-understand metaphors (like twenty-five tons = three full-grown male African elephants). This may take some creativity and quick research to do.

A. 10,000 liters
B. 250 feet
C. 25,000 pounds
3. **Learning Activity.** Describe your favorite childhood toy to the class using clear, descriptive, specific language. Avoid vague words.
4. **Presentation Preparation:** For your upcoming presentation, make a list of all the words or acronyms you need to define. Then—in your own words—give a simple definition for each aloud.
5. **Presentation Preparation:** Identify a metaphor you can use to discuss your topic or one of your main points. List the similarities between the actual concept and the metaphor.

Credit

1. Computer Copyright © 2015 by Audrey Mora. Reprinted with permission.

CHAPTER 11

Give Them a Good Story

With contributions from Joseph Alan Ullian

After studying this chapter, you should be able to:
- *Articulate the importance of using narrative techniques in your presentations.*
- *Identify the key components of a good story.*
- *Craft stories that are relevant to your audience's needs and values.*
- *Tell a story like you mean it.*
- *Incorporate humor into your stories in a relatable way.*

It was his turn to present, and the classroom of students settled down for what they inevitably anticipated to be another dry presentation. He was normally monotonous and relatively lifeless when talking in front of the class. Nerves would take hold of him and render him impassive. No anticipated that this time would be any different. His presentation started out much the same as his others—peppered with facts and delivered statically. But when he launched into a story about kids at his old middle school who had started their own fight club, á la the hit 1999 movie, the mood in the room changed. He retold the ridiculous antics of these sixth graders, who would fight in the bathroom for fun before lunch, and how they were inevitably caught: "They broke the first rule of Fight Club ... by talking about it, so there's no way there were going to get away with it." The audience began to laugh—not in raucous hysterics, but the mood lightened nonetheless. The audience eased up and leaned in to hear more, and the presenter's nerves started to melt away.

Storytelling is a powerful presentations tool. Not only does it liven up the room, but it also makes concepts easier and more palatable for your audience. Audiences are used to making sense of information and events through the structure of storytelling. Stories bring a realism and emotional connection that abstract facts and figures lack. They make your audience see, understand, feel, and remember your message more distinctly than lists of information do.

Help Your Audience Visualize

Storytelling should be one of the easiest techniques for a presenter to use. Watch a young child, and you can see that the gift of storytelling is one we have had since we were tots. Yet when many enter the realm of "professional presentation," they abandon their tale telling and stick just to the facts. In presentations in which we are trying to captivate, persuade, or at least hold the attention of our audience, a facts-only approach is bound to fall flat. Think of a teacher who stands in front of the class and communicates only straight facts for an hour without including anecdotes or personal examples. *Bo-ring.*

Now think of the best storytellers you know—the ones who can make you laugh aloud, choke up from sadness, or wince with fear. Their gift is that of *visualization*—allowing their audience to picture the story in their own heads and to feel as though they are "in it." This tactic is one that should be incorporated into your business stories.

So, how can you get your audience to connect to the story and visualize it well? Several suggestions can help you reach this goal:

- **Use clear, descriptive language.** Why settle for "It was a sunny day," when you can instead say, "The sun was streaming through the trees, showing off the bright green of the freshly emerged leaves. It looked like one of the happy scenes in an animated Disney movie ... just without the singing"?
- **Use metaphor and simile.** Describing the heat from the sun? Try, "The sun was beaming down on us like the type of bear hug that makes you feel loved but also a little suffocated."
- **Use traditional storytelling elements.** You have likely had stories read to you since before you could grasp the concepts in them. Call up classic narrative elements so the story feels "natural" to your audience.
  - **Context** – the setting and needed background information for your audience to understand the story.
  - **Protagonists** – the heroes and heroines. These are the people the audience should be rooting for, the ones they can identify with. If your story is about your audience members or their business, then they would make the most logical choice for this role.
  - **Antagonists** – the villains. Competing businesses, efficiency problems, and disadvantageous circumstances could all make for worthy narrative opposition.
  - **Plot line** – complete with a beginning, middle, and end.
  - **Conflict** – the main issue(s) the protagonist must overcome.
  - **Resolution** – the solution to the conflict. Perhaps the product, plan, or company you are pitching to your audience can provide the resolution your protagonists seek.

Stories have grabbing power. A list of ideas you may rattle off to your audience is just that—a list of ideas. While it may inform the audience and explain your company, the problems your audience faces, or the solutions to those problems, it will not grab and hold onto your audience the way a good story can. Good stories engage your audience.

Tell *Their* Stories, Too

Some well-placed anecdotes about yourself may add a little punch and intrigue to a persuasive pitch, but the most important stories you can tell are about *the audience*. After all, they're the ones you are trying to convince. Show them that you care about what's important to them by incorporating their story into your presentation. This really is the essence of the *right* story: making it about your audience.

Let's put this into practice. Let's say that you are trying to convince the technology office at your college to spend the money needed to improve your campus's wireless

Internet range and strength. You might believe it to be sensible to tell a story that exemplifies why college students need this improved Wi-Fi:

> The poor Wi-Fi reception on this campus is really a problem. The other day I was scheduled to give a presentation for my communication course. I had worked really hard on perfecting my PowerPoint presentation and emailed it to myself so I could retrieve it in class. Well, when I tried to open up my email on the classroom laptop, the page wouldn't load. Because we were in a basement room on the outer edge of the campus, I couldn't get Internet service. There was no Ethernet cord in the room to use, and no one else in the class could get an Internet connection. As a result, I had to present without my PowerPoint presentation, which resulted in an automatic point deduction and completely messed up all that I had planned to say and show. It was a disaster, all because of bad Wi-Fi.

Now, that story has nice description and—if told well—could be illustrative and captivating, but it misses the persuasive mark. This entire story is about the *presenter*; it doesn't speak to the needs and concerns of the audience. Even a compassionate person in the tech department might respond with, "Tough break. Next time try saving the PowerPoint to a thumb drive" (that would be my response, anyway).

The problem is that you haven't told your audience why *they* should care, why *they* should be moved to action. Remember, audiences want to know WII-FM ("What's in it for me?"). If you did your audience analysis well, you should have some idea as to what values your audience holds: speak to those. Here's an alternative story, now focused on your audience at the technology office:

> The poor Wi-Fi reception on this campus is really a problem. Last semester, I served as a tour guide for high-school juniors and seniors considering whether or not to come to this school. Someone from almost every group I led commented about how they couldn't get decent Wi-Fi coverage on their phone. This is really problematic. Students are getting the impression that we are a technological "dead zone." I know how hard you've worked to keep this campus on the cutting edge of technology, but if we don't have consistent and reliable Internet access across this campus, students won't care about Smart Boards and Blackboard. Getting better Wi-Fi *needs* to become a priority.

Would this definitely convince your audience to dole out a ton of cash to improve the Wi-Fi coverage? Maybe not—that would take more evidence and arguments—but the message is more audience-focused. It's less about you and more about the core values of your target audience.

Make the Point Clear

Your audience may respond to a good story, but they will easily tire of a story with no focus or point. If you are making the stories about your clients, those points will probably be inherent in the telling. It helps, too, to directly point out the "moral" of the story. Don't make your audience guess at your main point (they do enough of that in literature and poetry classes).

In the Wi-Fi example I just gave, the last two lines gives that point to the audience: "I know how hard you've worked to keep this campus on the cutting edge of technology, but if we don't have consistent and reliable Internet access across this campus, your hard work will be overshadowed by that deficiency. Getting better Wi-Fi *needs* to become a priority." That line could then be followed up with a discussion of your solution: a better Wi-Fi network.

Tell It Like You Mean It

In an interview with *Forbes* magazine about his call for more "enlightened leadership," entrepreneur Deepak Chopra (Goudreau, 2011) said that "in all my research, the greatest leaders looked inward and were able to tell a good story with authenticity and passion." To be a great presenter, you should be able to do the same.

Stories require enthusiasm and emotional connection. If the narratives in your own presentations still seem too stiff, follow these storytelling tips:

- **Use inflection.** That is, change the tone or pitch of your voice as you talk. When your voice never fluctuates or doesn't indicate the emotions of the story, those feelings don't get transferred to your audience. If the story is happy, sound happy. If it's sad, sound sad. Don't let monotony drag down your effectiveness.
- **Use a conversational rate.** Unless you are an exceptionally fast talker, use a normal conversational rate to convey your story. Going too slowly will make the story seem too stale and canned. Just be sure to leave slight pauses in between sentences so the audience has time to absorb what you have said.
- **Engage your audience.** Stephen Denning, author of *The Springboard: How Storytelling Ignites Action in Knowledge-Era Organizations*, notes that "A focus on the story alone, to the exclusion of the interaction between the storyteller and the listener, misses the point of storytelling. It is the interaction of the storyteller with the listeners and the communal meaning that emerges from the interaction" (137). Toward that end, keep your audience engaged. Make direct eye contact. Respond to their laughter, shock, or disapproval ("I know! I felt the same way!"). Keep them involved and engrossed. If the audience isn't absorbed in the tale, there isn't much point in telling it.
- **Don't over-rehearse.** Memorized stories run the risk of losing their authentic feel. In classes I have heard over-rehearsed storytellers span both ends of the inflection spectrum—some have been overly monotonous (they lost their narrative passion) and others delivered their stories in such a sing-song tone, I wondered if the presenters believed their

Look alive, Joe!

professional audience was actually a classroom of kindergarteners. Your normal, enthusiastic storytelling voice is best. Don't try to memorize the exact lines of the story, or you might lose that natural feel.

- **Look alive.** Think of when you are excited to tell a story to a friend. You probably don't stand perfectly still like a Marine at roll call as you relay the tale. If something is really big, you might stretch your arms apart to indicate the size. If something is odd or unusual, you might make a puzzled face. If something is funny, you might grin widely or even laugh a little. Do that in your presentation, too. *Professional presentation* does not mean *devoid of personality*. Keep your movements respectful (no middle-finger salutes) but lively.

- **Act like you believe it.** Better yet, just believe it. If you don't have and demonstrate conviction in what you are saying, you cannot expect your audience to believe in it either. Let your genuine enthusiasm shine, and your audience will be far more likely to engage with your tale and believe in its lessons.

Above all, tell a story like it's a story. Don't allow the conventions of formal speaking to dampen the narrative abilities you have been cultivating since childhood.

Make 'Em Laugh: Using Humor in Your Stories

Oftentimes the best stories—the ones our audience members will remember the longest—are the ones that appeal to emotion. If your story isn't intended to be maddening or saddening, then consider whether or not a bit of humor will fit.

You may believe that you just aren't a funny person, but you don't have to be a stand-up comedian to tell a funny story. The absurdities of life often provide enough humor to use in your tales. **Don't worry about punch lines; instead, use humor more subtly:**

- Tell stories with funny twists or descriptions (e.g., "When you're working in a team, you may get that one teammate who thinks he knows it all. Let's call him Super-Genius Sam").
- Make small comments that will make the audience smile (e.g., "My name is Jane Doe, and I am the new vice president of sales. My mom is so proud, by the way").
- Include dialogue that allows the audience to picture themselves there (e.g., "So I say to the poor unsuspecting customer, 'Um, sir, I'm not sure how to tell you this … but … your fly is down'").
- Act it out (e.g., "So, he turns around and tries to do a subtle little zip of the pants, but [you make a surprised face and tug at your zipper as though it is stuck] he gets his zipper caught on his shirt").

An important note: Humor can be powerful, but it can also be dangerous. Avoid humor that makes fun of other people. You can have a good-natured chuckle at other people's *behaviors*, but no bit of humor you use should feel like a personal attack on anyone. Every audience member will have different sensibilities, and making fun of someone—especially for traits they cannot control—will turn laughs to scowls all too quickly.

You may wonder, then, about self-deprecating humor. You can poke fun at yourself a bit, but don't mock yourself for a lack of confidence or poor presentation skills. Your audience won't want to listen to someone who admittedly has no idea what s/he is doing.

Humor should not be the primary reason you tell a story; stories should be included when they prove or exemplify something important. Nonetheless, humor can be a beneficial by-product of a narrative. If your attempts at humor fail, though, don't despair; the story should still have some logical appeal that made it worth including in the first place.

Stories as Powerful Presentation Tools

Stories have much to offer presenters, and even more to offer audience members. In presentations, it is of utmost importance to keep your audience's interest. If they lose interest, even the best facts and arguments made in a presentation will fail to sway your audience. Stories, though, can break up the monotony of fact-based lectures and data-driven doldrums.

Remember that presentations, at their core, are conversations—exchanges of ideas between *human beings*, not robots or computers. Humans like stories. Narratives can breathe life back into presentations and organize information around easily digested themes. Use that power.

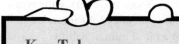

Key Takeaways

- Stories make concepts easy to understand and more interesting for your audience.
- Help your audience visualize your stories through the language and story elements you use.
- Tell stories that speak to your audience's needs, wants, and values.
- Make the morals of your stories clear to your audience by saying them overtly.
- Tell your stories in a lively and engaging way.
- Humor in your stories can be a powerful tool, but it should be used cautiously.

Questions and Activities:

1. **Reflection Question:** Who is the best storyteller you know (it could be someone from your personal life or someone in the media)? What qualities does s/he possess that makes him or her such a good narrator? What steps can you take to demonstrate those same qualities?

2. **Learning Activity:** Pretend you are a representative from a public-relations firm. You want to convince Company A to contract your company to do their PR work, because you believe your services will give them a competitive edge over Company B. Devise the elements needed to use a narrative format for your presentation by identifying the different components of their story below (since these are fictitious companies, you can create fictitious scenarios and "plots"):

   Protagonist: Company A

   Antagonist: Company B

   Context:

   Plot line:

   Conflict:

   Resolutions:

3. **Learning Activity:** Think of a funny story that happened to you or that you witnessed personally. Tell that story to the class, trying to follow the guidelines for good narrative delivery.

4. **Presentation Preparation:** Think of a story that you could use for your upcoming presentation. Be sure that it is relevant and illustrative of one or more of your main points.

Credit

CHAPTER 12

Involve Them and They Learn
The Power of Audience Participation

After studying this chapter, you should be able to:
- *Explain the importance of using audience participation in your presentations.*
- *Identify the different ways you can incorporate audience involvement in your presentation.*
- *Choose the type of audience interaction that will work best for your presentation.*
- *Facilitate audience involvement effectively.*

The great American forefather Benjamin Franklin notably said, "Tell me and I forget. Teach me and I remember. Involve me and I learn." **Presentations should include audience involvement**— after all, it is one of the three channels[1] for your presentation. Remember that your presentation should mimic a conversation, and—unless you are a terrible conversationalist—that means that there should be some back and forth, some give and take.

Sure, your audience always gives you feedback, whether or not they open their mouths. Their facial expressions, their body language, their eye contact (or lack thereof) are constantly communicating to you. But if your audience members really are the most important people in the room, then they deserve more of a presence than just a few sideways glances or silent nods of approval. In other words, **whether it's to get their feedback or to help them learn a concept, you should aim to** *directly involve* **your audience in your presentation.**

Encouraging audience participation is valuable for several reasons:
1. **It keeps them awake.** Lectures are boring. How many times have you tuned out your parents or your teachers when it was clear your input didn't matter one iota to their one-way sermons? Giving your audience a voice gives them a reason to pay attention.
2. **It helps you to adjust your message appropriately.** Despite your excellent audience analysis, you won't know *everything* about your audience while you plan your message. Letting your audience give their input into the presentation will help you continue to tailor your message to them, even as you give it.
3. **It allows you to make meaning together.** Facilitating expert Robert W. Pike (1994) makes an important point in his book *Creative Training Techniques Handbook* (so important, in fact, that he calls it a *law*): "People don't argue with their own data." Involve your audience in proving points so they can reach the same

---

1   As a friendly reminder, the three channels of AIMC are you (your delivery), audience interaction, and visual aids.

conclusions as you. It will mean more to them if they are involved in the proof than it would if you just told them the fact.

Audience interaction livens up listeners and makes them more engaged in what you have to say. An active and attentive audience is far easier to present to than a bored or grumpy one.

So Happy Together: Ways to Include Audience Participation in Your Presentation

Ready to try it, but don't know how? Here are some ways to work audience participation into your next presentation:

Questions

The most common type of questions presenters like to ask audience members is the "raise-your-hand-if" variety, but frankly, those are also the most boring, predictable, and detached type. **Ask your audience open-ended questions so they can *really* have a voice.**

For instance, if you are doing a presentation on how your classmates can improve their customer service skills, you could start by asking the audience if anyone has a good customer service horror story. Talk to that participant about his or her experience and flesh out the details of the incident. Then you can use that story as your guiding example through the presentation: "Fred, if you had tried this method, perhaps the customer would have cooled off a little and not gone to your manager."

Other interactive questions to try are knowledge or opinion questions. In your customer service presentation, for instance, you could tell your audience a story of a particularly difficult customer or scenario. But before you tell them the actual resolution to the problem or the suggestions you would offer to handle it, you could ask the audience what *they* would do. Yes, they may give you some crazy answers, but that's okay. Flesh out their ideas and allow the audience to debate a little, if you have time ("Do you all agree? You would lock the door on the customer and put up a 'Keep Out' sign?"). Then, you can judiciously give the "correct" answers: "Let's look at what the experts say we should do." Keep coming back to their suggestions to explain (kindly) why their ideas were ineffective (or perhaps to applaud them when their suggestions were ideal).

Libby follows up a hand-raising question with more direct audience engagement.

If you *really* want to ask a hand-raising question, you can; just be sure that you follow up the audience's response with some interaction: "Keep your hands up if you say *yes*. Now, everyone, look around the room. Most of you believe that Jane was justified in her reaction to the customer. Well, sorry, folks, but experts would say that all of you with your hands up are wrong."

Direct Application

Having your audience practice the suggestions you give them will help the information "stick." Direct-application exercises are quick ways your audience can enact or apply the lessons you are trying to teach. For instance, don't just *tell* your audience the correct way to shake hands in a business encounter; follow up your explanation by asking your audience members to shake the hands of the people next to them. Then they can critique each other's grip, eye contact, and facial expressions based on the criteria you gave them.

Demonstration

If you want to make a point that can be demonstrated easily in front of your audience, consider whether one or more audience members can help you make that point. If you wanted to show your audience how to properly greet a client in Japan, you might call up an audience member to act out the greeting as you describe it. If you're trying to sell your audience on a product, why not give the audience a product demonstration? To make firm believers, it helps to let a lucky audience volunteer or two to try out the product themselves firsthand.

Workshop Activities

Workshop activities are longer forms of audience participation. In these situations, the presenter *relinquishes control to the audience* (don't worry; it's not as scary as it sounds). Activities should only be done when you have the time to do them; don't try to squeeze one into a ten-minute presentation, or both you and your audience will feel rushed.

Activities allow audience members to work together and practice the skills or concepts you have taught them.

Workshop activities allow the audience to try out the concepts you presented on their own; they are means of direct application not tightly controlled by you. For instance, if you wanted your audience to practice responding to customer concerns by following the guidelines you gave, you might set them off into groups of three—one customer, one service representative, and one critical observer—to act out some scenarios you provide them.

While this activity happens, your job is to be a quiet (and, at times, helpful) observer. Roam around from group to group, listening in on what they are doing. Make some small interjections or corrections as needed, but mostly let the audience control their own participation. Then discuss the results as a full group again.

Choosing the Right Interaction

Which form of audience participation you choose will depend on your comfort level, your time limitations, and what makes the most sense for the content you are presenting. Either way, though, you should aim to include *some* level of participation in your presentation. If you do, your audience will be more engaged. That, in turn, will make them more likely to learn what you are trying to teach or buy what you are trying to sell.

Rules of Engagement: Tips on Letting Your Audience Participate Effectively

Involving your audience in your presentation may seem scary. What if they hijack the conversation? What if they ask you questions or bring up issues you're not prepared to answer? What if the audience gets too rowdy, and you can't get them to refocus?

All of these are valid concerns, but none of them are good enough to avoid participation. Follow the tips below to help you use participation effectively and preserve the integrity of your presentation's message:

Make It Fun...or at Least Engaging

Happy audiences are the best kind; they're less cynical, they're more engaged, and they associate their positive feelings with your presentation, company, or product. **Find an activity your listeners will enjoy doing or will at least feel motivated enough to complete.** Asking an audience of college students to start writing a cover letter during a presentation on effective job searching will likely result in a lot of blank stares, heads on tables, and unmoving pens. Let your audience engage their bodies, their senses, or their social skills; don't just give them more paperwork. All work and no play make Jack a dull boy … and you a dull presenter.

Make Sure It Serves a Purpose

The activities you select should be fun and engaging for your audience, but only if they're relevant to your presentation's intent. If, for instance, you are doing a presentation on how to use hand gestures effectively in workplace communication, you might misguidedly think to yourself, "What's a really fun hand gesture I could have my audience do? Jazz hands? The live-long-and-prosper sign? Flipping the bird?" I would hope that you would realize that none of these "activities" would benefit the intent of your presentation (and the last one certainly won't help with your professionalism). So, before you ask your audience to "wave their hands in the air if they just don't care," ask yourself, "As funny as this activity is for the audience, does it *really* help me meet my presentation's intent?" Unless your audience foresees being transported to a hip-hop concert circa 1995 the next time they walk into work, the answer is a clear-cut "no."

Give the Audience Guidelines

Just telling the audience to complete a workshop activity without any guidelines leaves the audience with many questions: "How long do we have to do this? How are we going to share the results? What are the rules for the activity?" Don't make your audience scramble to figure out what their role is; lay it out for them as clearly as you can:

> I want you all to pair up with the person next to you. Up on the screen is a recap of the four-step procedure we discussed for answering interview questions. I've given each of you a list of common interviewing questions. One of you will ask one of the questions on the paper, and your partner will then try to answer the question honestly using the four-step procedure. You can look at the screen for reference; this exercise is about making sure you *say enough* in the answer, not necessarily how fluently you say it. Interviewers, help to give your partner feedback after they've given their answer. Then switch and have the other person ask the questions. Keep going back and forth until I call time. You will have ten minutes, which means you should be able to get through a couple of questions each. You don't need to write anything down. Do this all aloud, and I'll come around and give you some feedback, too. Are there any questions before we start?

Give your audience clear instructions, rules, time frames, and other parameters for the assignment. Then ask if anyone has any questions, just in case you forgot to mention something you should have. **Clear guidelines will help to keep the participation orderly and purposeful.**

Keep Control, but Not Too Much

It's important not to let participation get out of hand, but **how much control you exercise over your audience during their involvement really depends on the nature of the exercise.** If you're asking individuals to answer open-ended questions, you should yield control long enough to let someone give his or her answer completely. Then you can re-take the reins to facilitate the next contribution. If you are doing a workshop activity—a more independently run participation exercise—you can map out clear guidelines for your audience and then set them off to their tasks. Don't hover over the groups or individuals, but do keep at least some presence so everyone stays focused and you can answer any questions. Check in periodically on how they're doing: "How are we doing over here?" Comment on their progress: "Great job on that answer; just don't forget to tie it back to the original question at the end." Shout out time-limit remainders to the entire audience: "Five more minutes, everyone. You should be on your last scenario." Let them know you're around, but stay out of their faces.

Make It Challenging, but Not Frustrating

Let's imagine your presentation focuses on how your audience can learn to hold their tempers when dealing with particularly grating customers. This would be an *ineffective* start: "How many of you believe that it's important to hold your temper when dealing with a customer?" Umm ... *everybody*. I would hope anyone paying attention would raise their hands. Who in the audience is thinking, "Oh, no. It's much more appropriate when you cuss them out and throw things at their heads"?

If the exercise you do is that incredibly obvious to your audience, there really is no point in you doing it (remember, you want to give your audience *new* information). On the flip side, you don't want to give them an activity that is so complicated they'll give up partway through from sheer frustration. Find the sweet spot somewhere in between, where your audience can gain new insight but still be able to complete the task. The best way to figure out if your questions or activities are too hard or too easy is to try them out on people similar to your audience and see how well they do.

Allow Opportunities to Process the Information as Groups

There are many individual activities that may be appropriate for presentations. In a workshop on dealing with teamwork, for instance, you might want to start by giving all audience members a self-test on conflict styles to figure out what their particular strategies are for dealing with discord in a team. But, when the entire workshop activity from start to finish is individual, it is less engaging for the audience. Participation exercises mean more when your audience members can talk about them with other people. After your conflict-styles quiz, for instance, you could put people into groups and have teammates compare their styles to each other. Then they could talk about how well they probably would or would not get along in a team.

Even for short direct-application exercises, you should still have participants talk about it as a group, whether they do so as one big group or in smaller groups. For audience members to be able to make meaning together, they need to have an avenue to communicate with each other.

As an added bonus, having audience members process aloud in groups allows you to eavesdrop on their conversations and find out how well they are understanding your points or how they feel about the topic.

Use Competition with Caution

Competitions can be helpful in motivating participants to get involved, but even if the prize is just a piece of pre-chewed gum, some audience members will let the adrenaline of the competition overpower them. If you want to use competition to liven up your audience, go for it. Just give very clear rules so there is no whining or arguing about whether or not this answer counts or whether or not what that team did was cheating. (I know you think your audience would be too old for this kind of immaturity, but I can tell you from experience ... they're not, no matter how old they are.) If the competition gets too crazy and the audience gets too combative with one another, feel free to stop the exercise, laugh off the tension, and try a different tactic.

Tell Them the Point

It may seem obvious to you how the exercise you just had the audience do fits into your presentation's intent, but audiences like to be hit over the head (metaphorically, not literally) with each point you make. Wrap up each exercise with a clear statement telling your audience how they can apply these skills, these findings, or this activity to what they are supposed to be learning or gaining from this entire presentation: "I know you only shook each other's hands for a short while, but use the feedback your partner gave you to help you adjust in the future. Getting the right grip, eye contact, and smile is important in making a good first impression."

Participation: Fun but Finicky

Incorporating participation into your presentation takes finesse. Take heart in the fact that most audiences are well behaved. They want to gain something valuable from your presentation, and they know that playing by the rules will help them get it. You likely won't need the facilitation expertise of Jerry Springer (or his bodyguards) to be able to pull off engaging participation activities. When audiences fall off track, gentle redirections will often be enough to bring them back. But if you do get a wild crowd that could rival that of a trashy TV talk show, look at the bright side: at least your audience will remember the presentation, and you'll have a heck of story to tell next time.

Key Takeaways

- Audience participation is an effective way to keep your listeners engaged and to more closely mimic the conversational style ideal for presentations.
- Use questions, direct-application exercises, demonstrations, and workshop activities to keep your audience involved in the learning or persuasion process.
- Choose amusing, purposeful forms of interaction of the right difficulty level that allow audience members to work together.
- Give the audience guidelines for their involvement, but don't exert too much control over how they do engage.
- Use competition carefully to ensure that audiences have fun and stay motivated, not get stressed out or start fights.

Questions and Activities:

1. **Reflection Question:** Consider a presentation you have given in the past that involved no or very little audience interaction. Explain the presentation's audience, intent, and message. Then identify types of audience interaction you could have included in that presentation to make it more engaging for the audience. Explain specifically how you could have done the activities.
2. **Learning Activity:** Choose a simple activity for your audience to do (like folding a paper airplane). Explain the steps or concepts to your audience, and then explain the parameters of the activity (time limits, guidelines, etc.). Let your audience do the activity while you practice facilitation skills. Check in with your audience to make sure they are on track, but avoid micromanaging or taking over.
3. **Presentation Preparation:** Decide on two audience-participation exercises you could use in your presentation. Choose the types of exercises that are best suited for the audience, intent, occasion, and time limitations.

Credits

CHAPTER 13

Calling an Audible

The Art of Adjusting to Your Audience

After studying this chapter, you should be able to:
- *Articulate the importance of adjusting to your audience throughout the presentation.*
- *Identify strategies for reading and responding to listeners' nonverbal cues.*
- *Adjust to audience members' interruptions.*

Presentations are like conversations, and as has been mentioned throughout this book, presenters must conform their presentations to their audiences—not just in the planning stages, but while delivering them as well.

Think of a typical conversation you have had. You were likely not the supreme director of where that conversation headed. That is, you probably had some items you wanted to talk about within the exchange, but exactly how the conversation progressed was not completely under your control. In dialogues, both parties are active participants, and thus both parties can influence the direction of the conversation. The same ought to be true for presentations.

Good presenters include and adjust to their audience members. The previous chapter has already discussed ways in which you can involve your listeners in your presentation, but beyond planned interactions, your presentation should be flexible enough to bend to your audience's will.

Let me give you an example of when my husband and I were shopping for new windows. We were trying to decide between two different companies for the job, and the sales associate for the first company was going through his preplanned sales pitch:

Because this sales associate didn't adjust his presentation to us, we ended up feeling intensely annoyed, and he ended up losing the sale. As my husband said to me after the sales associate left, "Even if we go with [Company A], we need to find another contact person, because I don't want to give *that* guy any commission."

Customers, clients, and audiences know that they are the most important people in the room and that you are there to meet their needs. They expect—and should have—presentations tailored specifically to them. Proper planning and audience analysis is a crucial first step in doing this, but on-the-spot adjustments are often needed to make sure that your presentation reaches its ultimate intent.

In football, the team has a plan for advancing the ball down the field before everyone lines up to make the play. But sometimes the quarterback has to make last-second changes to the game plan when they reach the line of scrimmage, based on the opposition's formation. It's called **"calling an audible."** In presentations, you may often have to make the same kind of in-the-moment adjustments.

I recognize that saying "Adjust to your audience" is much easier said than done, so let's look at some advice for various audience situations with some "Dear Aimee C.[1]" letters:

Dear Aimee C...

Afraid to Look

DEAR AIMEE C.: I am new at presenting, and the idea of having to pay attention to my audience is overwhelming to me. Isn't it enough that I have to remember what to say *and* try not to faint? How am I really supposed to do this?
   TERRIFIED OF PEOPLE

DEAR TERRIFIED: I know that looking at your audience seems scary, but direct eye contact will actually help put you at ease. Looking at one person at a time while you talk will make it easier—more like a one-to-one conversation—than it would be to scan over a sea of heads. If you focus on one person at a time, the same way you would in a dialogue, you'll be able to gauge whether that one person agrees or disagrees.
   And if you still struggle to read people well, then plan to stop often and ask, "Does anyone have any questions, confusions, or concerns so far?"

Confused Faces

DEAR AIMEE C.: I practiced my presentation today in front of a few of my friends, and they looked really confused when I talked. I thought I used clear language and good organization, but somehow it just didn't stick. I don't know if my friends just aren't as smart as I thought they were or if I'm doing something wrong. What do I do if my real audience gets that confused, too?
   SMARTER THAN MY FRIENDS

---

1   Aimee C. ... AIMC ... get it?

DEAR SMARTER: Did you try asking your friends what they found confusing? That might be a good place to start.

If you're convinced that your message speaks to your real audience's knowledge level, then proceed with that message. If your audience furrows their brows, looks around in confusion, or whispers to others to figure out what's going on, then stop. It's time to call an audible. Say to them, "It looks like some of you may be confused. Where did I lose you?" Then do your best to re-explain the points of confusion.

Bored, Bored, Bored

DEAR AIMEE C.: I tried so hard to make my last presentation engaging and exciting for my audience. Really, I did! And yet when I gave it, a few of my audience members just looked so bored. One was texting, one was staring off into space, and another even fell asleep! I was so frustrated! What should I do when this happens?
READY TO SCREAM IN THEIR FACES

DEAR READY: First and foremost, make sure your message and your delivery style are encouraging audience engagement and exuding enthusiasm. If you've done that, and you still have a few non-listeners, remember that presentations are contextual. Perhaps the time of day, the spot in which you presented, the weather, or their own bad sleep habits are causing this behavior. But even if the situation is not your fault, it is still your job to fix it.

Screaming into their faces—really, any screaming at all—is a bad idea. You must stay in control of your own emotions. Don't call them out directly or show others that you are annoyed by their lack of attention. Remember, you are not the one in the power position; they are. Your success depends on them, and chastising them or embarrassing them in front of others will not help you in your cause.

Instead, try more subtle tactics like walking closer to them as you talk; perhaps the increase in volume will jar them out of their stupor. Or you can try asking the audience as a whole if there are any issues or points you haven't raised that you should. Perhaps these audience members feel that your presentation isn't relevant to them, and an invitation for their feedback might get them more involved.

If one of your sleepers is a particularly important decision maker, try talking to him/her individually when the presentation is over and the audience has dispersed: "I'm afraid that you didn't see the value in my product today. Can I ask what didn't appeal to you?" If there was a problem with your pitch, you can now have a more engaged conversation about it. If the issue was just their own sleep deprivation, you can graciously accept their inevitable apology and offer to talk over your proposal again another time.

Ring-a-Ling ... It's for You

DEAR AIMEE C.: While I was giving my last presentation, something super-awkward happened: someone's phone started ringing really loudly, with a really annoying old-car-horn ringtone. I tried to keep on going, but everyone just kept looking around to see whose phone it was. And that stupid phone just kept going ah-OOH-ga, ah-OOH-ga, AH-OOH-GA. What should I have done?

    WISH I HAD SMASHED THE PHONE

DEAR WISH: Interruptions happen. Whether phones ring (or honk), people talk loudly in the hallways, thunder rumbles outside, or construction workers start jack-hammering outside your window, there will be distractions you can't avoid. The key, though, is to deal with them as best you can. Ignoring interruptions won't work; your audience's attention has already been diverted. Instead, acknowledge the distraction. If it's something that can be solved, solve it. If you can't, adjust to it as best you can.

    So, in the case of your never-ending ringtone, you could have stopped and said politely, "Does someone need to get that?" Most times the offender will fish out the phone, shut it off, and apologize profusely. Tell them it was no trouble (whether or not you think differently) and then move on. No criticisms, no jokes, and no sweat off your back.

    If the distraction is a noise you can't stop, then your job is to make light of the situation (don't show your stress), and adjust as best you can: "I'm so sorry this construction crew chose right now to jackhammer the sidewalk. They must be testing just how loudly I can talk. Can everyone hear me now?" Acknowledge your distractions, hide your frustrations, and adjust as needed.

Ugh. What Do You Want Now?

DEAR AIMEE C.: I am taking a presentations course, and the audience has free rein to interrupt anyone's presentation to ask questions or raise criticisms. Well, one girl in my class enjoys doing this way too much. She keeps interrupting my presentations and asking questions about topics I haven't gotten to yet or didn't even plan on covering. I am just trying to get through my presentations. How do I make her shut up?

    NEED TO FIND MY HAPPY PLACE

DEAR NEED: How do you make her shut up? You don't. You seem to be forgetting that presentations are not about you "getting through them," but about the audience getting something out of them. Clearly she's not getting what she wants from what you have to say. If she were, she'd "shut up." As frustrating as it may be to have someone throw you off course, interrupting audience members can show you the holes in your presentation and offer you the chance to fix them.

So, let's talk practical advice. If someone asks a question about a topic you have yet to cover, be polite in your reply: "I was actually going to get to how the product works after I talked about the market share. Would you like me to cover it now instead?" If you include a clear preview of the points you'll cover in your introduction, you'll be less likely to get questions out of turn.

If someone asks a question that you didn't plan on covering, answer it. You are the expert; you should know more about your topic than just what fit in your presentation. If the question is way off course, be judicious in your reply: "Well, we do have some ideas for social media marketing and a hashtag campaign that we can share with you. But our main goals for today are to introduce you to the product and show you why it's worth your investment. If you want to talk marketing today, I'm happy to talk with you about it afterwards."

Remember, be polite and make adjustments where adjustments are needed. You are a presenter, not the audience police.

Calling an Audible: Stop, Acknowledge, and Adjust

When presenting, you must pay attention to your audience; they are always giving you feedback on how you're doing. If their verbal or nonverbal communication says to you, "I'm not receiving your message the way you want me to," then you need to stop, acknowledge the issue, and adjust accordingly. You may not be able to pinpoint exactly what the problem is when it arises, but if you maintain the spirit of conversation, dealing with it will be easier: "It seems like you're not all on board here, but I'm not sure why. What are you thinking?" Show your audience you care and that you are there *for them* by making them the focus of your presentation.

Key Takeaways

- Successful presentations continually adjust to their audiences.
- Look at your listeners to gauge their nonverbal communication.
- Adjust to audience members' boredom or interruptions without criticizing or chastising them.
- Deal with interruptions in stride. Stop, acknowledge, and adjust.
- Hold your temper, and remember that the audience's needs come before your own desire to finish your presentation.

Questions and Activities:

1. **Reflection Question:** Think of a scenario from your own presentation past for which you should have "called an audible." How did you respond to the situation when it happened? What was effective about your response? Ineffective? What, if anything, would you do differently if the situation happened again?
2. **Learning Activity:** In class (or with some willing friends or family members), tell your audience an interesting or funny story that happened this week. Ask them to create distractions, interrupt with questions (some on topic and some off), and to overplay their emotional responses so they are easy for you to identify. Practice handling this audience feedback and continuing on with your presentation as calmly and seamlessly as possible, regardless of your audience's rude behavior or poor acting skills.
3. **Presentation Preparation:** Practice your presentation in front of a mock audience—a few friends, roommates, or family members—and ask them to respond nonverbally to your presentation without them telling you what emotion they are showing. Practice stopping, acknowledging the issue, and adjusting as needed.

Credits

CHAPTER 14

Question, Question, Who's Got a Question?

By M. Sandra DiFrancesco

After studying this chapter, you should be able to:
- *Explain the benefits of Q&A sessions for the audience and for the presenter.*
- *Prepare properly for questions and practice answers as part of your presentation preparation.*
- *Identify and apply the techniques for answering questions like a pro.*
- *Identify and demonstrate the most effective ways to handle the Q&A session.*

Preparation and practice are the keys for developing confidence for your presentation and for the question-and-answer (Q&A) period that follows.

It would be highly unlikely for the audience not to ask any questions after a business presentation delivered in the classroom, in our offices, during meetings, and to clients. Remember what we've been saying in this book: a presentation should be a conversation with your audience. Conversations usually include questions from the other participants.

For many presenters, the Q&A session can be a very exciting part of the presentation. For many others, it can be the most dreaded and nerve-wracking aspect of presenting—the stuff of their worst nightmares. For these presenters, they purposely avoid the question-and-answer period by quickly ending their presentation or by speaking for the entire time limit so that there is no time left for questions. Both of these escape tactics are bad ideas.

A Great Opportunity for the Presenter

It's important to remember that questions are a vital part of the presentation. They provide an opportunity for you to expand your main points, for clarifying any misunderstandings or confusing concepts, for summarizing your information, for reinforcing your message, for audience interaction, and for immediate feedback. Handled correctly, Q&A sessions can really enhance your presentation, make you more likeable and credible, and help you to achieve your intent.

Nothing can derail an otherwise good presentation more than being unprepared for Q&A. Just ask Miss Utah (2013), Miss Teen South Carolina (2007), or Miss California (2012)— they learned the hard way when their rambling answers to the interview portion of the contest went viral (Breslaw, 2013). Miss Utah badly flubbed a question about why women earn less then men. Her answer: "We need to figure out how to create education better." Miss Teen South Carolina was asked why one-fifth of Americans couldn't locate the USA on a map; she responded: "I personally believe ... that some people out there don't have maps." Miss California was asked the question, "What are your feelings on euthanasia?" Her response? "That's one of the things I'm not educated on so I need to look up what that means ... but I do know that's a vaccine."

Learn from these women's mistakes. **It's just as important to prepare and practice for the Q&A period as it is to practice the other key ideas you plan to present.**

Your Audience Is Not Your Enemy

Let's say you've been asked to give a major client presentation that will take place next week, and your nerves are beginning to take over. You've done your research, planned out your key points, and got your presentation down pat—and you know if you can pull it off that it could have a major impact on your company and on your career. But if you think your presentation *only* involves talking about all the material you've spent several days planning, you're wrong.

Very often presenters are afraid of their audience asking questions, and when the clients start to talk back or raise concerns, the presenters fall into an awkward, defensive, and sometimes argumentative position. They forget one simple truth: **your audience is not your enemy. They want to see you succeed.**

Remember, "It's *NOT* about you." Simply stated, curious and engaged audiences ask questions. They want to know more. This is

Your audience is not your enemy. Don't fear the questions when your audience needs to know the answers.

a good thing, as much as you may dread it. But like any other professional skill, how to best ask and answer questions is learned and perfected through planning, practice, and a great deal of experience.

Treat the Q&A Session as Part of Your Presentation

Since the Q&A period is a routine part of the overall presentation, there's no reason it needs to cause extra apprehension or anxiety. Q&A sessions can be handled effectively if you prepare ahead of time and maintain control.

Many presenters fear the question-and-answer session because they feel they are not in control or they will not be able to answer the questions. But ready or not, the questions are coming. If you are well prepared for the questions likely to come your way and know how to handle answering them effectively, they won't seem nearly as scary.

Dr. Henry Kissinger, the former secretary of state and national security adviser, famously quipped during a news conference, "Does anyone have any questions for my answers?" (Barks, 2012). The message was clear: he had a message to deliver, he was in charge, and he was going to remain focused. **You can't control the questions, but you can control your responses.** On the flip side: Sam Donaldson of ABC News, said, "The questions don't do the damage. Only the answers do." Let your statement of intent be your guide; provide answers that stick to the points you want to make.

Beyond knowing the answers, it's just as important to know how to handle questions with respect and confidence. "Uh, I'm going to, uh, respond to that question, um, by telling you, um, what we do best, um" is not very compelling.

When Should You Encourage Questions?

A major point that has been made throughout this book is that you must unequivocally understand that this is not *your* presentation. The presentation belongs to your audience. It's all about them. Every decision you make as a presenter must be geared around this question: how is what I'm doing helping my audience? This is why, **in most circumstances, you should encourage questions throughout the presentation.**

Holding questions until the end might make it easier for *you*, but not for your audience. They want to get their points clarified as you go along. Otherwise, they could still be trying to figure out what you meant in your first main point as you plow along to your third. Guess what? They didn't follow along (How could they? They were lost!), and all that talking you did after the first main point was for nothing.

Instead of taking the attitude that questions mean you are being interrupted and spun out of control, think of these questions as opportunities to make your presentation even better. Questions show that the audience is interested in what you have to say, and they can make the talk more lively and interactive. By allowing questions to be asked during your presentation, you have the advantage of knowing and responding to what your audience needs from you. You have the opportunity to clarify any "muddy" points, and you can be sure that your audience is awake, engaged, and paying attention. You will get a feel for what your audience wants to know, and that will give you greater confidence.

There are a few cases when it simply is not realistic to encourage people to interrupt you with questions throughout the presentation. Asking your audience to hold questions until the end is most appropriate if you have a very short time limit or if you're presenting to a very large group (fifty or more). If you do decide to hold questions until the end, you should allow 20 to 25 percent of your presentation time for questions. Even if you decide not to allow your audience to interrupt as they see fit, you don't have to wait exclusively until the end of your talk. You can point out exactly when you want to answer any questions by asking at specific moments, "What questions do you have on the topics I've covered so far?"

Whether you decide to take questions throughout your presentation

Connor interrupts his presentation to take a question from the audience.

(recommended) or at designated times, make sure you include in your introduction an announcement of when you will take questions. Be aware, though, that even if you try to corral questions to specific times, clients of importance may just ask questions whenever they want anyway. They know they are the most important people in the room, and they know that they deserve to have their confusions and concerns handled whenever they want.

Strategies for Managing Great Question & Answer Sessions

A poorly handled Q&A session leaves the audience with a negative impression of the presenter's core message, no matter how brilliantly it has been delivered in the main presentation. Don't let this happen to you.

Before the Presentation: Be Ahead of the Game

Build a Q&A session into your presentation. Visualize it as an opportunity for you to clarify your message and reinforce your key points. **Prepare and practice how you will answer the questions you are likely to get.**

- **Prepare questions in advance.** Responding to questions from your audience will be easy if you have anticipated the questions that might be asked and if you have prepared clear and brief answers. Position yourself being in *their* shoes, and brainstorm every potential question they might ask.
  - Anticipate the worst possible questions, the "So what?" questions, and the really off-topic questions. Use your audience analysis to help you think through your audience's mindset.
  - Write down at least the top ten questions. By anticipating these, you will have covered 80 to 90 percent of the likely questions that your audience will ask.
  - Work the *really important questions* into the content of your presentation, especially if they will make your message clearer. Don't wait for all the questions to be asked during the Q&A session, or you'll feel bombarded, and the clients will leave feeling that you were unprepared.
  - For the rest of the questions, prepare the best responses—short, concise answers. If you're in a team, make sure you all know and agree on those answers. In a short time, like Dr. Kissinger, you'll have the answers even before the audience knows their questions. For the ones you can't answer, prepare an "I don't know" answer. Give up the belief that you have to be perfect.
- **Practice your delivery.** How you answer a question is as important as what you say. Make practicing the answers to anticipated questions an integral part of your presentation practice.
- **Include a Q&A session in your practice sessions.** If you are lucky enough to find willing audience members for your practice sessions, encourage them to ask questions. Not only will this give you practice in answering the questions, but it will also help you figure out what types of questions your real audience may ask.

During the Presentation: Invite Questions Effectively

Invite your audience to ask questions in a way that shows your willingness to respond and your confidence in your ideas.

- **Don't ask**, "Do you have any questions?" **or** "Are there any questions?" midway through the presentation. These are problematic for two reasons: (1) these are yes/no questions that make the audience less likely to speak up; and (2) they are so broad that you may get asked questions on topics you haven't even covered yet. Make it easier on yourself by asking for questions more specifically: "What questions do you have on how the product works before we get into pricing and marketing?" This makes it clear to the audience that, if they want to know how much it'll cost or how you'll get the word out on it, they just need to sit tight … you're going to answer that question soon.
- **Nonverbally welcome questions as they are asked.** Set a tone and encourage questions by leaning or stepping forward toward the questioner. This helps you avoid the unintentional slow backwards step or the lean against the wall that can be perceived as a retreat.

During the Q&A Session: How to Answer Questions like a Pro

Handling questions well can help to enhance your credibility and is critical to a successful business presentation. Also remember that questions are a good opportunity for you to interact with your audience. The following steps will help you to respond more effectively to questions from your audience:

- **Show them that you're listening.** Great presenters remember that their listeners want their questions and comments heard and validated. Show the audience that you are an active listener and that you care about what they have to say. When you take questions and comments from your audience, really pay attention. Show interest by nodding your head, smiling, and maintaining eye contact. Rolling eyes, huffing, and dismissing an audience member are quick ways to lose a sale, opportunity, or support.
- **Listen to the entire question.** Please let the questioner finish; don't cut a question off partway through, no matter how eager you are to deliver your answer.
- **Don't say, "Good question."** Does that mean that all the other questions were bad ones? If this question was so good, why wasn't this point covered in your presentation? And why are you talking to your audience like they are children: "Oooh. You asked a good question. Good job!" Enough said. Instead, try phrases like these:
  - "I've been thinking about that very question a lot lately myself."
  - "You raise an interesting point."
  - "Thank you for asking."
- **Show positive nonverbal communication.** When taking comments from your audience, start every answer with a smile—a way to nonverbally say, "Thanks for your interest and contribution to this conversation," even if you are feeling very

differently inside. Listen to and look at the questioner, but then slowly move your eye contact around to include the rest of your audience in your answer.

- **Be brief and concise.** Don't give another mini-presentation to answer a question. You can certainly drive home some of your main points in your answer, but don't regurgitate the whole presentation you just gave.
- **Answer the question.** Not answering a question directly can gravely hurt your credibility. Whether you are trying to avoid the question or you just don't understand what was being asked, your audience will find your roundabout answer infuriating. If you don't have a good answer immediately, take a few seconds to collect your thoughts before answering. If you're not sure what the questioner has asked, paraphrase it back to the questioner: "Do you mean ..." When you are done with your answer, ask, "Does that answer your question?" just to make sure your response was on point.
- **Stay cool, confident, and controlled.** Treat all questions and questioners with respect. Maintain your composure at all times, even if the questioner's tone and attitude seems too aggressive. Under no circumstances, even if you disagree with your audience, should your nonverbal cues suggest that the questioner's contribution was not valued.
- **Defend the idea, not yourself.** When doing a sales pitch to a customer, for example, you might get a snide comment like "That's the dumbest idea I ever heard." (I know I've caught myself saying that a couple of times, especially when someone is trying to sell me something they claim will "change my life forever.") Remember that business is not personal, even if it feels that way sometimes. Keep the focus on defending your arguments, not yourself.
- **Never try to embarrass the questioner.** No matter how tempting it is—no matter how foolish the question is—avoid a disparaging answer. Even an answer of "we already covered that" can bruise the ego of many. Always treat each question with the utmost respect, or you will make an enemy and make the job of selling your idea harder.
- **Be truthful.** Never make something up, guess, or speculate. If you don't have an answer, don't fake it. Admit when you don't know: "I don't know the answer to that question, but give me your card, and I will get back to you." Just beware that if you rely on this tactic too much, you will lose credibility points.

What to Do When No One Asks a Question

Maybe you've been in a similar situation. You wrapped up what you thought was a pretty good presentation, and as you stood at the front of the room, nothing but blank faces stared back at you. No questions? You're shocked. Or you falsely feel you've done an admirable job and so conclude by saying, "No questions? So I guess that wraps things up."

An audience with no questions is *not* a good sign. If your audience is "into" your presentation, they'll want to keep the presentation going so they can learn more or flesh out the logistics of your plan or product. They'll do that by asking thoughtful, pointed questions.

If you never receive a single question throughout your presentation, it is likely that something went wrong. Maybe your audience doesn't know how to start, you've confused them by not giving them what they want, you've talked so long they just want to go

Avoid awkward silences in Q&A sessions by being prepared.

home (or go to sleep), or something you said rubbed them the wrong way and now they're irritated with you. Whatever the case, it doesn't look good for you.

Avoiding the Awkward Silence: What's One to Do?

Here are some tips for dealing with the no-questions dilemma:

- **Have your own questions ready**. Some audiences will be slow to ask questions. To get them warmed up, you may want to ask your own question first. For instance, if you're met with silence, offer, "One question I'm often asked is: how does …" and then answer that.
- **Ask the audience questions.** Investigate what went wrong by asking them directly:
  - "Is everyone clear on the plan and how it can benefit your company?"
  - "Does this product seem like a good fit for your company?"
  - "How do you feel about the ideas we've presented here today?"
  Don't fear asking these types of questions when you need to know their answers.
- **If your baiting didn't work and there truly are no questions, wrap it up.** It will be very awkward for you and the audience if you just hang around onstage after they've made it clear they're done with you. Leave your contact information with the clients, so, if and when they have questions later, they know you're available to answer them.

Tips for Handling Objections and Tough Questions

Objections are a normal part of the persuasion process. They are reservations or concerns about some aspect of a service or product. Whether you regard objections as obstacles or opportunities will determine how you respond to them. Begin with the right attitude. Many times, an objection is just a person's way of saying:

- "I need more information before I decide."
- "There's something on my mind that tells me I'm not sure this will work for me."
- "I need more proof to be convinced."

The key is to welcome objections and not dread them. You are learning your audience's needs, wants, dislikes, and fears—everything you need to know to get them to buy into your proposal.

A way to get a handle on many of the possible objections concerning your proposal would be to anticipate three or four concerns that the audience might have. Then, incorporate the answers into your presentation. You tackle these reasonable concerns from a position of strength by dealing with them as part of your pitch. The others that may pop up during your presentation should be handled in a polite and respectful way.

- **Don't pounce on the person.** Take the approach of being inquisitive, and calmly discuss the reason for the objection. Use phrases like "You've asked a question that I'd like to talk more about," "That's an interesting comment, so let me make sure I have a good understanding of it," or "Tell me more about your concern." This allows you to soften the objection, gain a bit more time to think, and proceed to a more effective answer.
- **Don't let dissenters rain on your parade.** Politely acknowledge the dissenter. When you encounter a person who strongly disagrees with you and refuses to shut up, respond with "Thank you for your opinion. I know there are different schools of thought on this issue. I am telling you what has worked for me." Don't argue. Validate the dissenter and move on.
- **Demonstrate empathy.** Verbally state that you appreciate and understand the person's concern. "Mr. Warren, I understand that you have social media problems you have to deal with. Let me address that directly."
- **Keep the questioners on track.** Many times I have seen Q&A sessions get derailed. What should be a focus on the validity of the big-picture ideas turns into a nit-picking session on the finer details of the plan: What colors should the logo be? What hours should the business be open? Should the product be packaged in plastic or in a box? In most cases, the better question should be, "Who cares?" If the point of your presentation is to introduce a new concept or idea, the most important question your audience needs to ask is "Does this idea or product work for us?" Ron Hoff (1997) notes that, "When answering questions, always come back to the ... simple, discrete message you want your audience to take action on. 'Yes, it will take a year to build the new stadium, but it will provide work for ten thousand people—maybe even members of your family. That alone should be worth a YES vote next Tuesday'" (p. 107).

Remain the Owner of Your Presentation. Conclude With Impact!

Finish on a strong note; never end your presentation with the last question. You'll end up trailing off with "Well, if there are no more questions, thanks for having me."

Instead, plan a two-minute wrap up for after your Q&A session is over. Take control afterwards. Save your concluding words (and perhaps your final slides) for *after* the formal Q&A. Give another quick summary. Restate your main points and end with a strong close. This way, the last thing everyone hears is what you *want* them to hear—a final call to action for your product, plan, or ideas. Your presentation will finish with a bang, not a whimper.

Key Takeaways

- Think of responding to questions as part of your presentation.
- Anticipate questions; write them down. Then plan and rehearse key points on how you would respond.
- Listen closely for understanding; don't interrupt.
- Ask for specific questions throughout the presentation, and then openly accept any and all questions in the final Q&A.
- Pause before answering and keep your focus on the question. Restate the question if necessary.
- During your answer, step forward and maintain eye contact with others in the room.
- Check that the questioner is satisfied with your answer when you're done.
- After the Q&A session, end with your closing remarks, thereby reinforcing the main ideas of your presentation.

Questions and Activities:

1. **Reflection Question:** Think of a time when you have had to field questions from an audience. How did you find the experience? How confident and prepared were you? What did you do well, and what did you do not so well? Having now read this chapter, what could you have done differently to improve your handling of the questions you received?
2. **Learning Activity:** Engage in a mock debate with a friend or classmate. Question each other's beliefs in a very critical way. Then practice responding to these questions as diplomatically and respectfully as possible.
3. **Presentation Preparation:** Play the role of devil's advocate and identify the ten most challenging questions you might hear from the audience (the really mean stuff) in your next presentation. Then research and formulate answers (don't write out the entire answer; just jot down ideas of how you would answer). Finally, practice your responses.

Credits

CHAPTER 15

Putting It All Together
The Art of Persuasion
By Stephanie Kelly and Ho-Young (Anthony) Ahn

After studying this chapter, you should be able to:
- *Identify and apply appropriate persuasive appeals to use in your argument.*
- *Establish your credibility as a presenter.*
- *Structure a persuasive presentation.*

Joey was in trouble. His laptop had crashed overnight, taking his history midterm paper, which was due in just a few hours, with it. Of course, Joey was smart enough to have a backup on his USB, but now he couldn't find that either. Maybe it fell out of his bag somewhere, or maybe he left it in the computer lab, but either way, after an hour of searching, it appeared to be gone.

Joey's history professor was tough and notorious for not giving extensions, even when students cried. Joey couldn't accept the zero without pleading his case, though. He rushed to school and was at his professor's office, waiting, when he arrived. Joey explained to his professor what had happened. He also showed the outline he was writing from (clearly dated as having been drafted weeks ago), his laptop (which showed nothing but the blue screen of death), and a stack of all of his previous grades for the semester to verify that he was an A student who was not prone to procrastination.

Much to his surprise, Joey received a twenty-four-hour extension on the paper. Though he may not have realized it, Joey received the extension because of his strong persuasive skills. He established his credibility by reminding his professor of his high standard of performance, he chose a logical appeal based on evidence rather than on emotion (because emotional appeals were already known not to work with this professor), and he backed up each claim with evidence. The union of these three elements in his presentation saved the day.

We encounter persuasion every day, whether we realize it or not: flyers all over campus asking you to join a club, online advertisements begging you to "Click Here," or student-government candidates pleading for you to vote for them.

In the business world, there are sales presentations, motivational presentations, interviews, briefings, status reports, training sessions—numerous forms of presentations. A key role in business is to get others to understand your viewpoint and agree with your idea, whether you are selling a product or service, motivating employees to support new cooperative efforts within the company, requesting a "buy-in" to corporate changes, or encouraging management to adopt a new way to accomplish a task. In a job interview, your goal is to persuade others that you are a "perfect fit" and that the company should select you over all the others.

There is one thing all of these persuasive messages have in common: they try to change what people believe or do, or they reinforce the beliefs, attitudes, and values an audience already holds. Persuasion helps lead people to the problem's solution—making the audience see how they can get from Point A to Point B. Therefore, any time *you* want to change or reinforce what someone believes or does, whether it be agreeing with your point or granting a favor, you are engaging in persuasive communication.

Persuasion is defined as "human communication designed to influence others by modifying their beliefs, values, or attitudes" (Simons, 1976, p. 21). However, not all persuasive attempts are successful. Think of how often you ignore or roll your eyes at the persuasive messages you hear. Knowing how to convince people of your perspective is a valuable skill. By having a strong audience analysis, the types of appeals your audience will appreciate, and the evidence to back up your claims, you will increase your power to persuade others.

Your Audience: Who Needs Convincing?

Following our trusty AIMC model, all preparation should start with the audience. Individuals are unique. They each have varying motivations to pay attention, abilities to concentrate, levels of involvement with the given issue, and beliefs about what is right and wrong. Moreover, their embedded attitudes and values may seem to clash with the ideas or actions you want them to adopt. Given this, the greatest (but more important) challenge for a persuasive speaker is relating the presentation to the audience. Keep your audience analysis results handy as you move through your presentation preparation; you will need them to ensure your appeals will have any chance of persuasive success.

Great Thoughts from a Great Greek: Aristotle's Elements of Persuasion

Way back in the fourth century, Aristotle made the case that all speaking (often called *rhetoric*) was persuasive. He theorized that there are three essential components in the persuasive process: ethos (speaker credibility), logos (logical arguments), and pathos (emotional appeals). A combination of all three approaches, tailored to your audience, is your best bet for persuading your audience effectively. Let us explain each of these areas a bit more:

- **Ethos** involves your own credibility. If people believe and trust you as a speaker, you will have a much easier job of

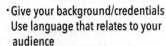

Ethos

- Give your background/credentials
  Use language that relates to your audience
- Cite credible sources your audience will respect

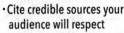

Logos

- Support arguments with proof
- Include shocking facts, figures, and statistics
- Organize arguments logically

Pathos

- Include impactful stories
- Display appropriate emotions
- Include figurative and powerful language

getting them to believe what you have to say. You should enhance your credibility so that your audience will feel like you are someone knowledgeable, trustworthy, and moral enough to follow. Joey used his previous work in the class to demonstrate his character. By showing that he had made all A's thus far, he established himself as a good student who wouldn't arbitrarily miss a due date. Thus, his own ethos helped to strengthen his arguments.

- **Logos** is a logical appeal. Logos relies heavily on the logical structure of your presentation: walking your audience through each point of evidence to reach the same conclusion. Logos also relies heavily on facts and data to make strong arguments. If you remember our initial example of Joey and his crashed computer, Joey used logos to help his case. By showing his history professor the timeline of his work and his now-defunct laptop, Joey included clear logic to prove that he was not lying.
- **Pathos** is an emotional appeal. A pathos appeal strives to elicit an emotional reaction from the audience that will shift their stance into alignment with your own. Storytelling and metaphorical language are often used to this effect. While Joey did not use an excessive amount of pathos in talking to his professor (because he knew his audience wouldn't appreciate that appeal), he likely used a little. Even the pleading in his voice gave hints at just how distraught Joey was at the prospect that he might fail the assignment because of matters beyond his control.

Which of these tactics you choose to emphasize should be based on your audience analysis. For Joey's teacher, logical and credibility appeals were the smartest moves. For others, emotional appeals might have more lasting impact. As best you can, learn about what "makes your audience tick," and make the appeals that have the best chance of success.

If you truly can't figure out which methods appeal most to your audience, plan to use a balanced approach of all three. If Joey hadn't known of his professor's dismissal of crying students, Joey might have started with an emotional appeal. But once he saw his professor roll his eyes and start to mentally "check out," he could have quickly switched over to his logical and credibility appeals (which clearly had more influence with his teacher). By having all three prepared, he would be ready to adjust on the spot to emphasize the best appeals for the listener.

Ethos and Speaker Credibility: "Whooooo Are Youuuuu?" Asked the Caterpillar

Although knowing the audience is the first step in building a persuasive argument, the actual act of persuasion begins with a person who has the power to influence: the speaker. The literature in psychology, marketing, and communication refers to this persuasive power as **source credibility** (believability of a message sender). It's how you use your ethos. There are many different characteristics accounting for source credibility (O'Keefe, 2002), such as:

- **Expertise:** Have you consulted credible sources? Great! Cite them.
- **Competence:** Does your topic relate to your major or your job? Great! Point that out! Then your audience will know that you have a skilled foundation for speaking on this topic.

- **Trustworthiness:** Be honest. When audience members may have valid points that counteract your argument, acknowledge those arguments yourself. It shows that you've done your homework and that you're not trying to hide anything.
- **Similarity:** "When I was your age ..." Have you ever sat through a lecture beginning that way? It's hard to relate to people who don't understand your frame of reference. Show your audience that you do understand them by pointing out what you have in common.
- **Liking:** Smile! Use some vocal inflection when you speak. Make light eye contact with your audience. If you look unapproachable or like you're angry that you have to be speaking, then your audience isn't going to like you or what you have to say.
- **Physical attractiveness:** Suit up! Okay, maybe you don't have to wear a full business suit for every presentation, but at least look like you've made an effort to look nice. Be sure that your outfit, hair, and accessories look like intentional choices rather than what happened to fall into place when you rolled out of bed ten minutes ago.

All of these tactics establish the speaker's credibility. **The more credibility-boosting tactics you can incorporate, the more credible you will seem.** Be sure to establish credibility early on in the presentation (when you introduce yourself in the presentation's introduction); that way, you're dealing with minimal skepticism from that point on.

You can't be an expert on everything all of the time, but you can do your research, dress the part, and smile. You don't have to be a doctor or have a PhD to have ethos. You just have to use the right tools.

Logos and Logical Arguments: What's the Message?

"The truth isn't the truth until people believe you, and they can't believe you if they don't know what you're saying, and they can't know what you're saying if they don't listen to you, and they won't listen to you if you're not interesting, and you won't be interesting unless you say things imaginatively, originally, freshly" (Sullivan, 2008, p.6). You might need to read this quote a couple of times (sure, it's a bit of a run-on sentence), but its essence is important: **you have to have a strong message to persuade effectively.** Let's look at the various aspects that go into a logical appeal.

Using a Logical Organization

At this point in preparation, you have your goal and you know how you need to approach your audience, so it's time to decide how to frame your message. The chapters on **What Infomercials Do Right** and **Speaking in Outlines** already gave you one speaking structure for a persuasive presentation—identifying benefits to your audience and listing them:

    I. Introduction
    II. Main Point #1: First benefit of your plan/product to your audience
    III. Main Point #2: Second benefit of your plan/product to your audience
    IV. Main Point #3: Third benefit of your plan/product to your audience
    V. Conclusion

If your arguments don't seem to fit into that structure well, you do have other options. Let's take a look at another standard persuasive message organizational strategy: Monroe's Motivated Sequence (German, Gronbeck, Ehniger, & Monroe, 2012).

Monroe's Motivated Sequence is a persuasive formula used in most commercials and can be adapted easily to your own persuasive presentation. The formula contains five steps:

1. **Attention:** Start with an attention-getter. This may be a statistic, shocking fact, question, story, etc. Just make sure that your audience is tuned in.
2. **Need:** Show your audience that there is a hole in their world. They may not have known it before you opened your mouth, but now they do. Something is wrong—and they need for you to offer a solution.
3. **Satisfaction:** So you do offer that solution. Tell them how to satisfy that need.
4. **Visualization:** Help your audience understand how much better their lives can be once they take your solution, or how much worse it's going to get if they don't.
5. **Action:** Tell them to take that solution.

Let's break down your typical Axe Body Spray commercial as a brief example of how this method works:

1. **Attention:** Pretty girls!
2. **Need:** A boy is shown who cannot interact with the pretty girls.
3. **Satisfaction:** Introducing Axe Body Spray! Now the boy can smell good.
4. **Visualization:** Now the girls are interacting with the boy because he smells good.
5. **Action:** Go buy Axe!

Okay, now let's expand Monroe's Motivated Sequence into the points of a persuasive presentation:

I. Introduction
- Begin—as always—by grabbing the audience's **ATTENTION.**

II. Main Point #1: **NEED** step
- Explain your audience's need. Show them the severity of the issue without overinflating the problem. Do not introduce your product yet; just show how the current state of affairs is insufficient.
- If doing a product pitch, for instance, you could show competing products, customers' dissatisfaction with those products, and the resulting hole in the market.

III. Main Point #2: **SATISFACTION** step
- Explain your product, plan, or solution, and how it can resolve the audience's need.
- Start with the big picture (selling the overall concept) before going into the details of the plan or product.
- Answer the audience's potential objections and show the strength of your plan.

IV. Main Point #3: **VISUALIZATION** step
- Explain the longer-term benefits of your plan or solution, or the consequences of not taking your suggestions.

- Use stories, examples, and projections to help the audience envision the future.
V. Conclusion
   - End with a clincher that is a call to **ACTION**. Tell the audience what they should do—right here, right now—to start implementing the solution.

It's important to note that while your organizational structure is part of your logical appeal, the content of that structure includes all three types of appeals: ethos, logos, and pathos. For ethos, the speaker should still establish credibility and cite credible sources. For logos, the presentation should include facts, solid arguments, and research. For pathos, the presenter should make direct appeals to the audience's emotions, particularly in the need and visualization steps.

Making Effective Persuasive Arguments

The earlier chapter on **Speaking in Outlines** already reviewed the basic rules for giving logical proof: tailor your arguments to your audience, and support every claim you make with reputable evidence.

In many cases, though, your attempts at persuasion will be met with resistance. Your intent will be a bit harder to meet if you discover that your stance will:

- Challenge facts—your audience is misinformed;
- Challenge values—your audience has traditions or customs that reject your stance; or
- Challenge beliefs—your audience has core beliefs about what is right and wrong that do not support your stance.

What does this mean? It means that you need to know which of those three scenarios you're facing to determine the best approach. You cannot effectively persuade an audience that you know nothing about. Make sure you have done a thorough audience analysis to figure out how your audience feels about your persuasive intent.

When you are in the message-planning phase of AIMC, prepare logical arguments to challenge your audience's facts, values, or beliefs. Here is an example: imagine that you want to persuade your peers to choose Google's Android over Apple's iOS.

- Challenge facts: if your peers are misinformed about the abilities of Android devices, debunking myths should be the focus of your speech.
- Challenge values: if your peers are part of the Apple culture, then your goal is to show them how Android devices can complement what they already do.
- Challenge beliefs: if your peers believe that Android's home company, Google, is corrupt, then your goal is to talk to them about Google's good deeds.

Remember, people's beliefs and attitudes are not easy to change. Don't expect persuasion to be simple. In fact, go into your presentation expecting everyone to be skeptical, confused, or apathetic. Be certain that your presentation focuses on what *the audience* wants or needs to hear, rather than on what *you* want to tell them.

More on Adapting to Your Audience's Values

A key point we tell our students is that **there are multiple paths to the same persuasive goal.** Your reasons for following through with your plan or endorsing your product may not be the reasons that work best for your audience. Meet them halfway and find out what will convince them.

For instance, let's imagine Francine wanted to convince her classmates to volunteer for a cleanup day on campus, aimed at removing litter, fixing broken benches and trashcans, and painting over graffiti. School pride is an important value for Francine, and that is *her* motivating force to participate in this event. Her classmates, though, don't share that same enthusiasm. Arguments focused on why it's important to have a beautiful campus won't speak to the audience's values. Instead, Francine should figure out what *will* move her audience. Perhaps this tactic would be more successful: "I know picking up garbage sounds like a lot less fun than hanging in your dorm room and watching Netflix. But I also know that a lot of you still need community service hours or volunteer experiences to boost your résumés. Cleanup Campus Day is an easy and convenient service project to do." Like Francine, let your logical arguments take the path your audience members are most likely to follow.

Knowing When Enough Is Enough

Sometimes you may be tempted to overshare information to establish your point because the information you find through research is so shocking and/or intriguing. But you cannot include *every* point you find or may want to make. The human brain can only process so much new information at once. **When audiences are bombarded with new facts and statistics, their working memory becomes gridlocked, leaving them unable to follow a speaker's argument.** This is called **information overload.** Causing your audience to go into information overload can be as bad as not having enough information to make your point, because, in either case, they cannot cognitively follow you to the conclusion of your argument.

Pathos and Emotional Appeals: How Do You Feel?

In professional presentations, it may seem like there is little place for emotional appeals, but in most cases, logic and credibility alone won't change thoughts or behavior. Human beings are simply not as rational as we think them to be. If we were, no one would smoke, drive fast, cheat on tests, or get wasted and streak naked across campus. **The fact is that humans are emotional, and for your persuasion efforts to be effective, you need to appeal to that emotion.**

Pathos does not mean that every—or any—presentation you give needs to be tear-jerking. But using pathos correctly does mean that your audience will feel a personal connection to your idea, product, or plan. Pathos can come in the form of storytelling and effective language use (both mentioned earlier in this unit), and from your delivery style (discussed in the next unit). Let us use this space to give some *other* tips on using emotional appeals effectively.

Using Humor Effectively

Humor is one of the more popular emotional appeals used in presentations. How many times have you heard the suggestion to start your presentation with a joke? Well, let us warn you that, while humor is a good idea (when it's appropriate), jokes are not.

Humor has the potential to be an incredibly powerful presentation tool. If your audience can laugh a little while they listen, they are more likely to pay attention and to have a positive impression of you and your ideas. Humor can also put your audience at ease, which, in turn, will help you to feel more comfortable and appear more confident.

Using humor, though, is not the same as telling jokes. Jokes are canned and often relate only tangentially (if at all) to the point of your presentation. When jokes fall flat (as is often the case), the presenter is left in an awkward silence that could make the most confident of speakers lose their nerve.

Humor, though, has no real consequence if it fails. Instead of planning out canned jokes to share, aim to tell *true* stories that fit into the points you are already trying to make. Think of how often you and your friends have laughed while retelling the events of a night out or an encounter with a stranger. Harness that power of story for your presentation—so long as the stories are appropriate for the audience and are relevant to your intent.

Then, if the humorous aspects of your story are lost on your audience, who cares? The point of the story—and thus the story itself—is still relevant. You can then continue on seamlessly, rather than having to resort to the awkward, "So ... um ... anyways ..." you would splutter out after your one-liner about the rabbi and priest walking into a bar inevitably bombs.

The point here: put away the joke books and avoid the one-line zingers. **Tell a few funny (and true) stories to inject some good-natured humor into your presentation.** So long as the focus remains on your persuasive arguments and not on your budding comedy career, you are likely to gain some favorability from your audience.

Using Fear Appeals Effectively

Another well-known emotional appeal is the fear appeal. **While a little fear may help to point out the seriousness of an issue (particularly in the Need step of a presentation following Monroe's Motivated Sequence), too much fear can cause audience members to shut down and stop listening in self-defense.** It's like when the commercials for starving children in Africa come on the television, and you immediately change the channel or walk away. You may care about the plight of these children (really, we believe you), but the images of bug-bite-ridden bodies and bellies distended from extreme hunger are just too much to handle.

In your presentations, choose visuals carefully, but also choose the way you word your arguments carefully. Avoid making extreme statements like "overexposure to the sun *will* kill you" or "people who don't study *never* find jobs," because this is likely to make your audience ignore the message. Don't exaggerate the consequences or evidence for the sake of an emotional appeal. Slight shock value can be useful, but too much shock value loses its actual value.

Putting It All Together

The best persuasive tactics are tailored specifically to the audience and intent, and they use elements of all three of Aristotle's components of persuasion: ethos, logos, and pathos. If you have followed the guidelines from the chapters preceding this one, you should already have some ideas as to how you can employ individual tactics that play to these areas of persuasion. You know how to find credible research, how to formulate effective arguments, how to organize your ideas, how to tell captivating stories, and how to show your concern for your audience by adjusting to them and responding to their questions. Now you can put all those elements together to formulate a message that will speak to your audience and help you reach your ultimate persuasive intent.

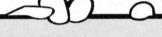

Key Takeaways

- Always start with your audience to determine the best persuasive tactics.
- Plan to use all three of Aristotle's elements of persuasion to have the best chance for presentation success.
- Boost your credibility as a presenter so the audience believes you are someone worthy of their time, attention, and trust.
- Organize your persuasive pitch logically, and formulate arguments that speak to the needs, wants, and hang-ups of your audience.
- Use emotion to sway your audience, but be careful not to use so much that your audience can no longer focus on your message.

Questions and Activities:

1. **Reflection Question:** In your presentations, which of the three types of persuasive appeals—ethos, logos, and pathos—do you use most often? Why do you think you make that choice? Which one do you need to emphasize more? In what ways could you do that in future presentations?
2. **Learning Activity:** Get into teams and elect someone to reach into his or her backpack, pocket, or purse and pull out an object. As a team, use Monroe's Motivated Sequence to write a sixty-second pitch convincing the audience to buy that product. Act out your commercials for your peers and provide one another with feedback on how well each team followed Monroe's Motivated Sequence.

3. **Learning Activity:** Play with ethos, logos, and pathos appeals by pitching a product. Choose a product and identify, in one sentence for each, your speaker credibility, a logical argument, and an emotional appeal.
4. **Presentation Preparation:** Consider the message you plan on using for your upcoming presentation. What balance do you have among ethos, logos, and pathos? Which of the three could you use more of? How will you work it into your message?

Credits

1. Putting it All Together: The Art of Persuasion Copyright © 2014 by Ho-Young Ahn and Stephanie Kelly. Reprinted with permission.
2. Copyright © 2015 by Audrey Mora. Reprinted with permission.

Unit 3

Delivery: You Are the Channel

A———Audience analyzed? Check! I—Intent identified? Check! M—Message planned? Check! What's left? Oh, right, the C—the channel, the delivery—the fun part!

If you remember from Unit 1, the channel is the means through which you share your message. In other words, the message is *what* you say, but the channel is *how* you say it.

An important type of presentation channel is the visual support you will use to prove or complement your message (PowerPoint and other visual aids), but we're going to save that discussion for the next unit. This unit will focus on the primary channel you use for *every* presentation you give: *you*.

Your voice, your mannerisms, your demeanor—all of these factors affect the way your audience perceives the message you are sending (Burke, Conway, & DiFrancesco, 2000). You could have the most brilliant research and the most interesting information to share, but if your audience would rather listen to nails on a chalkboard than the mind-numbing monotony of your voice, then your information will be lost to them. And, in those cases, you have no hope of ever reaching your intent, unless your intent was, "By the end of this presentation, my very bored audience will be lulled to sleep."

But monotony and boredom aren't the only hazards you need to avoid. In general, you need to make sure your delivery:

- doesn't inadvertently say to the audience, "I am not to be trusted";
- doesn't cast doubt on your expertise;
- doesn't distract or deter the audience from your message; and
- doesn't make you seem callous, disrespectful, or unprepared.

The readings in this unit are designed to help you avoid those misperceptions and help you grow as a presenter. If you've done your audience analysis well, planned a realistic intent, and researched and organized a message that works, your audience will *want* to listen to what you have to say; you will be giving them information they want or need. But poor presentation skills could distract them from listening well to what you have to say.

Now it is true that some people just have more monotonous voices than others. Some people just speak more softly. Some people have nervous tics, like "um," "uh," or an excessive use of "you know." Some people fidget, shake, and sweat in front of an audience. Yes, everyone likely has some bad presentation habits that need to be broken, and breaking them will probably not be easy.

Not easy, however, does not mean *impossible*. Good communication skills are *learned*. Some may seem to come naturally to you, and others will take persistence and honest self-reflection to change. But don't throw up your hands and presume that you "just can't" talk more confidently, gesture more purposefully, handle your nerves, or learn to speak fluently without memorizing. Just like with any other skill, practice makes perfect (or at least gets you closer to it). The more you present on a wide variety of topics—whether to a crowd or to yourself in the mirror—the more confident and engaging you will be.

Remember, too, that you are not expected to be perfect. In presenting, mistakes happen, and so long as you are able to recover and pull focus back to the message, that's okay. Your goal is not to be flawless (because who among us will ever reach that goal?); rather, your goal is to ensure that the way you present allows your information (and you) to be understood, trusted, and respected by your audience.

CHAPTER 16

I Am Presenter.
Hear Me Roar
Learning to Say It Like You Mean It

After studying this chapter, you should be able to:
- *Articulate the importance of "sounding like you mean it."*
- *Identify the ideal volume, rate, and enthusiasm for presenters.*
- *Reduce traces of vocal doubt in your voice through various language and inflection strategies.*

One of the most prevalent comments I hear when I ask students to watch videos of themselves presenting is something to the effect of, "Oh. My. God. Is that what I sound like? I hate my voice!" Indeed, we sound a lot different when we hear ourselves talking in our own heads than we sound to a camera or—more importantly—to our audience.

As much as you may not want to spend a lot of time honing and perfecting your voice, it is important to do so. The quality of your voice can not only make your content easier to understand for your audience, but it can also contribute greatly to how your audience perceives you and your expertise. Those with clear, pleasant, and fluent speech are perceived as more credible to their audiences (Burgoon, 1978), and those with poor articulation are seen as not (Addington, 1971). Your voice, then, is a crucial factor in whether or not you will reach your intent.

The key to effective vocal quality is to sound confident, talk conversationally, and show conviction. Let us start by looking at the basics—volume, rate, and enthusiasm—before delving into other tips on how to sound more confident:

Volume: A Little Bit Louder Now

Many of the presentations you will do in your life will involve small crowds rather than cavernous auditoriums full of people. For a small audience, in a small room, it is likely that your usual speaking voice will be loud enough to be heard. Nonetheless, **if you are standing up to present, then you should aim to project your voice louder than you would in a normal conversation.**

Why? Because part of the trick of finding the right vocal quality is learning how to "sound like you mean it." Using your normal conversational volume during a presentation will make you sound timid, as though you sort of want to say something, but you're not so sure you want *everyone* to hear it. Talking at a volume that allows your voice to fill the room and clearly mark your presence to the audience demonstrates a level of confidence that you need in order to be convincing. Let your volume say, "Hello! I'm here, and I have something important to say."

Not only should you begin by letting your volume bounce off all four walls of the room, but you should also aim to sustain that volume throughout the presentation. So often I see nervous presenters lose their courage mid-sentence and, consequently, let their volume trail off to just quiet mumblings to themselves. Don't let the mean and scary voices in your head convince you that what you are saying isn't worth projecting. Your audience is here to listen to you; they want to hear what you have to say. Don't make them strain their ears to hear the end of each sentence.

If you're not used to speaking at a loud volume, you may find your voice to be somewhat uncooperative when you present. Projecting your voice may take some practice before your throat will behave itself and not close up or get dry too fast mid-presentation. Talk loudly to yourself in your car (other drivers will just think your phone has a Bluetooth connection), belt out your favorite song in the shower (roommates be damned), and speak up in class when instructors ask for volunteers to answer questions (your teachers will love it). If you give them enough practice, your vocal chords will eventually get the hang of it.

Rate: A Little Bit Slower Now

But don't speak too slowly, please. That will become very boring very fast. An ideal rate will sound conversational—like you are simply talking about these brilliant ideas of yours—but it will be slow enough that the audience can digest the information you are giving them. In addition, you should use strategic pausing as you talk. If you were doing a reading in front of an audience, you would, hopefully, pause at every punctuation mark you saw—commas, colons, semicolons, dashes, and periods. Though you lack a script in a presentation, you should still punctuate your speaking with pauses to give your audience time to digest what you're saying.

Think of the fastest song you know (rap tunes are often good for this). If none come to mind, search YouTube for Reunion's "Life is a Rock (But the Radio Rolled Me)," and listen to it without looking at the screen or any lyric sheets. How many of the words did you have time to digest and really understand the first time you heard the song? Beyond the chorus, my guess is "not too many."

I have heard presenters talk that fast before. When nerves hit, and your body's fight-or-flight reaction is saying, "Flight! Flight! Choose Flight! Let's get outta here!" your

> ### Other Reasons to Press Pause
>
> Pausing is a powerful presentation tool. As long as it doesn't last too long (more than five seconds), audiences will find it natural in your speaking. Beyond aiding in audience comprehension, there are other benefits to a short pause:
>
> 1. Pausing allows you to collect your thoughts.
> 2. Pausing helps you to avoid filler words like "uh" and "um."
> 3. Pausing helps you catch your breath when nerves are taking hold.
> 4. Pausing wakes up the audience (sometimes silence is a great attention grabber).
> 5. Pausing can emphasize important points: Pausing. Is. Persuasive.

voice may speed off at a dizzying pace and leave your audience in the dust. You have to slow down, Road Runner. Pause at the end of sentences, pause to give lists, pause longer after each main point and sub-point. Give the audience a momentary mental break to think about what you just said. *Then*, you can move onto your next point.

If presentation nerves turn you into a speed talker, speaking at an appropriate rate might be easier said than done. Practicing in front of a video camera or even with a voice-recording device (many cell phones have "voice memo" features that could work for this) can help you determine how quickly you are talking. Or, if you are lucky enough to have willing audience members for your practice run, ask them to hold up their hand in a "stop" signal when your rate gets too fast. The more you practice talking at the right rate (even if you just tell nonsense stories to your audience or voice recorder), the more likely you will be able to avoid speeding through the real presentation.

Enthusiasm: A Lot More Lively Now

Picture the most boring instructor you know. Imagine sitting in his or her classroom and listening to yet another seemingly endless lecture on the philosophical musings of the ancient Greeks, the very long history of Mesopotamia, or the countless merits of genetic mapping. How does the instructor sound in your head? Does s/he sound happy to be there, discussing this topic with you, full of energy and full of life? Probably not—or at least it doesn't sound that way to you.

Here's an easy point to remember: **if you want the audience to be excited by your ideas, you have to be excited to present the ideas to them.**

Enthusiasm can be tough to infuse into your speaking if it's not already there. Some people just seem to have that energy, that dynamism, that spark that ignites a fire in the audience. Think of the truly electrifying presenters you've seen—the ones who come bounding into the room, grinning enthusiastically, with their voices booming over the audience. They have the crowd on their sides almost immediately. Their energy is palpable, and—more importantly—it's *infectious*.

To really capture your audience, you need to have that same energy. All of your innovative ideas, foolproof research, and impeccable logic will still be a tough sell to your audience if you are monotonously mumbling your way through the presentation. You have to sound alive, enthusiastic, and friendly.

Ron Hoff (1992) calls this presentation energy *chemistry*, and to him, the definition of *chemistry* is "Do you really want to see that person again tomorrow?" (p. 96). In most business presentations, this is the question your audience is asking. If they invest in your idea, buy your product, or hire you for a job, they will have to see you and work with you again. If you are devoid of emotion and personality—or at least seem that way when you present—you are not making the prospect of a long-term business relationship very enticing.

If you sound bored, your audience will be bored with you. Joe looks positively miserable to be here.

I recognize that nervousness is often the culprit for presenters' lack of enthusiasm. It's difficult to sound excited when you would rather curl into a ball and hide. There are some tips, though, that you can try to help inject more passion into your presentation:

- **Remember that your audience needs you**. If you've planned your presentation correctly, whatever you are saying or offering should have some direct benefit to your audience. Keep that in mind: **your audience needs you, and they want to hear what you have to say.** It's easier to sound more energetic and heartfelt when you concentrate more on helping your audience and less on your own nerves.
- **Focus on your ideas.** The voices in your head can get overwhelming at times. Trying to correct too many bad behaviors while presenting (stop playing with your pen, slow down, look to the left more, get your hand out of your pocket!) is enough to drive you batty. **The time to learn how to correct presentation behaviors is in your practice sessions; presentation time is the time to just focus on your ideas.** What do you need to tell the audience? What do they need to hear from you? Focus on telling them this information effectively, and your voice will sound much less overwhelmed.
- **Psych yourself up.** If you watch athletes before a game, you'll find they have a number of different methods for getting themselves energized before "go time." Some listen to music, some jump up and down and shake out their limbs, some huddle and have pep talks, some even pound themselves in the heads to ensure they are sufficiently awake. Regardless of the method (and please do any jumping, shaking, or head-pounding in a space *away* from your audience's gaze), the mentality is all the same: **get into a headspace that is full of determination and vigor for what's to come.** If you let your last thoughts before presenting be, "Oh, no. I don't want to do this!" you will find it hard to display genuine enthusiasm to your audience.
- **Talk with your audience.** Conversations are generally much easier to handle than presentations. If you create an invisible barrier between you and your audience in which you only talk and they only listen, your voice, indeed, might start to drone on and on and on. **If you inject conversation into your presentation, you will find yourself and your audience to be more comfortable.**

If you sound like you believe in your message, it becomes much more enticing for your audience to also believe in it. Find a method that makes you comfortable and enthusiastic so that your presentations are more reminiscent of the electrifying presenters you've seen, rather than the boring speakers you weren't able to escape.

"I Really, Really, *Really* Do Mean It": Removing Traces of Vocal Doubt

Students' voices quite often betray them by revealing their nerves. They sound, well, hesitant. To be believed, to be trusted, you must *sound* like the expert you are.

Demonstrating conviction, though, takes more than strings of "really" or "very." Just saying you "really, really, really think this is a great idea" or you "believe in this product very, very, very much," won't cut it. In fact, one study found that that people who overused intensifiers like "really" and "very" were seen as *less* trustworthy (Lind, et al., 1978).

Your audience will listen for the proof in the sound of your voice and the strength of your words, not in the number of repetitive adverbs you use.

Inflection: *"We Are the Right Choice for You?"*

Presenters who do not feel completely confident in their knowledge or who have difficulty talking definitively may use **uptalk**, which is a rising intonation at the ends of their sentences. Listen to someone who presents a fact they are not sure is true or states an opinion they think is unpopular; they probably inflect their statement as though it is a question. That is, the tone of their voice goes up at the end of the sentence; they use *uptalk*.

A small amount of uptalk is natural in speech and adds to vocal variety, but if your nerves, your lack of preparation, or your unwillingness to plainly state information to your audience causes you to raise your inflection at the ends of too many of your sentences, your audience will find it difficult to take your information seriously. After all, if even *you* don't appear to believe in it enough to state it as a fact, why should the audience believe it at all?

You may engage in uptalk more than you realize. Watch videos or listen to vocal recordings of yourself presenting to others. Ask yourself (or ask an impartial friend who is not afraid to tell you the truth), "Do I sound like an expert, or do I sound unsure or immature?" If you didn't answer *expert*, then it's time to start practicing your inflection and talking like you mean it.

Disfluencies: *"We, uh, are, um, the right choice for you."*

A *disfluency* is a disruption in the flow of your speaking. Choppiness, vocalized pauses ("uh" and "um"), and excessive reliance on filler words and phrases ("like," "you know," and "sort of") all qualify as disfluencies.

In a presentation in which you are supposed to be conversational—and, therefore, not perfect—a few disfluencies are not a big deal. The problem begins when the disfluencies become so prevalent that they are either distracting to the audience or they hurt your credibility. After all, it's difficult to believe that you are confident in the information you are presenting if your sentences are littered with very hesitant-sounding "uhs" and "ums."

Reducing your reliance on disfluencies is an important task, but it surely is not an easy one. I promise you, though, that it *can* be done, and I am living proof. When I was an undergraduate, I had to take a course in public speaking, and the pressure of talking to a crowd rattled me. I "uhh-hed" and "ummed" my way through the first couple of speeches I delivered. It

Avoid sounding as hesitant as Cesar and Ashley look.

wasn't until I had to watch myself on video that I even realized it was such a problem. So I committed myself to eradicating my reliance on fillers. I practiced each speech over and over again to get myself comfortable with the material, and every time I said "uh" or "um," I would stop myself and start over until I could get through the whole thing without any disfluencies at all.

In truth, that method helped—a little. What helped even more was when I started *presenting* instead of *public speaking*. In the context of a speechwriting class, my job was to deliver the speech as I had written it, as close to word-for-word as I could get it. It was in my later college years, my post-undergrad years, and especially in my graduate-school years that I really began to reduce the disfluencies. Why? Because I started teaching, and to teach well I had to prepare like a presenter, not a public speaker.

Teachers just *know* the material, rather than committing ahead of time to the words they will use to share it with the class. When I started talking to roomfuls of students about topics I knew and cared about, the disfluencies began to simply fall away. I was less nervous and less hesitant, because *I actually knew what I was talking about*. In my public-speaking course, I usually only researched and knew enough to write the speech. That, coupled with the added pressure of trying to remember exactly what words I was supposed to say, caused me to feel and sound hesitant.

This story should lead you to two conclusions: (1) trying to memorize the words you want to say to your audience will hurt your vocal quality and lead to more disfluencies; and (2) if you really do gain true expertise on your topic, you will be more likely to sound like an expert.

Language Use: "Well, we believe we are sort of the right choice for you—or whatever."

Just as the fear of presenting and the hesitation to speak frankly cause presenters to litter their speaking with disfluencies, that same fear and hesitation can also cause presenters to choose wishy–washy language. Let's look at some of the most common catchphrases in the world of indecisive language:

- *I Think, I Feel Like,* and *I Believe.* All of those words sound so hopeful and pleasant, but when you're delivering important information, audiences rarely want to hear them. They don't want to hear that you *think* you have a great product, you *feel* like you can help them make money, or you *believe* your idea won't be an utter failure. Audiences who are staking their time, their money, or even their reputation on you and your ideas want to know what you *know*, not what you *think*, *feel*, or *believe*.
- *Sort of* and *Kind of.* Many presenters who use these filler phrases don't do so because they are actually trying to hedge their statements, but they say them as a nervous tick (akin to "uh" or "um"). Nonetheless, telling audiences that your ideas are *sort of* great or your information is *kind of* solid is not particularly reassuring. Avoid the hedging and tell your audience what *actually and definitively is*.
- *… Or Whatever.* Few statements make my heart drop as much as when I hear a presenter follow his/her claims with "or whatever." If you make a statement that

you know is true, don't chicken out at the last second and tack on "or whatever." Stand by it unless and until you have a real reason not to do so.

Regardless of which sins of hesitation you may have committed in the past, make a concerted effort moving forward to use language with conviction. If you believe in yourself and your ideas—as I sincerely hope you do—you need to project that confidence to your audience. Otherwise, your hesitant language subliminally tells your audience, "Don't believe a word I say."

The Key to Saying It Like You Mean It? Practice Like You Mean It

When it comes to your vocal quality—or any aspect of presenting, for that matter—practice helps get you closer to perfect. The more you talk in a strong volume, at a reasonable rate, with genuine enthusiasm, and without vocalized hesitations, the more that definitive and confident voice will be a part of your "natural" speaking style. If you hedge throughout normal conversations or rely on fillers like "um," "like," or "you know," practice eliminating those behaviors in your everyday life.

Talk to yourself aloud. Read to yourself aloud. Talk to your friends. Talk to your family. Talk to strangers (just not the kind who want to give you candy). But more importantly, *practice talking effectively*. Eliminate the hedges, eliminate the fillers, increase your enthusiasm, raise your volume, and practice having conviction in what you say. If you work on improving your everyday voice, your presentation voice will naturally follow suit.

Key Takeaways

- For the audience to see you as credible, you must sound as though you are credible.
- The ideal vocal quality is confident and conversational.
- Project your volume, use a conversational rate with strategic pausing, and inject enthusiasm into your presenting voice.
- Practice confident speaking to remove traces of doubt in your voice and to sound like someone your audience will want to follow.

Questions and Activities:

1. **Reflection Question:** Search YouTube for poet Taylor Mali's performance of "Totally like whatever, you know?" Watch the video and reflect on your own speaking style. How much of Mali's speaking style sounds like your own? How about your friends' or peers' speaking style?

2. **Learning Activity:** Record yourself talking about your three best qualities. Then listen back to the recording (if it was on video, close your eyes or look away from the screen so you don't get distracted by your body language). If you didn't know yourself, what perception would you have of you based on your speaking style? Now respond honestly to the following questions:

My volume demanded attention	YES!	Yes	Maybe	No	NO!
I spoke slowly enough to be understood	YES!	Yes	Maybe	No	NO!
I paused long enough to let my words sink in	YES!	Yes	Maybe	No	NO!
I sounded excited and enthusiastic	YES!	Yes	Maybe	No	NO!
I sounded confident in myself and my ideas	YES!	Yes	Maybe	No	NO!
I sounded mature and professional	YES!	Yes	Maybe	No	NO!
I sound like someone I would want to hear again	YES!	Yes	Maybe	No	NO!

3. **Learning Activity:** Give a relatively impromptu presentation to others about your biggest pet peeve. Concentrate on "getting into it" and allowing your voice to communicate your frustration and annoyance.

4. **Presentation Preparation:** Choose a story you plan to tell for your next presentation, and deliver it to a willing audience member. Have that person critique your delivery style. What could you do vocally to increase your story's impact without sounding canned or overly rehearsed?

Credits

CHAPTER 17

Look at Me! I'm Presenting!
Learning to Look Like You Mean It

With contributions from Dyan Robinson

After studying this chapter, you should be able to:
- *Identify the two messages your nonverbal behaviors should send to your audience.*
- *Make effective eye contact with your listeners.*
- *Use appropriate gestures, movement, and posture to display your confidence and competence.*
- *Explain the benefits of smiling when presenting.*

It's hard for us to imagine now, in the age of sound bites and one-liners, that at one time moviegoers eagerly watched films without spoken dialogue. Before the age of "talkies," actors made audiences laugh, cry, and wince with fear through their soundless actions and facial expressions, much like a street mime draws in passersby without having to say a word.

The allure of silent-movie stars and of face-painted performers trapped in invisible boxes teaches an important lesson: **your nonverbal behaviors can communicate quite loudly to your audience.** In a presentation, you need to ensure that *your* nonverbal behaviors are communicating two clear messages to your audience:

1. I am confident in what I am saying.
2. You can trust me.

By definition, nonverbal communication is anything other than the words you say (which includes everything from the tone of your voice to the clothes that you wear). For this chapter, though, we are going to focus on the physical aspects of your nonverbal communication through five main areas: eye contact, gestures, movement, posture, and smiling. It should be noted that the suggestions to follow adhere to American customs and perceptions of nonverbal behavior. If your audience is comprised of a large portion of non-Americans, be sure that you research that culture's expectations for nonverbal behavior.

Look into My Eyes: Making Appropriate Eye Contact

Making eye contact with your audience lets them know that you care about them. It's not just that looking away makes you look less confident (which it does); it's that it prevents you from making a connection with your listeners. The presentation is supposed to be *for* the audience. As Eisenberg (1971) has noted, direct eye contact with another indicates that the lines of communication are open. **Looking your listeners in the eyes signals that they are important to you and that they are worth your individual time and attention.**

It's Not So Scary

If you are a nervous presenter, the idea of looking directly into listeners' eyes might seem intimidating. You may feel safer by looking instead at chins, noses, foreheads, walls, ceilings, floors, and projector screens. Often I see presenters let their eyes sweep over the audience's foreheads, avoiding direct eye contact as if their listeners were basilisks whose very gaze could instantly strike them dead.

While you may think that avoiding direct eye contact will make your nerves calmer, it will likely have the *opposite effect*. The next time you're facing a crowd of at least fifteen people, try this: let your eyes sweep over everyone (look at foreheads or hair, but don't lock eyes). The crowd looks big, right? Like, *really scary big*.

Now lock eyes for a few moments with one person in that crowd. Now look at another person in the eyes. Now, try another. I will venture to guess that being able to take the crowd one person at a time feels less overwhelming. Individual conversations are easier to handle than talking to a sea of nameless, faceless heads.

Make Better Eye Contact

So, if scanning and avoiding eyes is wrong, how do you make *real* eye contact? Put simply: you look individual listeners in the eye. I've said it before, and I will say it again: *presenting should be like a conversation*.

Pick one person and start talking to her for a while. When you get some recognition from her (the returned smile, a nod, a sparkle in her eye that says, "I'm with you"), you can move onto someone else on the other side of the room. Then chat it up with him for a sentence or two until he looks on board. This person-by-person method make these individual audience members feel valued and included (and will also help to keep you calm).

There is no one correct prescription for who you should look at first, second, and third. Instead, aim to make eye contact with people in all areas of the room. If you start by locking eyes with someone in the left section of the room, look at someone in the center next. After that, lock eyes with someone to the right. Keep looking at different areas of the room, but each time you do, try to find a new person to engage visually. This method will allow you to make genuine connections with multiple people without ignoring large sections of the room for extended periods of time.

The Power of the Eyes

I'm not exaggerating when I say that eye contact is *crucial* to the success of your presentation, especially when your intent involves persuasion. It should not surprise you, then, that good eye contact can help you demonstrate both of the nonverbal messages you want to send your audience:

Connor is using direct eye contact to show you that he cares.

1. **I am confident in what I am saying.** American audiences associate direct

eye contact with confidence and competence (Beebe, 1974; Droney & Brooks, 1993; Tessler & Sushelsky, 1978). Looking up, down, or all around says, "I don't really know what I'm talking about. Please stop looking at me."

2. **You can trust me.** Whether or not it's true, we presume that when people avoid eye contact, they are lying. At the very least, your audience might misread your lack of eye contact as a signal that you do not want to be talking to them. When we like people—when we want to have a positive relationship with them—we give them direct eye contact (Argyle & Dean, 1965). Looking your audience in the eyes says, "Hi. I'm here for you."

Eye contact is the most important facet of your nonverbal behavior. Without it, there is no connection between you and your audience. And, without that connection, you might as well have sent a written report instead.

Put Your Hands in the Air Like You Really Do Care: Using Appropriate Gesturing

Presenters without podiums to clench, notes to hold, or pens to click are often faced with a dilemma: *What am I supposed to do with my hands?*

If you are of the mindset that presenters are supposed to exhibit the utmost bodily control in front of their audience, then those silly little limbs of yours will feel completely in the way. And if nervousness hits, you may find your hands engaging in all sorts of ridiculous antics: playing with your hair, twirling your rings, cracking your knuckles, clenching your elbows, tugging at your shirt, rubbing the tops of your thighs, or just giving up and hiding in your pockets.

All of these actions are problematic because they contradict the first message your nonverbal behaviors are trying to send: "I am confident in what I'm saying." It's hard for your audience to believe that you're an expert on your topic (or on anything, really) when your flailing arms look like they're trying to fly you far, far away. Moreover, crossed arms or clenched hands make you appear physically closed off to your audience, thus calling into question our second nonverbal message: "You can trust me."

The better solution is *just to gesture* like you would in a normal conversation. If you are in a bigger space with a bigger audience, you might want to exaggerate your gestures a bit so everyone can "get the full show," but for most audiences and most venues you'll encounter, your normal conversational hand movements are fine. Gesturing will give your overactive hands something to do, and your hand movements will appear natural and purposeful.

Look at Joe and Sarah's hand placements. How do you think they feel? Probably not overly confident or enthusiastic.

Move It: Using Appropriate Movement

Standing still is boring. So often, presenters find one spot in front of the audience and get locked down for the remainder of their time. But you know nothing bad will happen if you leave that spot, right? There are no hidden land mines, no secret trap doors. You are free to move about the room.

Movement can be a finicky behavior to get right. No movement can make you seem less confident,

Movement matters; keep it purposeful.

like you were ordered to stand in one spot and now you can't seem to get your feet to move again. Too much movement begins to look like pacing, and that can make you look angry or perhaps even frantic. The ideal movement is slow and *purposeful*.

Try this: start in one spot in front of the room, stand still, and give your introduction. Then, as you transition to your first main point, move slowly across the room to a new spot. When you reach that spot, stop and solidly plant your feet to face your audience. As you talk about your first point (or sub-point), look at people in all three areas of the room. When you're ready to move your content onto to a new claim, move your physical position again to visually represent that transition to your audience. In other words, **use your movement to punctuate your presentation.**

Movement can also help the emotional feel of your presentation and aid in your connection with the audience. In most instances, a proper "social distance" of approximately four to twelve feet from your audience is appropriate. However, if you are telling a personal story or are taking questions from the audience, you may feel comfortable getting a bit closer, so long as you don't hover uncomfortably over them. Mindful movement can show your audience that you want to make a personal connection with them and that you are interested in what they have to contribute.

Stand Tall: Using Appropriate Posture

In the moments when you are not moving purposefully across the room, you need to *stand still*. Kicking your feet, shifting your body weight from side to side, rocking back and forth, or constantly moving from one place to the next makes you seem nervous—or like you really should have used the potty before beginning. Neither one says, "Look at me: I'm brimming with confidence in what I'm saying!"

Let me make it clear here that you are not expected to keep your body perfectly still while your head oscillates left and right like a room fan to look around the room. Let your body move naturally to make eye contact with your audience. But *constant movement* of your feet or your body can be very distracting to your listeners. Instead of them thinking, "Oh, what brilliant ideas this presenter has!" they are left to wonder, "Is this some new dance move I don't know?"

When you do move after a point or sub-point, pick a spot on the floor as your destination. When you reach that spot, stop and plant your feet so they face your audience. If you feel the nerves start to bubble up, try to channel that adrenaline through your gestures and through the enthusiasm in your voice, not through a snappy two-step or shuffle-and-slide.

Not only should you avoid looking antsy in front of your audience, but it's also important that you don't look closed off. Avoid crossing your legs, shifting your weight to one leg, or standing sideways to your audience. Doing so will make you look angry, bored, or unapproachable. Instead, stand square to the audience (that is, face them fully) and avoid dropping your hip to one side. Proper posture communicates both confidence and trustworthiness to your audience.

Smile!: Looking Happy to Be Here

The great Louis Armstrong once crooned that, "when you're smiling, the whole world smiles with you" (Fisher, Shay, & Goodwin, 1929). Well, Satchmo was right: smiling is contagious. If you begin your presentation with a friendly smile, you are likely to see many of your audience members smiling back at you. That warmth you'll get from them will help you to feel more comfortable and, therefore, *sound* more comfortable. The presentation will start to seem more like a conversation between friends (or at least acquaintances), rather than a stare-down between strangers.

Smiling shows confidence. Dan is showing—uh—something else.

Don't underestimate the power of a smile. It communicates both of the ideal nonverbal messages:

1. **I am confident in what I am saying.** Unless you are afflicted with the nervous giggles, genuine smiling generally denotes confidence (Ekman, Davidson, & Friesen, 1990).
2. **You can trust me.** People are more trusting of those people they like, and a smile makes you seem more approachable, friendly, and helpful.

Move to the Beat: Nonverbal Communication as Verbal Support

The right nonverbal communication not only communicates the two ideal messages—"I am confident in what I am saying," and "you can trust me"—but it also allows the audience to focus in on the content of the presentation. The best body movements and gestures *complement* what you are saying. Making eye contact to connect a point with a listener, using your hands to demonstrate your claims ("He's *this* tall!"), moving across the room to signal transitions between your ideas, planting your feet to focus in on an important explanation, and smiling to show the excitement the product or plan deserves—all of these nonverbal behaviors help to support the verbal content of your presentation.

People often use the phrase, "I'll believe it when I see it." Audiences think the same way. If you say your ideas are great, if you say you believe in them, if you say you're eager to help the client, you have to look the part for the audience to believe you. Practice in front of your mirror or in front of a video camera until you see that you actually look that part. Find out what presentation no-nos you commit that might be hurting your credibility or your trustworthiness, and work diligently to fix them. Remember, your presentation is a way to make a conversational connection with your audience. You need to look like you are happy and confident enough to do that.

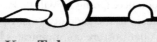

Key Takeaways

- Your nonverbal communication should communicate to your audience that you are confident in your message and that you are worthy of their trust.
- Use eye contact to make genuine connections with your listeners and display your credibility.
- Gesture conversationally, move slowly and purposefully, and demonstrate a confident posture.
- Smile! Show your audience you are happy to be with them and share your ideas.

Questions and Activities:

1. **Reflection Question:** Watch a video of yourself presenting. Turn off the sound and just pay attention to your nonverbal behavior. What are three aspects of your nonverbal behavior that are *effective*? What is the *one* (and only one) most important aspect of your nonverbal behavior that you need to work on before the next presentation? (Note: Hand gestures that seem perfectly normal and purposeful to the audience may look a bit manic on video. So long as your gestures are intentional—and not random or really just nervous tics—they are probably fine.)

2. **Learning Activity:** Give a relatively impromptu presentation to your audience (or a friend or two), describing the first car or bike you owned or rode. Use hand gestures, movement, and eye contact to "drive" home your points about what it looked like and how well (or not well) it rode. Aim to be animated!

3. **Learning Activity:** In your next conversation with a friend or family member (the kind of person who will forgive strange antics), try to use a different demeanor than you normally do. That is, if you are normally bubbly and smiley, attempt to look more straight-faced and serious. If you are normally even-toned, smile a lot more and aim to look more energetic. How does your friend or family member react to you? How does your demeanor change theirs?

4. **Learning Activity:** The next time you have to talk in front of any group of people or any class, make a conscious effort to smile more—start with a smile, end with a smile, and do lots of smiling in between. Take note of how many audience members start to smile back (or at least look slightly happier).
5. **Presentation Preparation:** Choose one or more main points from your next presentation to practice delivering. As best you can, mimic the basic room setup you will have for the presentation (how much walking room you have, where the audience and visual aids are in relation to you, etc.). Then deliver your main point(s) while moving purposefully around your space, looking in different areas of your "audience" and gesturing naturally. The more you practice your choreography, the less you'll have to remember to do it.

Credits

1. Eye Contact Copyright © 2014 by Isabel Chenoweth / Southern Connecticut State University. Reprinted with permission.
2. Hand Communication Copyright © 2014 by Isabel Chenoweth / Southern Connecticut State University. Reprinted with permission.
3. Movement Matters Copyright © 2014 by Audrey Mora. Reprinted with permission.
4. Keep Smiling Copyright © 2014 by Isabel Chenoweth / Southern Connecticut State University. Reprinted with permission.

CHAPTER 18

R-E-S-P-E-C-T, Find out What It Means to—Them

Demonstrating Respect for Business Clients

After studying this chapter, you should be able to:
- *Explain the importance of adhering to appropriate business customs when dealing with professional clients.*
- *Properly greet and speak to your professional clients in a way that demonstrates your respect for them.*

In her 1967 hit, Aretha Franklin belts out, "R-E-S-P-E-C-T, find out what it means to me" (Redding). But when it comes to dealing with professional clients, defining respect isn't about what it means to me or to you; it's about what it means to *them*. The customs and mannerisms you think are perfectly polite could very well appall someone else. Therefore, you must communicate with your audience's viewpoint in mind.

Now, I understand that saying that you have to be respectful of your audience may seem obvious, but when you are dealing with professional clients, as opposed to a room full of your classmates, the rules of the game change. In many cases, the Golden Rule of "Do unto others as you would have them do unto you" is a good rule to follow, but in the case of your clients, it may not be. You must remember that you are not your audience. You might be perfectly fine with skipping business formalities, using profanities, or even just talking a business deal out over wings and beer. That does *not* mean that your professional clients will appreciate the same treatment. To win their business, you have to learn to play their game.

When presenting, it can be hard to get out of your own head and think beyond the story you're trying to tell, but it is crucial to try to think like your clients. Picture how they see you, your team, and your presentation. How do they want to be greeted? What niceties are they expecting from you? What type of language—verbal and nonverbal—will make them most comfortable?

The lingering lesson of AIMC is that the audience should always be at the forefront of our minds when preparing or executing a presentation. If we have not reached them or spoken to their needs and goals, our efforts will all be for naught. But being audience-centered must extend beyond our construction of the message; it needs to be evident in how we behave toward the client.

In this chapter, we will review some of the basic elements of respect that you should employ in your presentation to a professional audience. I will concede that some of the advice to follow will seem nitpicky, but ask a group of business professionals for their business-meeting pet peeves, and you'll get a widely varied list. You don't want to commit the one interpersonal or professional sin that turns them against you before they've even considered your actual ideas.

Before the Presentation: Preparation Shows Dedication

Imagine you are throwing a party for a friend you love and respect. Would you invite him/her over at the last minute and then just drag random people off the street to sit around and stare at each other? I would hope not. You would show your friend how important s/he is to you by planning the party ahead of time and ensuring that it all runs smoothly.

You should demonstrate that same level of care and respect to your clients by ensuring that you are adequately—nay, *more than adequately*—prepared to put on a solid presentation that will speak to their needs and leave them with a positive impression. Not preparing properly disregards the audience and communicates to them, "You aren't that important to me." Everyone likes to feel important, especially people prepared to devote their time, attention, and possibly their money to you.

The Excellence Is in the Details

My father worked most of his career in retail management. His motto is one I hope you take to heart: "Don't make it hard for people to give you their money." For him, that meant ensuring there was enough staff to assist customers and enough cashiers to cut down on checkout wait times. For you, it means ensuring that you are fully prepared and that your clients can just sit down, relax, and concentrate on what you have to say.

There are a lot of small details that can make your clients feel welcome. Have chairs in place, papers stacked neatly, temperature controls set, and a title PowerPoint slide up. Perhaps you even want to step up your game further and have light background music playing as the clients enter, name tags on each member of your presenting team, and (for longer presentations) refreshments at each client place setting. None of these preparations alone will likely make or break the presentation, but often excellence is in the details. These little preparations let the client know that, "Yes, I am important to them. They do respect me and my time."

Above all, think through the presentation from the viewpoint of your audience. Ask yourself, "Is there anything else I need to be adequately prepared or to make this presentation as comfortable as possible for my clients?" If the answer is "yes," then keep prepping.

The Greeting: "Hey, I Just Met You, and This Is [Hopefully Not] Crazy"

No doubt you have heard the truism that "first impressions count" or that "you can never take back a first impression." While it may seem that your client's first impression of you lies solely in your presentation's opening line, they will actually be judging you well before you even get to deliver it. **The presentation really begins once you are in sight or earshot of the client.**

As a part of my former job as an administrator at a tutoring center, I used to interview and hire the teaching staff. Many times, I had mentally dismissed potential teachers before I even let them into the office to start the interview. Slouching in the waiting-room chairs, looking as though there were a thousand other places they would rather be than in our center, snapping gum at an obnoxiously loud volume—all of these behaviors were marks against their professionalism and how well I could believe that they genuinely wanted to work for us. Know that you are "on stage" immediately and that the audience's first impression of you may happen before you even open your mouth.

Properly Greet the Client

Don't let the first moment of meeting be awkward. If you are welcoming clients into a presentation space you have prepared, adhere to the following steps to ensure your greeting is smooth and respectful:

1. Meet the clients at the door. Stand and face them fully with open gestures (no crossed arms or legs).
2. Introduce yourself and anyone else with you while making direct eye contact and smiling to show you are friendly, confident, and approachable.

Shaking hands sets the right tone for your presentation. Doesn't Mike look happy that Sarah is here to listen to his presentation?

3. Shake right hands. Let your grip be firm (weak handshakes make you seem less confident), but don't try to fracture bones or inflict pain (overly firm handshakes may appear aggressive). Note: If the client does *not* offer his/her hand, skip this step; they may prefer not to touch other people.
4. Show the clients to their seats and ask them to "Please, sit down" or "Please, have a seat." If you or any of your teammates will also sit, wait for the clients to sit down first.
5. Offer available amenities to your clients. If you have beverages or snacks available, politely offer them to your clients. Don't ask vague questions like "Can I get you anything?" If they ask for an iced tea and a turkey sandwich, and you only have water and bagels, you'll have to be the bearer of bad news—not a positive start to the presentation.

Once you've made your stellar first impression, it's time to ensure that all the other impressions that follow will also be beneficial to you and your intent.

Delivering the Presentation: "I'm Here for You"

When all of your clients have settled in and are looking at you, it is time to begin. It is important that you communicate your gratitude for the opportunity to speak with them. By attending this meeting or presentation, the clients have done you a favor, and you need to show that you value their time and potential faith in you. Sample phrases to use include, "Thank you so much for giving us the opportunity to explain our product to you," or, "We really appreciate you taking the time to meet with us today."

Once you're ready to delve into the heart of your presentation, there are several elements that you should consider to maintain respect for your clients: your mentality, the words you use, checking in with clients, and maintaining patience. **Remember that, with any of these elements, the key point is this: If your clients feel disrespected, they'll move on.** Avoid the pitfalls that will trip you up and cost you the success of your presentation.

Your Mentality: It's Not Us vs. Them

Too often in presentations, speakers feel as though they are in an us-versus-them scenario. Their audience is a group to be conquered. The sale is a battle to be won. That kind of mindset gives the illusion that your clients are *against* you. Well, hop down from your horse and wipe off the war paint, Braveheart; no one's looking to take you out.

The truth is that most clients will want you to succeed; if they didn't, they wouldn't bother listening to what you have to say. Job interviewers *want* you to be the right candidate, company buyers *want* your product to be exciting for their customers, and committee members *want* you to have ideas that will work. You are *on their team*, so let the clients know that you are there to help them. They will respect you for it, and be more willing to embrace your presentation with an open mind rather than a slew of skepticism.

Use Appropriate Language: "Like, What the F, You Guys?"

In previous chapters, you have learned the ideal language and vocal quality to use in presentations. Beyond those tips, these suggestions will further help you to demonstrate respect to professional clients:

- **Avoid "you guys."** This is a common phrase that many people don't think twice about using in casual conversation, but it doesn't belong in a professional setting. Not only is "you guys" gender-specific (I'm not a "guy," thank you very much), but it is also too informal. Try "you all," "all of you," or simply just "you" instead.
- **Avoid profanities.** Some audiences won't care if you let a curse word or two slip by, but others will. In the realm of professional dealings, it's best to use less offensive language, even if one or two of your clients have been swearing like sailors since you first shook hands.
- **Avoid teen talk.** Relying on filler words—"like," "totally," "whatever," "super"— makes you seem immature and might make a professional audience question your credibility.
- **Remember your manners.** "Please" and "thank you" never go out of style. While every client may not be overwhelmed by your display of basic decency when you use these words, they will notice when you don't.

Checking in with Your Audience: Make Sure Everyone Is Still on Board

Earlier chapters have given you tips on responding to your audience's nonverbal cues. In most professional client situations, your audience is relatively small, which gives you greater opportunity to check in more directly. That is, **beyond gauging their nonverbal behaviors, you can also just ask your audience how they are doing.** They are people, too, after all. At key points throughout the presentation, make a point of checking in:

- "Are there any questions on how our product works before I move on to the pricing?"
- "So now that I have explained our product, tell me what you think. Is this something you would consider purchasing for your office?"
- "How is everyone doing? Do you need a break to stretch, or should I continue on to discuss the details of our plan?"

Remember to call an audible when it is needed, and adjust to your audience to make sure they're getting the information they need in a way they can understand and accept it.

Patience: Stay Calm, Hulk; They Wouldn't Like You When You're Angry

Presentations can be high-stress situations for presenters, particularly when one or more clients are being especially difficult. You must, however, keep your cool.

Remember, as frustrating as they may be at the moment, these clients are on your side. At worst, they're frenemies. But they are definitely not enemy combatants, so firing back with guns blazing will only end up backfiring on you. If you lose your temper and reply with a snippy tone of voice or passive–aggressive (or outright aggressive) remarks, you will be the one at fault (after all, you're the one "on stage"). Tsk tsk. We expect more from you!

So, what do you do when clients just won't relent? If they are clearly upset with you, start first by responding to the *emotional level* of their comments before responding to the content. Let's say that you are selling an electronic tablet to a client, and he rather rudely interrupts by saying, "I already have a laptop. Why in the world would I need another processing gadget that will probably break within a year? You think I'll just jump on the technology bandwagon and hand over my paycheck for nothing?" Yikes. Not nice, Mr. Client. Not nice.

But whether or not he plays well with others shouldn't stop you from being nice to him: "I can understand your skepticism. It's true that there are many similarities between this tablet and a laptop, but there are also some important advantages of a tablet that lead people like you to own both." **Start by showing your understanding and that the two of you are on the same team; then respond to the question.** He might be more apt to listen.

The Closing: "I Hope to See You Soon!"

In professional dealings, presentations are rarely a one-and-done scenario. If you convince clients to invest in your product, follow your plan of action, or even hire you for a job, you will have to work with these people again. The presentation is the start (or the continuation) of a working relationship.

When you are done presenting your arguments, make sure that you have answered everyone's questions thoroughly before drawing the presentation to a close. Keep in mind, though, that even though the official presentation is over, you are still "on stage" for your audience. Your instinct may be to let out a heavy sigh of relief, slump into a chair, or say exasperatingly, "Thank goodness *that's* over" once your presentation is done. But just as you needed to "be on" the moment your audience was in sight or hearing range of you, your presentation isn't *really* over until all your audience members are far, far away from you.

As everyone packs up to go, keep smiling, shake hands, and thank your audience again for their time and consideration. Make small talk. Offer to follow up. Give them your contact information. Ask if there is anything else you can answer or clarify. Without being creepy and overly pushy, let them know that you want to see them again.

As Ron Hoff (1992) notes, "We don't really think about making presentations. We put them in a much larger concept. We concentrate on building relationships" (p. 249). That is the essence of a good business presentation: it is one building block in a larger relationship. Ensure that you are likeable and amicable to your clients. Show them that you are someone they should want in a partnership.

A Multicultural Note: One Size Does Not Fit All

It is important to note that the advice above refers specifically to American presentation customs. While many pieces of advice transcend multiple cultures, some will not. Cater to your clients' culture and customs. As just one example of many, if you are meeting with clients from Japan (not people of Japanese ancestry who live in the US and demonstrate American customs, but people who actually live in, or are immersed in, Japanese culture), it is important that you do *not* make extended eye contact, particularly with those in a higher position than you. While for Americans that may show confidence and gumption, in Japanese culture that would communicate disrespect (Moran, Harris, & Moran, 2007).

Other cultures have different norms for offering food or drink, presenting gifts, using appropriate nonverbal behaviors, negotiating, dressing professionally, and many other issues that arise in presentations and professional dealings. Know your potential clients well. If you know you are doing international business or will be presenting to someone who actively practices a culture different from your own, do your homework. Know what is and is not considered respectful to them so you don't accidentally offend anyone.

Final Thoughts on Respect: Respect ≠ Brown-Nosing

I have students tell me that nobody likes a kiss-up. For the most part, this is true. But respecting your clients isn't about being sycophantic; it's about showing them the courtesy that they deserve. Remember that in order for you to achieve your presentation goals, you *need* your audience to be on board. Don't make it hard for them to be in your corner. Make yourself easy to like by showing them how important they are to you.

Let me share a final anecdote on respect: when my best friend's father passed away, I was amazed at how many people came to endure a two-hour wait in the cold rain to pay their respects to him and his family. A guidance counselor and English teacher, Lou had the opportunity to positively impact many people's lives, and that he clearly did. One of his students noted that "He always said whoever was in his office was the most important 'kid' in the building, and it was obvious that this was true, completely regardless of the person's achievements or aspirations." Lou was respected, because he knew how to make *everyone*—students, co-workers, neighbors, family, and even friends of his children—feel special.

As a presenter, you should aim to do the same for every audience you face. *Make them feel special*—like they are the most important clients you've ever had—whether they are your biggest or smallest account, whether you've just met them or have known them for years, and whether they are perfectly pleasant people or wretchedly bitter curmudgeons. Show your willingness to devote your time, attention, and understanding to them, because you appreciate *their* time, attention, and willingness to do business with you. Greet them warmly, treat them kindly, and work hard on their behalf. Aim to build a *relationship* with each of your clients; don't treat a presentation like it's a one-and-done encounter. If you show your audience that *they* are your first priority—that *they* are the "most important 'kid[s]' in the building"—you will see the respect you show them given back to you in turn.

Key Takeaways

- To show your clients respect, you must first consider what *they* would find respectful.
- Prepare for your presentations thoroughly, including the finer details like food, nametags, seating arrangements, etc.
- Greet the clients properly to make a positive and professional first impression.
- Show your clients that you are there for them throughout the presentation by keeping the right mentality, using appropriate language, checking in with them periodically, and controlling your temper.
- Make it clear to your audience that you hope to see them again.
- Study the cultures of your clients if they are different from your own to ensure you don't accidentally offend them.

Questions and Activities:

1. **Reflection Question:** How well can you keep your patience with difficult situations or clients/customers? Give an example of a specific time when you were able to keep your cool—or a specific time when you were not. What steps will you take in your next presentation to stay calm if a client is particularly difficult?
2. **Learning Activity:** Choose a different country or culture to research. Find out how to appropriately greet businesspeople in that culture, and present this method to the class. Explain the custom (what it is and why they do it), and then demonstrate how to do it properly.
3. **Presentation Preparation:** Jot down a list of at least two "extras" or "details" you can address to demonstrate respect for your clients in your next presentation.

Credit

CHAPTER 19

Being Nervous Is Normal. Deal with It.

By Mike Bay

After reading this chapter, you should be able to:
- *Understand the symbiotic relationship between the audience and presenter.*
- *Utilize the positive effects of nervous adrenaline on your performance.*
- *Identify stress-reducing techniques to minimize negative physical and mental effects of nervousness.*
- *Avoid risky behaviors that will adversely affect your presentations.*

For most of us, the thought of public speaking can elicit some uncomfortable emotions. I still vividly remember my first major presentation at a national conference in Las Vegas. I had been dreading this moment for months, and here I was, sitting alone in a corner of a massive conference room, reviewing my PowerPoint slides for the hundredth time. I heard only silence as I felt the audience's scowling faces aimed at me before I even said a word. My breathing became shallow, my heart rate elevated, my palms got clammy, and I suddenly wished I had grabbed a bottle of water (or two) from the breakfast table. After a polite introduction from someone I never met, I nervously ambled to the front of the stage and made some awkward introductory remarks. As I reached the end of my opening summary, I made a startling discovery: the audience wasn't there to judge me. I was there for the audience.

I soon realized that I was simply participating in an exchange of ideas and information. This was not a test or a trial, and I didn't have to command the stage like a Broadway performer. Soon, my forty-five minutes flew by, and I actually found the experience to be quite invigorating. The feeling of dread had lifted.

The lesson here is simple: **once you become more concerned with your audience's needs rather than your own, you have cleared the first hurdle in overcoming your fear of speaking in public.**

Nervous? Good!

Let me reassure you that if speaking in front of people makes you feel nervous, then congratulations—you are completely normal. I hope you find this diagnosis reassuring, because there are no techniques that will make you completely immune to these sensations. There is no guaranteed cure-all, and you shouldn't want there to be.

Nervousness can be a good thing; you need to accept your nerves and embrace the positive impact it can have on your performance. When the butterflies start fluttering (or maybe even violently flailing) around in your stomach, your body is indicating that you care about how you are perceived and that you want to do well. Those are both wonderful qualities for a presenter.

As stress levels rise, adrenaline is released into the bloodstream, increasing your breathing rate and sharpening your senses. This helps you to appear more energetic and engaged. When your roommate keeps you up for half the night watching TV, or you feel a bit under the weather, the adrenaline will help your body kick into high gear and help you get the job done.

Even after teaching hundreds of classes and presenting at dozens of conferences and workshops, I am happy to say that I still feel nervous before I speak. If you are one of the "lucky" few who don't get nervous, I would question how much the presentation meant to you, and I would certainly question how much it meant to your audience.

While there is a bright side to nervousness, anyone with shaky hands, sweaty palms, and a squeaking voice knows that there is also a dark side. Being nervous can quickly escalate into fear, panic, or even a complete meltdown if you don't address how to deal with your nerves effectively. By developing a realistic set of expectations, combined with plenty of preparation and practice, you will be able to harness this nervous energy and provide the audience with a positive and lasting experience.

Presenters Are Not Perfect

Perhaps the most common source of stress is caused by an unrealistic expectation of what a *professional presentation* is. We are all familiar with the image of a well-rehearsed politician behind a podium making dramatic, emotional appeals to a large and diverse audience. These are *speeches,* and they are very different from what you are being asked to do.

I once saw a student forget to introduce himself at the beginning of a presentation. As soon as he realized it, his shoulders slumped, his eyes fell to the floor, and he continued his presentation looking like someone just punched him in the gut. It struck me that he felt that he had to be *perfect* in order to get a good grade, despite my best efforts to refute this expectation. No wonder he was so nervous!

After he sat down, I asked the class how they would have reacted if, once he realized his mistake, he simply said, "Oh, by the way, my name is Tom." They all agreed that they would have laughed and quickly moved on. Your audience is interested in the information you are sharing, not in how many errors you make.

The goal of a professional presentation is to communicate specific information to an audience in an informative, organized, and engaging manner. **Perfection is not an expectation.** If you make a mistake, it's not the end of the world. By looking your audience members in the eyes and talking

Don't let little mistakes derail you. Connor needs to laugh and move on.

to them, you are engaging in a conversation, which is far less daunting than delivering a memorized speech to a crowd of foreheads. Mispronouncing a word or temporarily losing your train of thought will not change the tide of a political election or trend on Twitter. Simply laugh it off, pause to gather your thoughts, or ask the audience for help ("What was I saying?"). They will appreciate the humility and your willingness to reach out to them. I would even argue that an "imperfect" presentation would be seen as more real and personal than one that comes across as too polished or over-rehearsed.

Train Your Brain: Presentations Take Practice

A successful presentation is a physical activity that requires sufficient practice to coordinate your thoughts, words, and movements. Proper preparation is absolutely essential if you want to reduce the amount of stress you may feel before and during your presentation. However, most students do not practice effectively.

Professional athletes spend the majority of their time practicing and preparing their bodies for the relatively small amount of time that they actually compete. If your "rehearsal" consists of closing your eyes and running through the presentation a few times in your head, you will be unlikely to reduce your stress levels, and you may even reach your "meltdown point" on presentation day when your body reacts negatively to these new and stressful stimuli.

Think about it: which tests make you the most nervous? Probably the ones that you didn't study for. If you know your material and have practiced with your visuals like it was the real thing, the presentation will feel less stressful. You'll find it easier to be in the moment and converse with your audience if you don't have to think so hard about what you are supposed to say.

Recording and reviewing your rehearsals is an invaluable tool for minimizing stress. Try to recreate the environment as accurately as possible by finding a space that allows for sufficient room to move. Ask a classmate, family member, or friend to operate the camera/smartphone. In addition to facilitating the recording, they can also act as an "audience" member for practicing eye contact. They can even provide valuable feedback during and after your performance.

I realize that this is not an ideal way to spend your free time, but if you want to reduce your nervousness and improve your performance, it is one of the best tips I can provide.

OK. It's Go Time!

Despite all of your preparation, you are still likely to experience some buildup of nervous energy leading up to your presentation. Although it's entirely normal to *feel* nervous on presentation day, you don't want to *look* nervous. Imagine how concerned the audience would be if they saw their company's CEO biting her fingernails and anxiously pacing back and forth before presenting

Have a friend record your rehearsal. Then watch the "game tapes" to see how you did.

the fourth-quarter earnings report. Your presentation may not be as high stakes, but you still want to avoid making your audience nervous for you. You need to gain your audience's respect, not their pity.

To help reduce nervousness and promote a calmer, more confident appearance, please note the following suggestions:

1. **Take a walk.** If possible, it's a good idea to try to expend some of this extra energy by taking a brisk walk around the building. Extreme nervousness is really just a buildup of adrenaline that your body no longer knows how to channel properly. So, instead of releasing this extra adrenaline through shaking, sweating, and swooning, it's better to do something physical before the presentation. The easiest solution? Walk it off. But don't slowly shuffle your way down the hallway or outside, thinking, "Oh, no. Here it comes!" like you are marching to your doom. Move quickly, like you are in New York City and the people behind you will mow you down if you don't step lively. This tip won't get rid of all your nervousness, but it will help to "take the edge off."

2. **Find your inner Zen.** If you must sit before you present, keep your body open and calm as best you can. Avoid crossing your legs; your nervousness will make them more likely to fall asleep. Keep your arms at your sides to minimize tension, and occasionally stretch out your fingers and wrists to keep the blood flowing to your hands (this will help to keep them from noticeably trembling when the nerves hit). Sit upright and keep your shoulders back to reduce tension in your neck. From this position, take a few long, slow breaths to help settle your nerves and get some needed oxygen deep into your lungs. The calmer and looser you can keep your body, the calmer you'll feel when you get up to present.

3. **Don't write a script or try to memorize.** It's tempting to think that preparing every last word will help calm your nerves, but it won't. It will only make the nerves that much worse when you inevitably forget a word or phrase and get thrown completely off course.

4. **Hold a conversation with someone else before the presentation about something other than the presentation.** Just brooding about what's to come will not help your nerves. Last-minute "studying" also won't help. Cramming may work for tests, but it does not work for presentations. In the moments before you are to present, either you know it or you don't.

5. **Look your listeners in the eyes.** Scanning over your audience members' heads makes it look like there are a lot more people in the room than there actually are. If you make eye contact with one person at a time, for a few seconds at a time, the presentation becomes less like

Mike and Sarah take a brisk walk and talk about something pleasant before their big presentation.

an overwhelming address to a crowd and more like a very manageable series of one-to-one conversations.

Drug-Free Is the Way to Be

Unfortunately, some people still feel the need to numb their nerves through the use of drugs or alcohol. This is simply not an option. Your audience will know that you're "off," and your credibility as a professional is lost. As with most things in life, the quick "fixes" will not provide the desired results. As a presenter, it is important to appreciate that someone thought enough of you and your abilities to provide this opportunity. If you feel that chemicals are required to deal with the situation, then perhaps they were wrong to put their faith in you.

Please Stop Undressing Us with Your Eyes

Nervous presenters will try almost anything, including picturing their audience members naked. Despite the fact that it's pretty creepy for you to imagine us all in our skivvies, it's also counterintuitive to everything you have learned about the importance of the audience and your ability to connect with them. Let me identify two major problems with this whole nakedness concept:
1. The mentality behind it is that your audience is threatening to you. Thus, stripping them of their clothes will make them be more vulnerable and you more powerful. But your audience is not your enemy. Please don't mentally take their clothes off like a bully pulling another kid's pants down on the playground. It's just not nice.
2. Look around the room or think of the types of people you will present to in the working world. Do you *really* want to see *all* of them naked? What could make it harder to make eye contact (or even look in the audience's general vicinity) than picturing the businesspeople in your audience (people like your parents and grandparents) with no clothes on? Yikes! You might not even want to open your eyes.

Please, don't mentally undress your listeners. A clothed audience will be much easier to deal with than a naked one.

What's the Worst that Could Happen?

Remember, being nervous is normal. Even if you follow all of the above advice, nerves won't just go away. The key is to channel them appropriately.

Mistakes happen, and that's okay. Your audience won't care, and they won't remember the little blunders along the way, so long as you gave them a message worth hearing. They want you to succeed; they are on your side. Accepting these facts will go a long way toward diminishing any irrational fears of presenting to others. I remember sitting on the plane heading home after my Las Vegas conference, wishing I had known that earlier.

Lisa's Tip: "Don't Give Up"

It seems cliché to tell you, "Don't give up!"—but I'm going to say it anyway.

Many times I have seen students' nerves take hold and twist their tongues into metaphorical knots. Their racing brains can't focus, their mouths can't form words correctly, and they begin to feel mentally and physically defeated. Sometimes they just race through to the end of the presentation and bow out ungracefully. A few times I've witnessed a complete surrender: "I'm just going to sit down now." My response? "No, you're not!"

I don't like quitters, and neither does your audience. You are *human*. You are bound to make mistakes. So what if you completely blanked out in front of your audience? So what if it sounds like a cat actually "got your tongue" and is gripping it in its claws? So what if you want to crawl into a hole and come back out in a few years when the memory of this day fades? Here's some harsh reality: this isn't about *you*. You need to *get over yourself*.

Presentations are about the *audience*. Laugh off your mishap and focus in on what you need to tell the people sitting in front of you—whether or not you say it as eloquently or cleverly as you had planned.

Is your mind still blank and you still can't think of what to say? *Talk to your audience*: "My goal was to introduce you to a new product I've developed to help students better organize their desks. Let me just ask you, though, what are *you* most interested in knowing about it?" Let their questions guide your presentation. Yes, you'll be completely out of order from what you had anticipated saying, but *at least you will have shared the information*. (It will probably only take a question or two from the audience to help jog your memory about the points you initially wanted to make, anyway.)

Remember, too, *you are your harshest critic*. Yes, obviously your audience noticed that you were a wee bit nervous when you stood silently gaping like a deer in headlights in front of the projector's beam. But that shouldn't be the only takeaway they get from your presentation. If you give up and silently retreat offstage before you've really shared the meat of your presentation, then that is *all* they will remember (because it's all you've *given* them to remember). If you can salvage some of your content, the audience has something else to focus on: the information you originally wanted them to have.

So here comes the cheesy, inspirational go-to line again: "Don't give up!" Your audience deserves to hear the information they showed up to hear. Adjust your tactics to make sure you share that information with them before you retreat offstage to slump your head in your hands or belt out a muffled scream into your well-tailored suit jacket.

Key Takeaways

- Focusing more on your audience (and less on yourself) will help to reduce your nervousness.
- Nervousness is normal, and, when channeled correctly, it can improve your enthusiasm and liveliness.
- Presentations do not need to be perfect to be effective. Erase the notion that perfection is your goal.
- A lack of preparation causes nerves. Practice more to feel more comfortable.
- Do what you can to avoid excess nervousness when you present (take a brisk walk beforehand, keep your body calm, avoid scripts, don't brood or cram, and look your audience in the eye), but avoid chemical fixes and bad advice.

Questions and Activities:

1. **Reflection Question:** Think of the last presentation you were really nervous about. Why do you think you had so much trepidation about the presentation? Which specific tips do you think would have helped you keep calm the most? Why?
2. **Learning Activity:** Find a prewritten speech, like Abraham Lincoln's Gettysburg Address. Try to memorize it and deliver it to an audience. Notice how much more nerve-wracking it is to attempt to deliver a memorized speech than it is to deliver a presentation.
3. **Learning Activity:** Tell a story to the class. Start by not making any eye contact with anyone. After a minute, begin to look at your listeners in the eyes, one at a time. Notice how much more comforting it is to look at others like you are in conversation than to ignore your audience completely.
4. **Presentation Preparation:** This one should be obvious. Practice your presentation without memorization and without over-rehearsing each and every word. Practice like you are delivering the real thing (use visuals, good vocal quality, and nonverbal behaviors, etc.) at least three times, and make adjustments as needed.

Credits

1. Being Nervous is Normal. Deal with It Copyright © 2014 by Mike Bay. Reprinted with permission.
2. Little Mistakes Copyright © 2014 by Isabel Chenoweth / Southern Connecticut State University. Reprinted with permission.
3. Recording Copyright © 2014 by Audrey Mora. Reprinted with permission.
4. Take a Brisk Walk and Talk Copyright © 2014 by Isabel Chenoweth / Southern Connecticut State University. Reprinted with permission.

CHAPTER 20

How to Practice for Presentation Success

By M. Sandra DiFrancesco

After studying this chapter, you should be able to:

- *Apply effective practice techniques for communicating key ideas, not memorizing words.*
- *Understand that practicing is one of the best opportunities for managing your anxiety by building your confidence.*
- *Recognize that the goal of practicing is to identify your strengths and discover weak areas you can work on to adjust and strengthen.*
- *Apply the ten guidelines of practicing to your own presentation practice.*

Practice takes hard work; all good players and good presenters know that. But practice also improves performance in every field of endeavor. The greatest athletes, musicians, actors/actresses, dancers, and other standouts spend countless hours perfecting their crafts. Presenters should be no different.

Excuses about Practicing

All too often, presenters create a false sense of preparedness by chanting a wide array of excuses for not practicing. Sometimes it's because they've just waited too long and there's no time left to practice. Other times, there are other reasons: the idea just seems boring, they feel embarrassed or too silly to practice out loud, they think they know their material like the back of their hand, or they truly feel that they'll be more enthusiastic when they stand in front of their audience if they don't practice beforehand. For some people, the problem seems to be that they believe practice is unnecessary, because they've deluded themselves into thinking, "I've never had a problem talking with people."

Excuses won't help you get better at, or calmer about, presenting. Too many people feel that they don't need to practice because they already "ran over" their presentation in their minds, but thinking about a presentation is not the same as practicing it. People who claim to be better speakers by preparing *less* are kidding themselves or are just trying to validate their laziness.

Most nerves hit when presenters realize just how unprepared to speak they actually are. It's like when you think you can easily ace a test, but then when it's test time and you actually see the questions, you realize you're in serious trouble. If, however, you practice and become familiar with your material, you will be more confident and feel good about what you are presenting. It's a mystery to me why more people don't practice.

Memorizing is a Bad Technique for Handling Nervousness

Practicing should never be about memorizing or perfecting the art of reading your speech out loud. Don't do it. It's a bad idea. Really! Memorization and reading are recipes for disaster.

For some, speech writing and reciting is a safe tactic to use. Sure, you could memorize what you are going to say to feel prepared, but why would you? This is a conversation with your audience, not a Shakespearean drama. Writing and then memorizing all those words is a tedious chore. It also sets you up for increased anxiety and the likelihood that you will forget a lot of what you planned to say. Picture how your presentation will look: there you are, eyes closed, your forehead all scrunched up as you struggle to memorize all the words you have to say for your success. You're so preoccupied with trying to remember your script that you no longer focus on the ideas behind the words—and you forget all about your audience. You need to get out of your head and actually have a conversation with your audience.

Not only is memorization a bad technique in and of itself, but it's also a bad strategy for handling nervousness. You are putting yourself under even more pressure to remember every word you want to say. How can you *not* be nervous about forgetting *all* those words? Honestly, this type of practicing would be agonizing and gut wrenching for even the most seasoned presenters. All those words to remember. And what happens if you forget even one word?

Do not confuse practice with memorization. Practice allows you to feel more comfortable with your message and its delivery. Memorization focuses all your attention on remembering every last word, rather than on your audience and your intent. You don't want to screw up or have things go wrong; it's understandable. But when you memorize, a lot does go wrong for both you, the presenter, and for the audience. There are better ways.

Make the audience be your priority. Practice by internalizing your key points and testing out your delivery, but avoid getting stuck to a script that would bar you from effective audience interaction. Practice until you are prepared enough to be competent and confident.

Be careful about **over-rehearsing,** when you become so rigid that you don't embrace interacting with your audience for fear it might "screw you up." If the audience is primary, responding to them is never screwing up. View your presentation as a communication opportunity and a chance to interact, share ideas, and provide information to others.

Practice Your Way to Success

Based on the assumption that you have done the preparation, researched, and become familiar with the material, your next step is to follow the advice outlined in the rest of this chapter. The best advice is not to wait until the day or morning before to start practicing. If you rush frantically to practice at the last minute, or if you practice only once, you're almost guaranteed to stink up the room.

Follow these tips to avoid scriptwriting and memorization and instead practice effectively for your presentations:

- **Learn the material first.** Not in relation to the points you're making in your presentation, but just to learn the material. It seems a lot of students practice with notes, their research, or a fully written-out speech in front of them because they don't actually know the material yet. Aim to learn about the topic itself, not to commit to memory just the facts you plan to include in your presentation.
- **Plan out the main points.** Use the basic presentation outline discussed in **Chapter 9: Speaking in Outlines.** Only write down a few words or phrases to help you organize your thoughts. Use this bare-bones outline to practice for the first few times to help you keep your thoughts organized.
- **Start Early.** Practice is not the last step of your presentation prep. It's a trial run to see what can be made better. You practice your presentation, evaluate it, make changes to it, and then practice it again. **Everything doesn't have to be in perfect form before you start to practice.** Practice is a way of evolving and improving, not a way to cram timing and information into your head.
- **Divide your material into bite-sized chunks.** If it's easier for you, you can practice in increments. Every practice session does not have to be a full trial run of your entire presentation. Actors and actresses don't practice the entire play every time. They break it into scenes and practice each scene until everything runs smoothly. For theater folk, that means getting every word right. You shouldn't attempt to commit words to memory; you should just aim to get the gist down before moving on.

   Practicing in increments—the attention-getting opening, the key ideas of each main point, the memorable closing—can also help determine the length of your presentation. Time your presentation during every practice. This way you'll know exactly how long your material is. You now have the opportunity to adjust it by scaling down some information or by adding more examples and details.

- **Practice whenever you have down time.** Practice in the car while you're driving, in the morning while you're eating breakfast, at the gym, in the shower, before you fall asleep. You should never say it exactly the same way twice, but having the basic ideas you want to express down pat will do wonders for your confidence.

Maximizing your Practice Time

Many feel they are the busiest people around—busier than anyone else. They barely have time to prepare, much less find several times to practice. But practicing is a non-negotiable part of your preparation. **The amount of time you set aside to practice a presentation is directly related to that presentation's success.** Plan for the times when you will practice.

Of course, it's always your decision to take risks and shortcuts. You can go through things in your mind, quickly look over your outline, look at your slides, and hope that the best will happen—but it probably won't. It might be their sixth sense, but **audiences know when you haven't put in the time.**

Ten Guidelines for Presentation Practice

Here's a little something to keep in mind: there are effective and ineffective ways to practice. It's important to note that just going through the motions of practice isn't enough. What does that mean, exactly? It means that **you need** *deliberate, effortful* practice with constructive feedback and self-reflection to make improvements along the way. If you follow the guidelines below, you will feel more prepared and confident on the day you present.

Sorry, slackers! There are no shortcuts around these steps:

1. **Don't practice with the goal of memorizing.** Take the pressure off yourself. Every word does not need to be pure poetry.

2. **Visualize your success.** Visualize yourself doing well. Imagine that your audience is fully engaged with what you are saying. If you can present confidently in practice sessions, you will be much more likely to present confidently in front of your audience.

Shedeen practices in front of friends who will give her honest feedback.

3. **Practice over several days** rather than multiple times on the day you are to speak. Starting your practice early will give you time to make changes and allow your concepts to "sink in."

4. **Do full "dress rehearsals."** Practice your presentation the way you will give it—standing, aloud, with passion, making eye contact, using your visuals, and moving around. Have at least a couple of full "dress rehearsals" where you present the entire presentation without stopping or skimming over the details. Get comfortable putting all the pieces together.

5. **Practice with variety.** Practice a bit differently each time to discover better ways to say something. You need to deliver your material while standing and saying the words out loud without skimming over the details. Do this at least three times. That's it!

6. **Practice with an audience.** Practice in front of willing friends or family members to smooth out your presentation and get feedback. Have them make notes on what content is confusing or what is particularly good. Have them critique your vocal quality and nonverbal communication. Have this audience ask you questions as part of your Q&A. While it may be embarrassing to practice in front of others, it's far better to make your mistakes in front of a "fake" audience than it is to make them in front of the real one.

7. **Devote extra time to practicing your opening and closing.** Remember from Chapter 9 how critical it is to have a strong start and an inspiring conclusion.

8. **Practice by recording yourself.** Put yourself in the audience's shoes and ask yourself if your performance would have moved you to action. If your answer is "no," then you have the opportunity to fix what needs fixing. Seeing yourself present also helps you to see strengths you weren't aware you had. Athletes rely on watching tapes of themselves to improve. They know that their own deluded perceptions may be faulty, but the videos won't lie.

9. **Your mirror is your friend.** There are a lot of differences of opinion about practicing in front of a mirror. You may believe it to be a narcissistic behavior, or you may fear that your attention will be on admiring yourself instead of paying attention to your presentation. I tend to be one who disagrees with this. Even after you have practiced in front of a live audience, you can continue to practice in front of your mirror. You will be able to hear yourself and see yourself using appropriate gestures, good eye contact, and effective body movement. Seeing yourself as the audience sees and hears you will allow you to make decisions about how to improve and enhance your presentation.

10. **Practice to "own" the material; don't practice for perfection.** Your job is to be an expert, not to be locked down to specific words or phrases by your need for perfection. Practice one more time after you feel you have done the presentation well. When it's time to present, you will feel secure with your material, and you will be able to focus on the audience and be "totally in the moment"—making connections, engaging your listeners, and feeling good about how you are doing, whether or not your words are sheer perfection.

These suggestions may seem like a lot of work, but your audience's thundering applause will make all your practicing efforts worthwhile.

Reflective Practice

You will read more about self-reflection in **Chapter 22: I. Am. Awesome!**, but a short note about it here is important. Reflective practice is learning from experience. It's about thinking about how you did in practice and about what you can improve for next time.

By practicing early and practicing a lot, you allow yourself more time to reflect, to evaluate your performance, and to ensure that you focus on the aspects of your presentation that matter the most. The goal of this self-reflection is for you to identify both your strengths and weaknesses as a speaker and to make a plan for improvement. Doing that—thinking reflectively about your performance—adds far more value to your practice sessions than just practicing for the sake of "getting it in your head."

Practice Makes—Well, If Not *Perfect*, Then at Least *Better*

In her book *The Presentation Secrets of Steve Jobs: How to be Insanely Great in Front of Any Audience*, Carmine Gallo (2009) says that "Steve Jobs makes a presentation look effortless, but that polish comes after hours and hours of grueling practice." Jobs wasn't the only presenter to understand the importance of practice. Presentations coach Richard Peterson (2014) says that if you "rehearse your presentation once in real time, out loud, [you'll] enjoy an 80% advantage over other presenters, because they're not rehearsed."

Many people will need more than just one full practice session. Beginning speakers and those who have a high degree of anxiety should spend more time practicing. And the more critical the speaking situation, the more practice time is recommended. Show the significance of the occasion by preparing fully for the presentation.

David Weiner (2005), author of several psychology bestsellers, including *Reality Check: What Your Mind Knows but Isn't Telling You,* states that "when you practice anything—be it a business, sales or scientific presentation or even Beethoven's 'Moonlight' sonata—you essentially carve a path for it in your brain. Without practice, your brain can take any of tens or hundreds of paths to reach its final destination." If you want to feel more confident in what you are saying and how you are saying it, practice is key.

Be in the Moment

When you've internalized the key points of your message, when you know the ideas you want to share so well that you aren't thrown by questions and misdirection, then you can truly be in the moment.

Cesar practices like he means it.

Presentation day will be a time to relax and be on "the top of your game" if you practice, practice, and practice once more.

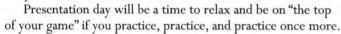

Key Takeaways

- The best cure for nervousness is confidence, and confidence comes with practice.
- Practicing small chunks of your presentation, one at a time, allows your key ideas to sink in.
- Practicing early and often gives you time to reflect and to work on the "kinks" and things that need fixing.
- Becoming more comfortable with your content and yourself allows you to focus more on your audience (your priority) when it's time to present.

Questions and Activities:

1. **Reflection Question:** Make two lists: the first should be the presentation skills you feel you already have, and the second list should be the presentation skills you want to improve. This will be a checklist for how you have improved over the semester.
2. **Learning Activity:** What did you notice from your first "dress rehearsal" of your presentation? What areas were ideal (the ones that made you say, "Yes, I rocked it!"), and which ones need improvement? Write these down to help you focus on what needs more practicing.

3. **Presentation Preparation:** This one should be obvious. Practice your presentation without memorization and without over-rehearsing each and every word. Practice like you are delivering the real thing (use visuals, good vocal quality, and nonverbal behaviors, etc.) at least three times, and make adjustments as needed.

Credits

CHAPTER 21

Break out the Good Clothes
Tips on Appropriate Business Attire

By Meg Sargent

After studying this chapter, you should be able to:
- *Understand how dressing appropriately for the audience and occasion affects first impressions and professional credibility.*
- *Differentiate between business formal and business casual attire.*
- *Explain and apply the guidelines for adhering to different types of business attire.*
- *Identify crucial grooming considerations that are part of a professional image.*

If you added them up, how many hours would you say you will have put into your college education by the time you graduate? Hundreds? Thousands? Whatever your number, I'm sure it's impressive. Now consider this: within seconds, others will sum you up based on little more than your physical appearance and mannerisms. From that first impression, they will make judgments and draw conclusions about your character, credibility, and potential. And once these impressions are formed, you have to work *that* much harder to prove otherwise. It's therefore in your best interest to make that first impression as positive as possible in your presentation, and one simple way to do that is to dress appropriately.

What you wear has two important communication effects we will explore: (1) clothing affects how your audience perceives you; and (2) clothing affects how you see yourself.

- **Audience Perception.** "Dressing for success" is one of the key components of making a positive first impression. Attire is actually considered a component of nonverbal communication because of the ways in which it can communicate about you and how you feel. A sloppy appearance, messy hair, and wrinkled clothes send the message, "I don't care" or, "this is not important to me." Your audience would be justified in taking your poor attire choice personally, even if you don't see your "whatever" look as disrespectful. How we dress tells others how important we think the occasion and audience are to us. There is a reason you dress up for most weddings and funerals—it demonstrates respect for the importance of the occasion and the people you came to honor. You want your attire to communicate, "I am giving you (and this situation) the respect you deserve."
  Your audience will also look to your attire to get clues about your intelligence or ability level. Study after study has shown that when someone is dressed up, they are perceived as more competent in their field of expertise (e.g., Heitmeyer & Goldsmith, 1990; Kerr & Dell, 1976; Kwon & Johnson-Hillery, 1998). One study (Craig & Savage, 2013) even showed that formal attire for the presenter (in their case, a college instructor) was associated with increased audience learning.
- **Self-Perception.** Not only does dressing up let the audience take you seriously, it also helps you to take yourself seriously as well. How you look has an effect on

how you feel. Wearing business formal attire is likely to increase your perception of your own authority, trustworthiness, and competence (Peluchette & Karl, 2007), and aren't those fantastic feelings to have going into a presentation? It's a simple equation: dressing like a professional will make you feel like one.

Dressing for the Audience and the Occasion

Dressing appropriately does not necessarily mean that you have to wear a suit. As we will explore shortly, there are different levels of attire found in the business world. The two we will explain more in detail are business formal and business casual. Which one you choose will depend on a number of factors. Ask yourself, "What do I want to communicate to my audience? And how can I use my appearance as an effective channel of this message?" Both of these questions go a long way in cutting through the clutter as we stand in front of the closet or mirror. Just as you should tailor your presentation to your specific audience, so too should you tailor your clothing.

Think about your audience and the speaking occasion. If you are presenting to a group of professional clients to pitch an idea or product, you need to dust off your suit and nice shoes. If you are holding a computer workshop for casually dressed students, business casual would likely be fine. If you're unsure what the norm should be, consider this question: what would your audience expect you to wear? Consider also what your audience will likely be wearing and ensure that your attire is a step up from theirs. As we tell our students, it should be obvious from your attire that you are the presenter.

From College Casual to Business Professional

So how do you dress to impress? Sit up straight, tuck in your shirt, dust off your shoes, and let's consider some essentials for both men and women. Before we give specific advice for men and women's attire in the workplace, let's first define the different levels of attire:

- **Business Formal Attire.** Although this style continues to decline among white-collar workers, it remains the preferred look for job interviews and industry-specific environments such as banking, financial-service companies, law firms, and accounting firms. Despite its overall decline, a more formal look still makes an ideal first impression and is suitable for any type of office profession—from an entry-level administrative assistant to a lawyer. For both men and women, this attire consists of classically tailored dark suits in neutral colors, coordinating dress shirts or blouses, and conservative leather (or vegan alternative) shoes. Both men and women should also appear well groomed.
- **Business Casual Attire.** Do not confuse *business casual* with *casual* or *careless*. This is simply one step down from a full-on suit. Trousers, skirts, button-down shirts, and appropriate shoes are still required. Men and women have more flexibility with their attire choices when following business-casual guidelines (including more color and style options), but many everyday comfort clothing items are still not allowed (e.g., no sneakers, UGGs, jeans, sweatpants, yoga pants, capris, T-shirts, sweatshirts, zip-up hoodies, tank tops, etc.). Appropriate personal grooming is still expected.

Now that the terms have been defined, let's explore how you can actually dress in these styles:

Business Professional Attire for Men

Hair should be conservative cut and style.

Facial hair should be short and neatly groomed.

Remove piercings and hide tattoos (when possible).

Wear a classically tailored dark suit in a solid color (navy, gray, or black) or subtle pinstripe.

Wear a white or light-colored long-sleeve button-down shirt. Shirt sleeve should extend half an inch below suit jacket sleeve. Tuck in shirt completely.

Tie should be a conservative color and design. Should touch the top of your belt. No clip-on ties. Choose a knot size appropriate for your stature.

Limit jewelry to gold or silver dress watch and one ring.

Wear a dark-colored dress belt that matches shoes. Avoid clunky or showy belt buckles.

Pants must match jacket. Pant leg should touch front of shoe and fall above back of heels. Pants should be fitted but not tight.

Wear calf-length, dark-colored socks that match shoes. Subtle patterns are okay.

Wear dark-colored leather (or leather-like) shoes with medium polish. Can be loafers, tied shoes, or low boots, so long as they have the right sheen and are made of the right material.

Business Casual Attire for Men

Hair should be conservative cut and style. Facial hair should be short and neatly groomed. No hats or head coverings allowed, unless for religious purposes.

Remove piercings and cover tattoos when possible.

Can wear a sport coat or suit jacket without a tie, but jacket is optional.

Wear a collared shirt or sweater with solid or minimal color and pattern. Only top button may be undone. No polo shirts or T-shirts.

Tie not required, but may be worn with long-sleeved shirts only. Patterns and colors must be conservative. Tie length should touch the top of belt.

Limit jewelry on hands to professional-looking watch and one ring.

Wear a leather (or leather-like) belt that coordinates with shoes. Avoid oversized, gaudy, or flashy belt buckles.

Wear well-pressed suit pants, trousers, or khakis. Pants should touch top of shoes, but not fall below bottom of heels. Pants should be fitted, but not tight.

Wear calf-length trouser socks that match pants. Subtle patterns are okay.

Conservative dress shoes (Oxfords, loafers) in leather or suede or similar alternative. No athletic shoes or sandals.

Business Professional Attire for Women

Hair should be neat, clean, and out of your face. Keep hair in a natural color and style.

Makeup should look natural and accentuate features, not make them the focal point.

Jewelry should be of decent quality and classic design. Avoid dangly, gaudy, or excessive amounts of jewelry.

Suit jacket should be in a neutral color in a traditional design and cut. Jacket should not pull or pucker when buttoned. Ensure the jacket is made of suiting material (it should be lined on the inside).

Wear a blouse or camisole underneath the jacket in white or light colors. No cleavage should be visible.

Limit jewelry on hands to a conservative watch and one ring per hand. Avoid costume jewelry.

Wear full-length dress slacks or a knee-length skirt that matches suit jacket. Bottoms should be fitted but not tight. Avoid high slits in a skirt and stretchy materials, like spandex.

Must wear neutral-colored, sheer pantyhose with a skirt. Avoid fishnets, patterns, or opaque tights.

Avoid open-toed shoes. Choose basic leather pumps with a low heel or flats. Avoid platform shoes. Colored shoes are fine, so long as they are not fluorescent, overly busy, or distracting.

Business Casual Attire for Women

Hair should be clean, neat, and out of your face. Should be in a natural color and style.

Makeup should be flattering and natural; never heavy, loud, or distracting.

Can wear trendier jewelry than in business professional wear, but accessories should not be overly gaudy or overdone. Avoid multiple bracelets that may make noise when you gesture.

Can wear blazer or modern jacket in varying colors. Or, you can wear cardigan sweater, sweater set, or blouse with subtle pattern. Blouse should not pull or pucker and should be tucked in.

Clothing should not reveal shoulders, stomach, back, thighs, or cleavage.

Dress pants, pressed khakis, or knee-length skirts are appropriate. Capris, shorts, or jeans are not. Bottoms should be fitted but not tight. Professional, conservative dresses are okay, but sundresses are not. Avoid high slits in a skirt and stretchy materials, like spandex.

Must wear neutral-colored, sheer pantyhose with a skirt or dress. Avoid fishnets, patterns, or opaque tights.

Avoid open-toed shoes. Choose basic leather pumps with a low heel or flats. Avoid platform shoes. Colored shoes are fine, as long as they are not fluorescent, overly busy, or distracting.

Grooming and Attire Tips for Everyone: Basic Business Guidelines for Men and Women

Regardless of what level of attire you are wearing, there are some hard and fast rules you should always follow when it comes to your appearance in a professional presentation:

- Clothes should fit properly. If you have a hard time buying clothes that fit well "off the rack," buy the larger size and bring them to a tailor.
- Clothes should be clean, neatly pressed (invest in an iron or garment steamer), and stain-free.
- Fix loose or missing buttons, hanging threads, or frayed edges.
- Ensure your outfits are free of lint and pet hair.
- Shoes should be polished and scuff-free. No chunky platforms, heels over four inches, or sneakers.
- Accessories should be minimal and tasteful.
- Skin (cleavage, back, stomach, shoulders, and feet) should be covered. Studies have shown that women of status are seen less favorably when they dress provocatively (Howlett et al, 2015).
- Tattoos should be covered when possible.
- Piercings (beyond one per ear) should be removed.
- Use perfume or cologne very sparingly or not at all; some people have allergies or sensitivities to fragrances.
- Fingernails should be clean and well groomed.
- Empty your pockets so there are no hip bulges or jingling coins or keys.
- Aim for fresh-smelling breath (no coffee or smoking breath), but don't chew gum once in sight of the audience (and definitely don't chew gum as you present).

Suit-Buying Tips

Many college students don't come into school already owning a business-appropriate suit. If you are shopping for a suit for the first time for your presentation (or for a career fair, interview, or other professional opportunity), here are some handy tips to try:

- Get professionally measured. At many suit shops, the sales staff is able to do this for you. Taking the time to get your precise measurements will help to ensure you have a suit that will fit well.
- Choose a neutral suit color. Charcoal gray and navy blue are often the best choices; they are strong but not overpowering. Choose black only for high-powered positions. Men should particularly avoid brown suits.
- Get your suit tailored. How well your suit fits has an effect on how your audience perceives you. One study (Howlett et al., 2013) found that participants rated men in tailored suits as more confident and successful than men in off-the-rack suits, even though the differences were relatively minor.
- Suit jackets often come with a label sewn onto the sleeve's cuff, white stitches on the back vents (bottom) of the coat, and pockets sewn shut. Using small scissors, carefully snip and remove the threads and label.

Picture Perfect: Putting the Finishing Touches on a Professional Image

There are multiple interpretations of what constitutes "appropriate attire," but, ultimately, the formula is quite simple: **consider the audience and occasion, and match your appearance appropriately.** Your audience will find you more credible and competent, and may therefore feel more motivated to give you their attention and consideration.

So, whether for a class presentation, a meeting with a client, or an employment interview, how you present yourself makes a difference—sometimes a big difference. If you want to be taken seriously—and after all the work you have put into prepping your presentation, I'm sure you do—then you need to look the part. Your polished appearance will be the perfect complement to your polished presentation.

Key Takeaways

- Dressing up allows your audience to see you as more competent and confident.
- Dressing up allows you to feel more competent and confident in yourself.
- Your attire should reflect your professionalism and your respect for your audience.
- Follow the guidelines for the different levels of business attire to ensure that clothing and appearance help you to give a positive impression.

Questions and Activities:

1. **Reflection Question:** Reflect on the last time you dressed up for a professional occasion (a presentation, career fair, job interview, etc.). How did more formal attire make you feel? Did it change your demeanor or the way you carried yourself? How?
2. **Learning Activity:** Practice your next presentation in different outfits to see the difference in how clothes make you feel. Say the intro and your first main point in your pajamas. Then say the second main point in your bathing suit. Finally, say the last main point and the conclusion in your business suit. How did the different clothes make you feel?
3. **Presentation Preparation:** Pick out your outfit for your next presentation. Consider the clothing that will demonstrate your professionalism and credibility in front of your audience. Make sure all items fit properly and are neatly pressed and free from stains.

Credits

1. Break out the Good Clothes: Tips on Appropriate Business Attire Copyright © 2014 by Meg Sargent. Reprinted with permission.
2. Business Professional Attire for Men Copyright © 2015 by M. Sandra DiFrancesco. Reprinted with permission.
3. Business Casual Attire for Women Copyright © 2015 by Isabel Chenoweth / Southern Connecticut State University. Reprinted with permission.

CHAPTER 22

Vetting the Venue and Other Acts of Self-Defense

By Frank Tavares

After studying this chapter, you should be able to:
- *Explain the importance of visiting your presentation space ahead of time.*
- *Choose an appropriate room setup and presentation space.*
- *Understand the limits your presentation space may present, and know some possible solutions.*
- *Recognize potential technology issues and solutions.*

The Countdown

It's 9:45 Tuesday morning. You've got the ten o'clock presentation ready to go. You're the second on the list of presenters, so even if you're a couple of minutes late, it will not be a problem. You've practiced more times than you'd like to admit. The PowerPoint slides are pro. Things are looking good.

The hotel has named its meeting rooms after various US presidents. It makes it easy to remember. You're in the one named POTUS #23: The Harrison Room—B. You know it's on the third level, and press the elevator button with confidence. In less than a minute, you're on the third floor. To your left, there's a sign for the Cleveland Room. To your right, the Garfield Room—(named for the president, not the cat). But there's no Harrison Room.

You look for a directory. It's hidden behind a pillar. You run your finger down the list of names, but they're not in alphabetical order. They're presented by suites, and towers, and levels! Help! Finally, "The Harrison Room—Level Three, West Wing." You find the star on the map marked "You Are Here," and discover you're in the *East* Wing.

Ten minutes. You can still get there in time to sit at the table with the other panelists and not be the one who rushes in late, out of breath, interrupting the start of the first presentation.

And you make it! Just seconds before the moderator introduces the panel members. Fantastic!

You've done it! No one knows how you almost blew it. You smile in acknowledgement as you're introduced, and are stunned when you're asked to present first.

You open your laptop. "Should I stand?" you ask the moderator.

"Well, that would make sense," she says.

You carry the laptop to the podium and realize that if you don't keep a hand on it, it'll slide right off the top, making the kind of memorable impact you'd rather not make.

You grab the cable to connect to the ceiling projector, but it doesn't have a plug that'll fit your machine. One of the panelists sees your plight and rescues you with an adaptor. You manage to connect it, but realize the projector is off. You look around trying to find the controls.

"Does anyone know how to turn it on?" you ask.

Someone in the second row points to the wall behind you. "Try the button that says 'ON.'"

You poke at it, and it changes from red to green. Maybe everything will be all right. But nothing happens. You poke the button again, and the light turns back to red. This time it's flashing. You poke it a third time. Nothing. You poke the other buttons—"laptop," "doc cam," "volume." Still nothing.

"Well," you say, gesturing toward the screen. "If you could see my slides, the first one has the title and a great outline of my major points. Oh, and a picture of my dog."

No one laughs. And perhaps that's comforting, because you weren't trying to be funny.

This is where we should say, "Then you wake up! It was all a dream."

But truth be told, if you sit through enough professional presentations, you will see this exact thing happen and wonder why the presenter just didn't come better prepared.

A Little Paranoia Is Not a Bad Thing

Being familiar with the site of your presentation needs to be on your to-do list. It seems like such a simple thing, but it can make a huge difference when it comes to facing the audience with the confidence of a professional.

This is especially important if you're in a strange location. Campus meeting rooms, conference centers, hotels, or auditoriums—every space is a different adventure and can present different challenges. Arm yourself with the knowledge of familiarity. Being a little paranoid about the unknowns of a presentation space and the limits of the facility is a helpful thing.

Before your presentation, visit the room. Know where it is and how you'll be able to get to it. If it's in a location not within walking distance, know where you'll be able to park or where someone might drop you off. Know how much time it will take to get there so you won't be sweating, literally or figuratively.

Ideally, it would be great to see the space the day before you're scheduled to use it. If you can sit in the audience—or pop inside and stand for a moment in the back—watch how others maneuver behind a table or a podium, or how they roam freely about the room as they talk to the audience.

In the perfect world, you can stay behind after the room clears to practice on your own. But that's not always possible, and you may be lucky if you only see the venue a short time before you're expected to be there. Regardless, any time you can visit it before your presentation will let you know what to expect.

In some cases, if you just can't get there, see if it's possible ahead of time to get a friend or fellow presenter to take a photo or two of the space—with or without a selfie—and text it to you.

Once you find the site, notice what's near it. Are the restrooms close? Is it on a noisy corridor that will prevent you from leaving the door open? Will latecomers be disruptive because the door is noisy or located at the front of the room where everyone's eyes will be diverted each time someone stumbles in?

Look at the adjacent presentation rooms. Are they sound-isolated? Will you have to compete against the laughter or applause of the audience next door?

Pay attention to the size of the room and the number expected to attend. That can dramatically affect your relationship with the audience. If it's an intimate conference room and you're standing near the head of the table, there will be a very different vibe than if it's a lecture hall. Knowing what to expect can put you in the right frame of mind.

Some of these things you won't be able to change, but you'll be able to prepare yourself for how you might handle them. We'll talk about a couple of specifics in a minute.

Self-Defense for When You Won't Be Able to See the Space Ahead of Time

Anytime you're watching a presentation—in a classroom, meeting or conference room, or auditorium—get in the habit of imagining how *you* would present there. That way, even if you can't see a venue ahead of time, when you walk in, it may still seem familiar.

Imagine: "If I had to present in here ..."

- Where would I stand?
- How could I move?
- Could I change the room around?
- What are the options for tech?

If you consciously practice this every time you're watching a presentation, you'll be able to figure out your options quickly when you walk into a strange room for your own presentation.

The Control Freak in All of Us

When it comes to the room, there are some things you won't be able to control. It might be the shape of the room, the color, or the lighting. It could include the seating. Is it theater seating or separate chairs? Is it a classroom with chairs that have writing surfaces? Are there tables? Can they be moved? How about the lighting, or tech switches, or temperature controls? Where are they? Do you have access?

As hard as it may be, you have to take a deep breath and summon up the strength not to let the things you cannot control make you crazy. But there are some difficult site characteristics that you might be able to compensate for if you're aware of them ahead of time.

Where, Oh, Where Could You Be?

There are a number of potential room types and setups. Here are some of the more typical presentation spaces you might encounter:

- **A Meeting Room** at a hotel or student center. Moveable chairs, with a table up front and a podium. Room may or may not have tech available in it. If it does, there's probably a screen on the wall behind the table. In a room like this, if there aren't more than a couple of dozen people, you can move freely to separate yourself from the podium or to move in front of the table where other presenters may be seated.

- **A Conference Room.** Usually has with one large table or smaller moveable tables configured in a rectangle or a U. Presenter might be standing at one end addressing those seated around the table, or, in some cases, expected to present while seated yourself. It's a more intimate setting: easier to make eye contact, smile, and talk to people "one-to-one," even though they are a part of a larger group.
- **A Small Auditorium.** More constricted. Seats are fixed in place. The presentation is done from a stage of some sort. It can distance you from your audience, but it can also make it easier for them to see you. Hard for you to move among the audience.
- **A Large Auditorium.** Fixed seating. You may be limited in how you can move— i.e., you'll be out of the spotlight or away from a stationary microphone.
- **A Classroom Setting.** Audience often in chairs with arms that provide a writing surface, or at a small desk. Sometimes classroom chairs may be fixed in place. Often you'll present from the front of the room, but movable chairs give you the opportunity to have people slide into a circle so you can be seated with them. Often that's a way to create a more intimate space and involve members of the audience (no place for them to hide).

The Podium Trap and the "Dais Moat"

Podiums are not inherently evil, but, depending on the room, getting stuck behind one can limit your interaction with the audience.

If you stay behind the podium or are stuck behind a table of presenters, it creates a barrier between you and the audience. You can see them and they can see you, but it's like waving from the castle ramparts at your subjects on the other side of the moat. The forced separation makes it harder to be connected to them.

There *are* situations that prevent you from moving away from a podium or a presentation table: The room is so large that you need a microphone, and the microphone on the podium or at the table is fixed. If you move away from it, only those in the first few rows will be able to hear you. Or, worse yet, if the session is being recorded and you move away from that fixed microphone, no one watching the video or listening to the audio will be able to hear you.

Uh oh. Dan has fallen into the podium trap. Get out while you can, Dan!

Most of the time, however, you can (and should) move away from the podium or out from behind the table to lessen the space between you and the audience. If the room is small enough and/or you don't need a microphone at all, moving away from the podium helps to strengthen that connection. Depending on the configuration of the room, you can walk about, keeping the audience interested and awake as they follow you.

Even if you need a microphone, most can be detached from the mic stand, allowing you to hold it as you roam freely. If you have a wireless mic, the only thing you'll need to worry about is how close you can come to the speakers. If you wander in front of—or under—one of the public address speakers, the mic may punish you with the shock of audio feedback. You've all heard it. It can range from a reverberant tone that starts to get louder to a piercing whistle. Microphone feedback is not a good thing. It is sometimes even painful.

This is something you can test before your presentation, when the room is empty. Move with the microphone, recite the alphabet, or sing your favorite karaoke, and look for those feedback hotspots. Make a mental note of where you can stand and where you can't, and, during your presentation, picture a wireless fence and don't attempt crossing that line.

The Glare of the Spotlight—Not So Glamorous

The spotlight can be trouble in two instances. The first is bothersome for you—getting caught in a multimedia projector's high beams. When visiting the venue, turn on the projector and pull the screen down. **Figure out where you can stand and walk so that you will stay out of the projector's light beam.** Sure, being in the spotlight will make you feel special, but it also makes it hard to see the audience—or anything, for that matter.

The second instance is another glaring situation into which you might stumble—presenting in front of a window. A recent wedding provides a surprising example. The couple had visited a number of venues and finally chose a beautiful space, in a rural setting, that overlooked a natural lake, open fields, and a pristine forest. It was a beautiful, sunny summer day. The room, with floor-to-ceiling windows, was bright and airy. Before the ceremony, a number of guests stood at those windows admiring the view. Tall grass in a field was swaying in the breeze. The pond even had swans! When the ceremony was about to begin, the guests went back to their seats. Everyone was smiling as the wedding party walked up the center aisle towards the window with the finest view. As soon as the guests turned to watch the ceremony, they realized they could not see the faces of the couple, the wedding party, or the person presiding; everyone was in silhouette! The wedding sounded wonderful. The guests were touched by the vows and delighted to hear the couple taking this step. But everyone seated in the audience was squinting into the sun, holding a hand or a program as a visor, trying for any glimpse of the participants' faces and expressions.

While it may not be in a wedding, you might find yourself in a similar situation. Picture yourself in the expensively decorated conference room of an organization that prides itself on its location by the water, below the mountains, or over a cityscape. It can be breathtaking to look at the view, but for those looking across the table at anyone talking in front of the windows, it is painful.

In that wedding venue, once the couple walked up that aisle, it's not likely anyone would have pushed them towards a different wall. But in that conference room, when it's your time to share what you've been working on over the previous week, sometimes it's possible to stand and move a few feet to a spot out of the glare.

If you've seen the presentation space ahead of time, think about how you could handle a situation like this.

The Power Play

If you're planning on using a laptop, tablet, or any electronic device as part of your presentation, even if you think it's fully charged, make sure to bring your power cord, and know where the A/C outlets are. Sometimes you'll arrive ready to plug in the power and find that the closest outlet is beyond the reach of the six-foot cord that comes with your device. If that's the case, bring your own extension cord.

"My own extension cord?"

Yes. On your next visit to a big box store, buy a ten- or twelve-foot extension cord and throw it in your presentation safety kit, along with extra batteries, the remote control for your PowerPoint, cables, cable adaptors, and a couple of whiteboard markers just for fun. You never know, and it's better to have them with you than not.

We All Want Tech to Be Our Friend

We often believe that presentation technology will make our presentations stronger. The PowerPoint slides we've designed so carefully, the YouTube video we've embedded among them, the website we plan to demonstrate, and the audio we want to play at the beginning to set the mood—all of these things can add to a presentation.

The sad truth, though, is that, no matter how you've prepared, sometimes tech is just not your friend—the missing cable, the corrupted file, the iffy Wi-Fi connection, the misplaced flash drive, the dying battery. Each of you can add to this list with examples from

Sometimes tech is just not your friend. Be prepared for it to fail so your presentation isn't derailed.

personal experiences as an audience member or a presenter. Tech *will* let you down, and it will often be at the most inopportune and embarrassing times. Have you ever uttered, "But it worked fine when I tried it in rehearsal?" Of course you have. If it hasn't happened to you yet, it will. It's just the nature of tech. Its promise is beguiling, but remember: deep down, it's not your friend.

So yes, prepare as much as you can. Practice, create a checklist of things to bring, but always be ready with a backup plan—a Plan B.

The Miracle of a "Plan B"

Many presentations will survive just fine if you've built in a backup plan. This can be as simple as

- printing out copies of your most important PowerPoint slides that you can share as a handout (print multiple slides per page);
- preloading a web video on the desktop of your tablet or laptop to which you can switch if an embedded link refuses to react;
- emailing a copy of your presentation to yourself in case the file you have gets corrupted; or
- moving to your next point without spending more than a few seconds trying to get the technology to cooperate.

If you've practiced for such inevitabilities, many attendees will not even realize you had a problem, and even those who do will quickly forget as you pull their attention to the next point you wanted to make. **Don't draw attention to the glitch any more than the glitch itself.** Don't apologize or try to explain why something isn't working; just jump past it.

Could you do your presentation if the power failed just before you stood? Could you do it if you didn't have your laptop? Could you do it if you discovered that your tablet could not read the presentation file?

In any of those instances, maybe you wouldn't be able to make all of the points you had in your outline, and maybe you wouldn't be able to show some of the most colorful examples you had hoped to share, but if you have a Plan B, *and* you've practiced it, you'll still be able to finish your presentation.

Plan B Isn't Just for Tech Failures

There can be other unexpected glitches. Sometimes your presentation is changed to another room at the last minute. Or the room is set up differently from what you saw earlier. Or the number of people sitting in the space is smaller or larger than expected. **Adapting is the key.**

If you find yourself in a space that's now unfamiliar, don't make a point of it. Don't tell the audience you're not prepared for the change in layout. Don't tell them what you *won't* be able to do. Adapt the best you can, and without complaint. If you know your material, and have practiced it, you will be able to deliver most of what you had planned. And few, if any, in the audience will be aware of what may have been changed or left out.

If a handful of attendees are spread throughout the room or lined up in the back, it's okay to ask them to gather in the front. On some occasions, if the chairs are moveable, you might invite them to sit with you in a circle. That can encourage a comfortable informality—for you and for them—and the conversation with your audience can flow more easily.

If there's an overflow, and you can reach a person overseeing the facility, it may be possible to do a last-minute switch to a larger space nearby. It may mean you start a few minutes late, but most people will be good-natured about picking up their things and walking down the hall, or even up the stairs. If moving isn't an option, you might ask that extra chairs be brought in. But often, with a larger-than-expected audience, you might just be stuck with SRO (standing room only) and some disappointed audience members.

Saving Yourself from the 3:00 a.m. Panic

We've looked at a number of things, some you already knew and perhaps a couple you hadn't really thought about. Maybe there are a couple of things that you'll now add to the worry list that can keep you awake the night before your presentation. Sorry about that.

But! If you scout out the space ahead of time, you might be able to erase some of these worries from that list. For instance:

- If the door to the room closes with a disruptive slam, try to leave it open. If the corridor is noisy and that would make it worse, station someone by the door who can close it quietly behind anyone coming or going.
- If the room setup creates a "Dais Moat"—whether with a podium or front table— think ahead of time about the options that let you move closer to the audience to keep them interested and occupied.
- If you see a potential glare problem, present away from the window so those looking at you will not have to squint.
- If you're planning on using any tech, from PowerPoint to a microphone to a Wi-Fi connection, determine the presence and placement of equipment, cables, plugs, and controls.
- Check the projector and equipment controls. Connect your laptop or tablet ahead of time so you'll feel confident handling the equipment. And turn the controls on and off when everything is connected to see how they work.
- Make sure you practice resetting the controls and connections. Know how much time you'll need to reset everything if there is a tech failure during your presentation, but also determine ahead of time when it's time to abandon Plan A and jump to the lifeboat of Plan B.
- Practice removing and replacing the microphone from its stand.
- If you can identify technical problems in advance, find the person responsible for fixing them. And if they can only be fixed during your presentation, consider asking the staff to wait until you're done with your Plan B. Sometimes the disruption caused by the repair is just not worth it.
- If a tech support person can only work on a problem during your presentation, try to physically distance yourself from them. Let them work on the control panel or the cable connection or on a ladder by the projector while you divert the audience's attention by standing on the opposite side of the room from where the repair is taking place. Try to move the distraction out of the audience's line of sight.

Owning the Space

If you survey the presentation site ahead of time, you will identify many of the potential problems—and possibilities—of working in that very particular venue. Remember that, even if there are things about the space you cannot control, fix, or adjust, you can still "control the space." You can still find a way to connect to your audience so they will watch you and listen to you and hear what you have to share with them. If you scope it out ahead of time, even if the space presents some challenges, you can work to neutralize those challenges. Walk the perimeter. Sit where the audience will sit. Stand where you plan to stand. Begin a practice run-through, and take it as far as is practical. Make notes about the problems you need to solve and questions you need to answer.

Doing these things ahead of time will give you the ability, confidence, and strategies to present as the knowledgeable and prepared person you have become.

Key Takeaways

- Vetting your venue before presentation day will eliminate a lot of stress and help you plan for the presentation you want to have.
- Control what you can to make the space work for your audience and your intent, but learn to work around those aspects you cannot change.
- Avoid the "Dais Moat" by walking in front of the podium or presenting table; eliminate physical barriers between you and your audience.
- Make sure neither you nor your audience stares into a glare.
- Bring a presentation safety kit to all your presentations with items that will help you deal with difficult venue situations.
- Be ready with Plan Bs for your potential technology and room issues.

Questions and Activities:

1. **Reflection Question:** Consider the presentations you have given or seen. Identify a time in which the presenter had a difficult presentation space (because of the amount of room, seating arrangements, lights, noises, or some other complication). How did the presenter deal with the difficulties? How effective were their actions? What other ways could the person have dealt with the space issues?

2. **Learning Activity:** Set up the classroom in different configurations—desks in a U, desks in rows, desks pushed together to make group tables, etc.—and talk to the class. How do the different space arrangements change the way you can interact with your audience? What are the strengths and weakness of each setup? When would you ideally use each kind of setup (if ever)?

3. **Presentation Preparation:** Visit the site of your next presentation. If you can, arrange tables, seating, and equipment until you are happy with the setup. Take a picture or sketch out a diagram so you can remember which setup worked best for presentation day. If you cannot move the furniture during your visit, take a picture of the space and sketch out a simple diagram of the space, including the available furniture and technological hookups, so you can plan your presentation space on paper before the presentation.

Credits

CHAPTER 23

"I. Am. Awesome!"
Engaging in Effective Self-Reflections

By David John Petroski

After studying this chapter, you should be able to:
- *articulate the importance of engaging in self-reflections.*
- *identify the key components of a successful self-reflection.*
- *conduct and write self-reflections that effectively make connections to, critique, and analyze your behaviors.*

Quite a while ago, I was working on a project with some friends of mine who live across the country. A lot of our work and communication is done by email. At one point, we were trying to coordinate a face-to-face meeting at a regional conference we were all planning to attend. I sent out an email to let everyone know when and where we'd meet. When the time came for the meeting, I showed up at the spot I had emailed about, but I was the only one there. I was furious! Didn't they care about the project? Even if they had good reasons, couldn't they have let me know that they wouldn't be able to make it? I was ready to read them the riot act the next time I spoke with them. How dare they stand me up?

About a week after the conference, I spoke with one of my friends. After a few minutes of small talk, I asked pointedly, "Where were you at the conference? I waited for you." The conversation stopped dead. My friend sounded confused: "Were we supposed to meet? I didn't realize that." Not to let her get off that easy, I said, "Yes—just like I said in the email I sent the week before the conference." She pleaded ignorance. Just to drive the point home, I pulled up the email from my "sent mail" folder so I could point out the date I sent it. That's when I saw that the email was only addressed to one person in our group. And to top it off, the address I had entered had a typo, so it clearly wouldn't have made it to any of my friends. Here I was, ready to jump to conclusions that my teammates were to blame when it was my fault the whole time. Next came a lot of apologies, not just for the false accusations, but also because the team's progress had been held up by my error. What an embarrassment!

It may seem like an ordinary thing, maybe even a bit dumb, but at the heart of my issue with the email was lack of reflection on my part. Thinking back on this incident, I didn't even consider that the problem was caused by something that I'd done. My conversation with my friend marked an important point where I stopped looking at what others did and focused more on what my role was in that situation. That moment of reflection, reconsidering the frustrating misunderstanding with my friends, helped me to develop a new strategy for collaborating through email. From that point forward, if I don't receive responses to my emails, I check to make sure I've sent the email correctly, rather than assume I'm being ignored. In fact, when an email is important, I now make it a point to double-check email addresses before I click *send*. The point is this: reflecting on my own behavior led to improved communication on my part.

What Is Self-Reflection, and How Does It Help?

The critical point to remember is that self-reflection is an opportunity for you to consider your own thinking, behavior, and learning processes. It lets you piece together what happened to you and helps you try to make sense of your role in that situation. Ultimately, it's the means to help you learn from your experiences (good and bad). With self-reflection,

Joe, Rheanna, and Ashley hold a postmortem meeting to reflect on how they did as a group in the presentation.

you can spot possible mistakes or problems you had in a situation and recognize what you can do better or differently (or even the same way) to make it easier to handle a similar situation in the future.

Self-reflection also helps you identify things that can serve as an agenda for your future learning and action. With my email example, I adopted a new method of handling email in the future—double-checking email addresses and checking the sent folder to ensure my message was sent appropriately.

Most of what you use self-reflection for in the classroom is specifically related to what you're learning. In a presentations course, it is likely that you will be asked to reflect on your presentation performance—what you did well and what still needs improvement. You might even be asked to reflect upon the readings in this book (that's what those handy **Reflection Questions** are for at the end of each chapter).

What about outside of school? By learning how to effectively self-reflect, you are developing an important thinking skill that will help well beyond what you do in the classroom. Self-reflection is actually a common practice in business, particularly where complex team projects are concerned. Businesses often engage in a "postmortem" meeting where all of the participants in the project talk about what went right and what went wrong. They try to talk about ways they can improve the process so it's easier or better the next time they have to do a similar project. As an example, Greer (2012) advises project managers to use the following set of questions to guide the postmortem process (see box below). By the way, these are also good questions to ask of your teammates when you do group work in classes. The postmortem process is a usually more in-depth than this, but the questions give you an idea of how businesses engage in self-reflection.

Project "Postmortem" Review Questions (Greer, 2012)

1. Are you proud of our finished deliverables (project work products)? If yes, what's so good about them? If no, what's wrong with them?
2. What was the single most frustrating part of our project?

---

3. How would you do things differently next time to avoid this frustration?
4. What was the most gratifying or professionally satisfying part of the project?
5. Which of our methods or processes worked particularly well?
6. Which of our methods or processes were difficult or frustrating to use?
7. If you could wave a magic wand and change anything about the project, what would you change?
8. Did our stakeholders, senior managers, customers, and sponsor(s) participate effectively? If not, how could we improve their participation?

What Makes Good Self-Reflection?

Let's be practical. At this point in your career, most self-reflections happen in the classroom. Instructors ask you to talk or write about what you've learned—a lot. What do they look for? More importantly, how can you write self-reflections that are going to help you most? After reviewing more than fifty rubrics for classes that require reflections, I've identified three areas of emphasis that come up consistently: **making connections**, **self-criticism**, and **analysis**. Each of these three areas also represents the way a well-known scholar defines and frames *reflection* (Dewey, 1991; Boud et. al, 1985; and Moon, 1991; respectively).

Three different perspectives on the nature of reflection			
	Dewey (1991)	Boud et al. (1985)	Moon (1999)
Focus	Making Connections	Self-Criticism	Analysis
Outcome	Apply what you know to you're trying to do	Using experiences to develop new understandings and appreciations, particularly related to your own behavior	Thinking about complex problems with no obvious solutions

What follows are the key points raised in the rubrics by instructors who ask students to use self-reflection in their assignments. If you use these points to guide you in your own self-reflection, it will help you use the process more productively. At the very least, doing this will help you learn class material better. The added benefit is that it will help you learn a bit more about yourself—like what you do or know best, what your limits are, or what you may need to learn more about.

Making Connections

Self-reflection assignments that ask you to make connections are essentially looking for you to work out the relationships between ideas and concepts. These links may or may not be obvious, but the point of the self-reflection is essentially to get you to connect the dots. Examples of questions that ask you to make connections are:

- What did this experience tell you about effective presentation strategy?
- In what ways did you apply the concepts from the textbook in your presentation?
- Can you explain some examples when you've applied this technique in the past?

- What concepts do you know better because of your experience?

Here are several points to consider when your self-reflection emphasizes *making connections*:

- The best self-reflections discuss multiple connections between this learning experience and content from other courses, past learning, life experiences and/or future goals. These kinds of questions ask you to make clear links between what you already know and what is happening in class or other learning experiences.
- Solid self-reflections include an analysis of the connections between experiences and learning goals. So it's not just about linking to what you know, it's also about linking to what you're supposed to be learning. Based on that analysis, you try to predict future behaviors/decisions. ("Next time, I'd do this instead …").
- Experiences from outside of class can be extremely helpful for making connections between concepts and how you use them in practice. So when you try to explain how you see concepts applied, you can draw examples from your everyday life to illustrate what you're talking about.
- The very best reflections push for further analysis and insight resulting from what you may have learned from readings other than those assigned for class. (Yes, this means looking deeper into important things on your own!)

When writing responses to these kinds of questions, one of the best strategies is to use your syllabus, readings, and class notes as a guide for your self-reflections.

- **Syllabus**: The syllabus should identify critical points you are expected to learn in class. These become important connection points between your learning goals and your experience.
- **Readings**: Readings focus attention on specific ideas. As a rule of thumb, the most important ideas come directly from concepts you've read about most. If you are reflecting on your own presentation behaviors, consider what this book or other supplementary materials say certain behaviors communicate and what suggestions they offer for improvement.
- **Class notes**: Lectures explicitly state what's important, so your notes become the key to making connections. Discussions and exercises may also aid in reflection. Even being an audience member to your peers can help you identify how you are similar or different from the other presenter and what changes you should therefore make.

Self-Criticism

An important part of self-reflection is being critical of your own work, even though this is really hard to do. We're all pretty good at pointing out what we're good at, but the real benefit of self-reflection is discovering your weaknesses so that you can improve them. Examples of questions that ask you to engage in critical self-reflection are:

- What did you do well in your presentation?
- Thinking about your presentation, what is the most urgent area in which you need to improve?
- If you were going to deliver this presentation to the same audience again, what would you do differently?

The difficulty with assignments like these is that they ask you to be critical of your own behavior, which is not easy. **Just remember that you can't improve if you don't honestly assess what you're doing.** Here are a few thoughts to help you approach this form of self-reflection productively:

- Make an effort to understand concepts by *openly* examining your own experiences in the past as they relate to the topic. If you're trying to learn from your experiences, you have to be willing to consider what you've done wrong as well as what you've done right.
- The best self-reflections demonstrate an *open, non-defensive ability to self-appraise*, discussing both growth and frustrations as they relate to learning. If something was hard or uncomfortable for you, why do you think that was the case? Try to get at the root cause of the difficulty rather than dwelling on critical labels. Rather than making a blanket statement like, "I'm a terrible speaker! I stumble over my words all the time!" you might consider that you may not be comfortable with the topic or that it just may be an issue of needing more practice. If you can identify the specific problem—I am having trouble speaking with confidence—there are direct actions you can take as a response.
- One of the pitfalls of self-critique is that if you dwell too much on what you've done wrong, you can easily get discouraged. To work against this, make sure that you get into the practice of making notes about the things you did well along with the things you need to work on. Keeping in mind the things you're good at is a way of encouraging yourself to keep up the good work and increase your presentation confidence.
- As you look for areas of improvement, it's important to keep realistic goals for yourself. There are some things you can "fix" more quickly than others. For example, if you came across in a presentation as not being well informed, you might need to research and plan more. Easy fix. However, if something is really challenging for you, it may be best to take small steps at remedying the situation. For instance, if your nervousness is obvious to your audience, saying simply, "I will stop being nervous" will not make a good immediate goal; that sort of issue needs to be worked out over time.

When you're faced with the task of writing a self-critique, whether it's on a form, in a journal or paper, or even as part of a discussion, there are some straightforward ways to keep your critique focused:

- Give the most attention to the parts of your work that are most significant. For example, improving poor organization and faulty research are much more important than polishing phrasing or eliminating disfluencies like "uh" or "um." In general, your reflections should prioritize structure and content over the minute details of delivery. After all is said and done, no amount of polish can clean up a message not worth presenting.

- As you reflect on experiences, particularly presentations, be sure to concentrate on things that you can and should control, like your content and delivery. By contrast, it doesn't make sense to spend a lot of time reflecting about things that you can't fix or that are irrelevant. Students often remark, after viewing their own presentations, that they hate the sound of their voice or they don't like the way their hair looks. Who cares? This should be an exercise in self-improvement, not self-deprecation.
- When an assignment asks you to reflect on your work with a team, more often than not your instructor wants to know what *your* role was in the team. Complaining about your teammates and what they did or didn't do is just a distraction from what should be the real focus of your self-reflection: *you and your behavior*. Ultimately, any points you raise about work you complete as part of a team should be followed immediately by the answer to the question: "What could *I* have done differently?"

Analysis

One of the more difficult components of self-reflection is analysis. To reiterate what was discussed in Table X, the analysis aspect of self-reflection concentrates on thinking about complex problems that usually don't have a single, clear solution. Example assignment questions that ask you to engage in analytical self-reflection are:

- How would you change this presentation if the audience were different?
- If you were to give advice to a friend about how to present (this information or to this audience), what would you suggest?
- Based on your experience, what is your action plan for improvement as you move forward?
- What is your biggest weakness in this presentation? What specifically will you do to improve?

As you start to consider an analytical approach, it's important to recognize that this mode of reflection pushes you to think beyond the obvious. Put simply, the goal of analytical self-reflection is to deeply explore your experiences, draw inferences about the "big picture" of a situation, and discover how you might be able to use that experience to guide your decisions and actions in the future.

The following ideas should help you think through the reflective process from an analytical perspective:

- Don't just say what happened. You need to consider what worked well and what didn't. Try to move beyond blaming others or yourself. A better strategy is to focus on describing what happened and the consequences of that action (or inaction).
- Strong self-reflection moves beyond just describing the experience to the consideration of the specific ways the experience contributed to your understanding of yourself, others, and/or course concepts.

- With regard to problem solving, it's important to trace through how you worked through the solution you came up with. What did you do that might have been expected? On the opposite end, what did you do that was novel or unexpected?
- The best analysis asks you to regularly refer to your understanding of the discussion topic, outline next steps in improving your work, and evaluate how you will use your understanding to move forward. Quite simply, you talk directly about the ways you can make adjustments to your work in future revisions.
- If you are asked to create an action plan as part of your analysis, try to focus on specific and achievable goals. One to three action items is probably appropriate because you want to be realistic about what you'll be able to accomplish in the near and long term. For example, your reflection might lead you to the conclusion that you need to rehearse more. Put in a simple statement, you might write the action item, "I need to rehearse more, so next time I will practice no fewer than five times." Another example could be: "I need to make better eye contact, so I will practice my next presentation with my stuffed animals as my audience, and I will keep rehearsing until I can consistently keep my gaze at their little button eyes." In both of these examples the action is simple, descriptive, and doable.

Strategies for Writing Self-Reflections

Here are a few additional thoughts about how to approach self-reflection assignments, like journals, in classes, regardless of the subject:

- If you're writing in a journal, consciously make an effort to describe what happened first. What did you experience or read about? Then discuss what you think about that. What connections can you make? What discoveries or realizations come to mind? Sometimes it's even useful to label the parts of the journal entry as "What happened?" and "My Take." (Tavares, 2012)
- Try to separate your emotions from what you are doing. It's okay to acknowledge them; they are important. We may need to vent our frustration, anger, or embarrassment, which is fine. That helps get a handle on them. However, in the context of your written self-reflection, it is better to focus instead on the behaviors that bring up those emotions in the first place.
- Always think about the "long game." Try to consider how the things you're thinking about now relate to what you will be doing next time—or far into the future. This leads you to a much deeper analysis that can lead to a concrete plan of action.

Press Record: How to View Your Own Presentations

A tricky part about presentations, regardless of the context, is that you can't see yourself present. Much of the time, you're so wrapped up in trying to hit all the key points and connecting with your audience, you probably aren't aware of the details of how things are going. If that's the case, how can you ever think about what's working and what isn't? In writing, it's an easy process. You can go back and reread what you've written and check to see whether you're getting the job done. However, with presentations, you're in performance mode and not likely thinking about refining your technique.

The most straightforward way to address this is to videotape yourself presenting. Even if it's just taping a practice session before the main presentation event, it will give you the opportunity to look back on what you were doing during the presentation from the perspective of your audience and reflect on what went well or not. No, this isn't easy. The first time I watched myself on video I was about ready to run from the room screaming, "No! That's not true! That's impossible!"

So often people hate the video-watching experience because they focus too much on their appearance, the sound of their voice, or other aspects of themselves that are not particularly helpful for improving their presentations. This is not an exercise in "OMG, I can't believe how frumpy I look on camera." If you focus on superficial points, you will completely miss the presentation nuances you can fix. Put your own insecurities to the side, and pay attention to how you are actually presenting. (And really, you should just learn to love yourself the way you are.)

You shouldn't stress too much about watching yourself on video. But if you are stressing anyway, consider the points below, all adapted from Olivia Mitchell's (2014) article, "How to Survive Watching Yourself on Video":

- **Presenters often do better than they think.** Your imagination can be a dark and scary place when nerves take hold, and you probably think you did worse than you really did. Watching yourself on video will likely confirm that the audience didn't really notice the sweating, shaking, and nausea you thought were plainly obvious.
- **Get feedback from someone who was there live.** Watching a video version lets you hone in on behaviors your audience may not have seen (they are busy actually listening to you, after all). Ask your confidant what was and was not obvious during the actual performance.
- **It will be strange to watch and hear yourself.** You don't look or sound the same way on video that you do in real life. You just don't. The difference may be jarring, but do your best to detach yourself from the image on the screen and watch as though you are critiquing a stranger.
- **Don't stress the small stuff.** When you're not focusing on content like your audience, you may focus too heavily on critiquing minor behaviors, like how much you move your hands or how many times you stumbled over your words. Unless it was truly excessive (and your buddy from the presentation can help you determine that), make like Elsa and "Let It Go."
- **Look for the overall picture.** How do you

Cesar is bravely watching himself present and keeping note of his strengths and weaknesses.

look overall? Are you nervous? Confident? Are you too "red"? Too "blue"? Just the right shade of "purple"[1]? Listen to your voice and look at your movements. What kind of presenter do you appear to be? Once you have an overall picture, then dissect which specific habits are making you appear this way.

- **Focus on the positives.** Don't just make a laundry list of all the presentation sins you committed. Watching objectively, what are you doing well?

Once you've surrendered to the notion that the best way to reflect on your presentation technique is to use a video recording of yourself, here are a few suggestions that may make the experience more productive. When watching your own presentation video, try these steps to reflect effectively on your performance:

- Watch the video with a pad next to you, and take notes on what you see. Don't be afraid to pause or rewind so that you have the chance to jot down your thoughts. Don't labor over this. Just note a quick tag to serve as a reference point. The idea is to collect your initial impressions so that you have specific things to look at and consider with a more careful review.
- As you write down the notes, record a time reference so that you know where to look for that part if you want to see it again. If I'm thinking, "Wow! I did a great job transitioning between those ideas!" I really want to be able to go back to that to see what I did.
- If you're viewing the video on a computer, just open up a text document and keep your notes there. If you're like me, I often find it a pain to go back and read notes I took a while ago because my handwriting isn't that clear. Taking the notes directly on the computer makes it much easier look back at later.
- If you had specific goals (or a grading rubric) for the presentation, use that to guide your attention. If content and organization, for instance, are the most important goals (or worth the most points), watch specifically for those issues first. Then watch for delivery and style.

Final Reflections on Self-Reflections

Self-reflection is an invaluable tool as you learn to grow and develop as a presenter. Without adequate reflection, you are bound to make the same gaffes over and over again. As management consultant Margaret J. Wheatley (2005) said, "Without reflection, we go blindly on our way, creating more unintended consequences, and failing to achieve anything useful" (p. 262).

Self-reflection is a tool that should be employed often throughout the presentation process. Use it in your planning, in your practice sessions, and after the actual presentation itself. Even if you never have to give that same presentation again, it is likely that you will present again. Having a clear handle on your strengths and weaknesses will help you focus your energies better for the next time you stand in front of an audience.

---

1   See introductory chapter, "The Magic Key to Presenting," for more information on red, blue, and purple presenting styles.

Key Takeaways

- Self-reflection is an essential critical-thinking skill needed to improve your presentation preparation and performance.
- Postmortem meetings allow teams to reflect on their collective performance together.
- Good self-reflections require that you make connections, critique yourself, and analyze your behaviors.
- Videotape yourself presenting so you can watch from the perspective of your audience and critique your presentation more objectively.
- Without self-reflection, you are bound to repeat your mistakes. Reflecting and formulating plans for improvement will help you learn from those errors.

Questions and Activities:

1. **Reflection Question:** What is the importance of self-reflection for improving presentation performance? Why is it important to write down the things you did well along with the bigger things that need to be improved? In what ways have self-reflections—whether written down or not—helped you to improve in your presentations or other communication skills?

2. **Reflection Question:** Using what you have learned in this chapter, reflect on all that you have read thus far in this book. Choose *three* major points that have made you stop and think. What are they? What impression did they make on you? Why? And, most important, how do these points relate to you and your experience in making presentations? What will you do to apply them to your own preparation and presentations?

3. **Learning Activity:** Watch a video of yourself presenting, and take notes on what you like about your performance. Create a list called "The Ways I'm an Awesome Presenter" (or something similarly positive). Read it to yourself before every practice session and final presentation session to boost your confidence.

4. **Learning Activity:** Watch a video of yourself presenting, and take notes on what you need to improve for your next performance. Make three columns: "Important Things to Change," "Less Important Things to Change," and "Things I Can't Change." Your first column should be much smaller than the other two. Then devise an action plan to change one or two of the items in the "Important Things to Change" column.

5. **Presentation Preparation:** Self-reflect on the last presentation you gave. What were your greatest two strengths? What were your greatest two weaknesses? Devise a *specific* action plan for improving those two areas of weakness.

Credits

1. I. Am. Awesome! Engaging in Effective Self-Reflections Copyright © 2014 by David John Petroski. Reprinted with permission.
2. Postmortem Meeting Copyright © 2014 by Isabel Chenoweth. Reprinted with permission.
3. Watch Videos of Yourself Copyright © 2014 by Isabel Chenoweth / Southern Connecticut State University. Reprinted with permission.

Unit 4
Designing and Using Visual Channels

I t's obvious to say that we live in an increasingly technological world. The paper-and-marker flip charts of the olden days of *Mad Men* have been replaced with the bright lights of projector screens and multimedia slides. The receipt-spitting adding machines that sounded like they were literally "crunching numbers" have been overtaken by the silent yet versatile spreadsheet. And the handouts that used to require a team of specialists to make can now be created by any novice with access to readily available computer programs. As a result, the business world and business presentations are going visual.

In the course of most professional presentations, your audience will expect some visual pizzazz. This is not to say that you should add flash just for the sake of a little flash (this isn't a magic show), but you should recognize that many of your audience members are used to processing information visually. They often have to see it to believe it.

Unfortunately, the visual pizzazz that many presenters try to use in their presentations only distracts from the message. This is because these presenters know how to use the software programs to create the visuals, but they don't know *how to create visuals that communicate well.*

Remember, in AIMC, your visual aids are part of the channel. They are the ways in which you communicate your message to your audience, and, just like your own mannerisms and tone of voice, how you communicate this message through visual aids will reflect on the larger points you are trying to make.

Much of what you read in this unit will, therefore, concentrate on how to make visuals well. You will learn how to design your visuals effectively for your audience, message, and intent, and how to present them to your audience. This unit, however, will not cover in-depth how-to guidelines for the software programs you may need to make these visuals. If you and technology are not exactly BFFs, use the resources available to you to learn how to navigate the programs you need to use. Google and YouTube can teach you how to use almost any software program available far better than we could if we were to write out the steps in this book.

Our concern here is that you approach visual-aid construction from a *communication perspective.* Just because Microsoft PowerPoint lets you fill each slide with mini novels and make pictures twirl, spin, and bounce onto the screen doesn't mean you should. Just because layout software like Microsoft Publisher, Apple Pages, or Adobe InDesign lets you cram pictures and cartoon ClipArt onto every last square centimeter of a handout doesn't mean you should. There are better ways to let your visuals *complement* your message and communicate your message to your audience. Those are the lessons that will follow.

CHAPTER 24

Picking the Right Visual Channel for the Job

After studying this chapter, you should be able to:
- *Decide when you should and should not use a visual aid.*
- *Differentiate between visual channels and visuals.*
- *Choose the visual channel and visual types that work best for your audience, intent, and message.*

"Seeing is believing"—that's how the old phrase goes, and it certainly applies to the realm of presentations. When audiences want verification of your facts, figures, or explanations, they often want to *see* the proof. If you argue that a classroom is in disrepair, your audience will want to see a picture of that space. If you contend that profits are increasing, your audience will want to see the graph that depicts that trend. If you say that the adrenal glands are located above the kidneys, your audience will want to see a diagram of the human abdomen with those parts labeled so they can see just how "above the kidneys" you mean.

These examples embody the essence of good visual aids—they aid the audience in understanding or believing your presentation through a visual channel. Throughout this unit, we will use the term *visual aid* to define any visual material that supplements what you are saying in your presentation beyond your own verbal and nonverbal behaviors. Before we talk specifically about the various options for visual aids and how to decide among them, let's first talk about when and when not to use visual aids.

Show and Tell—or Just Tell?: When to Use Visual Aids

If you remember back to Chapter 5, the channel (the C of AIMC) has three different categorizations: your own delivery, audience participation, and visual aids. Of those three categories, visual aids make up the only one that is truly optional. That is, just because visual aids *can* be used, that doesn't mean that they necessarily *should* be used. So how, then, are you supposed to know when to use a visual aid or when to leave it out of the presentation?

There are many good reasons for including visual aids when presenting:

- They can enhance your credibility as a presenter.
- They can make your presentations more interesting and engaging for your audience.

- They can make it easier for you to communicate complex information effectively.
- They can help to reinforce your verbal message.
- They can help the audience to understand, use, and retain information.
- They can add emotional impact or dramatic support to your claims.

While all the benefits above are certainly true of good visual aids, you should not interpret that list as a green light to use any and all visual aids you can find. These advantages only apply to the *right kinds* of visual aids—those that make sense for the presentation and have been well designed. Random or poorly designed visuals can likely have the *opposite* effect of each of the benefits listed above.

So, what is the measure of a worthy visual aid? The basic rules for visual aids appeared in Chapter 5, but they are worth repeating here. For a visual aid to be of any value to the presentation, it must be audience-focused. Specifically, the visual aid should do at least one of the following:

1. Help the audience understand or remember a concept.
2. Help persuade the audience.

This means that many visuals that presenters often like to use—random ClipArt cartoons, stock images that lack emotional appeal, and videos of people saying exactly what the presenters could have said themselves—are merely fluff or filler. Just as the message of your presentation should focus only on the content that helps you fulfill your intent, your visuals should adhere to similar admittance criteria. The point here is simple: **if a visual aid neither aids in the audience's comprehension and memory nor aids in persuading the audience, then it should not be included in the presentation.** Period.

Let's look at each of these criteria more closely:

Helping the Audience Understand or Remember a Concept

Visual aids can help you clarify and demonstrate the information that you are trying to impart to your audience. Offering a visual channel (a visual aid) in addition to the oral channel (your speaking) will increase the likelihood that your audience grasps and remembers the concepts you are presenting. Let's say that you are discussing the double-helix structure of DNA, something hard for non-expert listeners to envision. Showing a picture of a DNA strand would help the audience understand exactly what you mean by "double helix."

Presenting numerical data also often needs visual accompaniment to achieve audience understanding. Spewing off endless numbers to your audience is ineffective. See? A double helix! Unless your listeners are brilliant mathematicians (and so few are), they won't be able to remember what you have said or know how to effectively translate what it means. Instead, numbers are often best served in visual format. So, if you were presenting the previous fiscal year's sales numbers to a board, you would have more clarity and impact by using a pie chart than by listing off the revenue for each quarter.

When preparing your presentation, think through each concept you want to share. Is there a visual aid—a picture, illustration, graph, video, etc.—that would better explain or exemplify this information? If there is, then put it in. Your audience will appreciate the visual interest and the cognitive help it provides.

Helping Persuade the Audience

The second way in which a visual could be used effectively is to aid in the audience's persuasion. Think back to the last presentation you saw on the dangers of drinking and driving. You were probably shown a picture of a drunk driver's smashed car. Many schools even bring damaged cars to school grounds and host "mock accidents." In these instances, you don't really *need* to see the smashed car to understand how an accident looks. That image, though, is intended to affect your heart more than your head. It is a means of evoking *pathos*.

You can similarly use images to affect your audience emotionally. If you wanted to convince your audience to join a club on campus, you might show a picture of an event the club hosted in which people are smiling. You would hope that those positive images might transfer to your audience's impressions of the organization.

It should be noted that while negative imagery (like the totaled cars in the drunk-driving talks) can be effective, showing images that are too disturbing or unsettling might turn your audience off. Trying to convince your audience to adopt vegetarianism by showing slaughtered chickens or to support the pro-life stance by showing aborted fetuses is *just too much*. Such a significant number of your listeners will turn away, close their eyes, audibly complain, or stop listening that your persuasion will be ineffective. Slight shock value can be useful, but too much shock value loses its actual value.

Seeing Is Believing: Types of Visuals

Now that you know when to use a visual, it would help to tell which visuals to use. As a point of clarification, we can look at visual aids in two categories: the visuals themselves and visual channels. *Visuals* can include photographs/cartoons, diagrams/illustrations, charts and graphs, and videos. *Visual channels* are the means by which you compile and present your visuals (PowerPoint presentation, handout, etc.). Let's talk first about the specific types of visuals you can use, and then we can discuss which channels make the most sense for your visuals.

The right visual can make a point more powerfully and much faster than most presenters could do by simply describing it aloud. **We live in a visual culture, and audiences often embody the credo that "seeing is believing."** If you are talking about the devastation caused by a natural disaster, your audience will want visual proof. If you are discussing budgetary shortfalls, your audience will want visual proof. If you are trying to explain how a motor functions, your audience will want visual proof. The trick is to figure out which type of visual will best suit your audience's needs for the greatest logical and/or emotional impact.

The list of potential visual types is long and varied, so, for here, we will focus on four common categories: photographs, diagrams, charts/graphs, and videos.

Photographs

When to Use: To show visual proof, demonstrate a concept, or provide persuasive or emotional support.

Points of Caution:
- Pictures must be clear and have a high resolution.
- Avoid graphic pictures that overplay gruesomeness or shock value; your audience will simply look away.
- Ensure that the images haven't been digitally altered. If the image seems too unreal to be true, it just might be.
- Avoid photo collages; they are too overwhelming. Show one picture at a time.
- Make sure you have copyright permission and/or cite the original source.

Diagrams

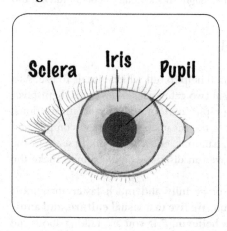

When to Use: To aid in audience understanding; to show processes, parts of a whole, and relative locations; to substitute for pictures when real photos would be too complicated or graphic to show.

Points of Caution:
- Must be easy for audience to understand.
- Only label and highlight parts relevant to message (edit premade diagrams yourself to follow this rule).
- Keep images as simple as possible.

Charts/Graphs

When to Use: To aid in audience understanding; to present numerical data.

Points of Caution:
- Make it as simple as possible.
- Avoid legends and keys; put labels directly on parts.
- Use headings that say the main point of the chart/graph, not just the topic.
- Avoid excessive 3-D; two-dimensional images are easier for your audience to digest quickly.
- Use distinct colors so printing or projecting doesn't make colors blend.

Videos

When to Use: To show movement, action, or processes that cannot adequately be shown through still images.

Points of Caution:
- Only use when necessary; don't use videos when you can explain or demonstrate yourself.
- Keep videos with audio short (less than ten percent of your total presentation time).
- Must be high quality and easy for audience to see.
- If you make it yourself, it must look professional.

Finding the Right Channels

The individual visual types listed above are often not shown as isolated images. Generally, in presentations, your visuals are part of a larger visual channel. The most popular one for presentations is a slideshow, but we will also consider handouts (ranging from single pieces of paper to bound presentation reports), document cameras[1], and low-tech channels like whiteboards, chalkboards, or flipcharts.

---

1   A document camera is a device true to its name: it is a camera hooked up to a projector that projects your documents (or other visuals) onto a screen.

	Ideal Uses	Benefits	Disadvantages
Slideshows	To show multiple successive images during a presentation.	Easy to use. Can be prepared ahead of time. Can include all visual types.	Too often misused. Must have A/V hookups. Tech can—and often does—fail. For some presenters, inhibits audience interaction.
Handouts	To give to audience as presentation takeaway. (Not for use during presentation.)	Easy to prepare with common software programs. Helps audience remember presentation afterward.	Grammar/spelling errors are immortalized for audience. Cannot be used during presentation, or it will pull focus from you. Cannot include videos or other dynamic elements.
Document Camera	Good for projecting limited numbers of visuals.	No worries about computer or software issues. Simple to use and easy to zoom in and out of image. Can project 3-D objects to audience.	Some images may get washed out by camera/projector. Limited camera scope means parts of visuals may be cut off. Transitions between visuals are less smooth than with computer slideshows.
White-boards, etc.	For on-the-spot explanations, visualizations, or direct interaction with small audiences.	Allows for audience interaction and adjustment. No prep needed—just a marker or piece of chalk required.	Not prepared ahead of time = greater chance for errors. Audience comprehension is subject to your penmanship. Only simple/crude images can be created in time restraints. Cannot be zoomed in if some audience members can't see it.

The visual channels you choose to use should depend on your audience, your presentation intent, and the content of your message. Consider the amount and types of visuals you need to show your audience. If you only have one very simple pie chart to show to a small audience, you might just be able to quickly sketch it out on the whiteboard. If you have a couple of images for one main point but not for the other points, the document camera might make the most sense. If you are covering a lot of information that it is crucial for your audience to retain, you may need to use a slideshow for the presentation itself and then provide the audience with comprehensive handouts.

The important point here is to make the channel decisions that are most sensible for the presentation you are giving. Don't feel that you need to break out PowerPoint for every presentation just because *that's* the norm. Use it when it is the right thing to use for your audience.

AIMing for the Right Visual Aids

The rest of this unit is designed to help you learn more about the visual aids you may use in a presentation. Our goal is for you to understand how to communicate effectively through visual aids.

When planning and designing each visual aid you will use, you need to follow the guidelines of AIMC. In addition to keeping in mind how your visual fits into the overall planning of your presentation, consider that each visual aid has its own intent, message, and channel (the audience for the visual should presumably be the same as the audience for the presentation itself). For instance, if you are designing a brochure, consider the following:

- Who is the *audience* for this presentation, and thus for this brochure?
- What is the *intent* of this brochure? That is, what do I want my audience to gain from having read it?
- What is the *message* I should use to reach that intent? What points and arguments do I need to make in the brochure—whether I include words or use only visuals?
- What is the *channel* I should use, or the ways in which I can visually communicate my message? Which types of images should I include, and how should they look?

Use the AIMC process for all your visual aids—whether they are visual channels or the visuals themselves. Make sure that whatever you show your audience is shown to them with purpose.

The remaining chapters in this unit will help you focus more specifically on different aspects of visuals aids: visual design, numerical data, slideshows, presenting with visuals, and handouts. While we cannot cover specific guidelines for every visual type without making this book much longer than you want it to be, keeping AIMC in mind will help. Use your critical-thinking skills to determine which types of visuals work best for your presentation and how you can design them most effectively.

Visual aids are tools. When used well, they can communicate clearly, convincingly, and even artfully. Choose the right tools, and use them well.

Key Takeaways

- Only use visual aids in your presentation when they help the audience understand or remember your point, or when they aid in persuasion.
- Choose the right visual types—photographs, diagrams, charts/graphs, and videos—for your audience, intent, and message.
- Use the visual channels that make the most sense for the number and scope of the visuals you've chosen for your presentation.
- Use AIMC as your guide when choosing and designing your visual aids.

Questions and Activities:

1. **Reflection Question:** Consider some of the visual aids you have used in past presentations. How well did those visuals adhere to the usefulness rules for visual aids—that they either help the audience understand or remember a point, or that they aid in persuasion? Give specific examples of the visuals you used and how they did or did not adhere to one of those two rules.
2. **Learning Activity:** Watch a video presentation (either a sample provided by your instructor or a TED talk online) in which the presenter uses visual aids. Identify the audience, intent, and basic message of the presentation. Then consider the visuals shown. Did the presenter use the right visual channels? Did each of the visuals serve a purpose for the audience? Be specific in your answers.
3. **Presentation Preparation:** Consider each of the main points you want to cover in your presentation, and the evidence you plan to use. Make a list of the types of visuals you want to include, taking into consideration the visual types that will work best for the points you are trying to prove or demonstrate. Then decide on the visual channel that would work most effectively for your visuals.

Credits

1. DNA Double Helix: National Human Genome Research Institute / Public Domain.
2. Toronto Clean Up in Brimfield: Russell Klika / U.S. Army / Copyright in the Public Domain.

CHAPTER 25

Make It Pretty, Professional, and Purposeful

Basic Guidelines for Visual Design

By M. Sandra DiFrancesco

After studying this chapter, you should be able to:
- *Understand why good visual design is important.*
- *List key guidelines that should be followed when preparing visuals.*
- *Apply basic design principles to the visuals you create.*
- *Describe the benefits of using visually driven material to supplement your presentation.*
- *Utilize simple typographic, color, and layout principles.*

Although it is often thought that your presentation simply consists of the words you choose to speak, effective presentations are much more than that. The typical academic, conference, sales, or work-related presentation consists of you (the presenter), the content of what you have to say, and your audience. And, in some cases, your presentation might be best delivered with accompanying visuals.

Visual aids can serve as effective tools to supplement your presentation and add to the total experience for your audience. They can help you capture your audience's attention and maintain their interest. But to do that, they need to be designed effectively.

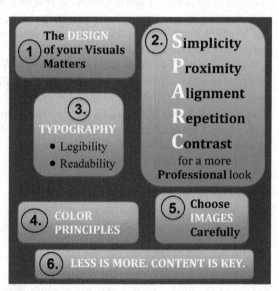

Infographic for how this chapter is organized.

The Design of Your Visuals Matters

Good news! Not a graphic designer? No problem. You don't have to be a design professional, or employ the services of one, in order to create appealing visuals. With the advent of desktop publishing software like Publisher and even Word (and a color printer, if you're making handouts), you have the means to create your own professional-looking material. If you really know what you're doing, you can also use industry-standard software packages like Adobe Illustrator, Photoshop, or InDesign to create even more personalized and creative designs. Whether you have access to basic programs or your computer is equipped with advanced design software, you have the PC tools to make your presentation visuals. What you need now is some basic training in the fundamentals of design to ensure you make them effectively.

This chapter will not make you a professional designer. Sorry. There are hundreds of tips and tricks that you can read about in other design books, but most are for graphic designers who design for a living. Our intent is to give you clear, basic concepts and concrete tips for creating visuals that look more professional, unified, engaging, and organized.

The key message throughout this discussion is that **design is about making communication as easy and clear for the viewer/reader as possible.** Effective visual aids should be simple, relevant, and supportive of the message of your presentation.

Preparing Visual Aids

The first step is to get started early so that you have time to create visuals that will truly support and enhance your presentation, not just provide relatively pretty "fluff." The key for effective visual communication is to represent your message in a clear and compelling way. And this is where the problems often start.

I have seen far too many students' visuals jam-packed with way too many words all cluttered together. Often the fonts they use are difficult to read (either too small or too flowery to serve a purpose). I have seen color palettes that varied so widely that they were fit for a circus flyer. Some use overly bright or fluorescent color choices more appropriate for a kindergarten class than a team of business professionals. Some try to go more "professional" and use the black-text-on-a-navy-blue-background combination that is nearly impossible to read. And the problems go on and on. What they are lacking are the fundamentals of good visual design.

In general, having good design will make it

1. easy for your audience to see and decipher the visual; and
2. easy for your audience to understand the point of the visual quickly.

Bad design overcomplicates images, making them difficult for your audience to learn from. It should not take more than a few seconds for your audience to get the gist of your presentational visuals (unless the confusion is intentional). If it takes longer to figure out and digest the image, your design has been insufficient.

Your presentation aids must be clear, clean, uncluttered, organized, and large enough for the audience to see and interpret correctly. Poorly designed presentation aids can damage your credibility as a speaker. Conversely, high quality visual design will contribute to your professional image and to your audience's acceptance of your message.

Good Design Lights a SPARC in Your Audience

While more in-depth graphic-design courses can teach you a litany of rules, there are five basic principles of design we will focus on here. Since visuals are an important component in communicating messages in a meaningful way, an understanding of basic visual-design principles can assist in preparing attractive and clear visual material.

In her brief 2004 book, The Non-Designer's Design Book, Robin Williams (the visual designer, not the comedian) identified four basic principles of visual design: proximity, alignment, repetition, and contrast. Williams had originally reordered those principles to create the acronym CRAP, but we are adding a fifth element—simplicity—to the list. So, with some slight rearrangement, our guiding design acronym will henceforth be SPARC.

Really, regardless of how we order the letters, the key point here is that, although these principles are being discussed individually, they are really interconnected. Applying one without the others will not make a significant difference in effectiveness. All five pieces of the SPARC puzzle must be in place for the resulting visual to be appealing and logical. Following SPARC will not guarantee *perfect* design, but it will certainly lead to *better* design. It will help to put intent behind your design and go beyond the uneasy test of "Well, I like it."

S Is for Simplicity: Less Is More

You have no doubt heard the phrase "Less is more," or perhaps even the more aggressive "Keep it simple, stupid." Simplicity is a crucial element of good design. **Crowded visuals make it too difficult for your audience to see all the elements easily, and the overabundance of components muddles the overall message.**

Eliminate all the "junk"—all the visual swirls, circles, squares, variety of colors, different textures, extra pictures, or other "stuff" that is superfluous to the message. Eliminate the clutter. Use only a few different colors, fonts, shapes, and stylistic elements so your visual's intent can come across clearly.

Simplicity sounds easy, but it's actually hard to achieve. The goal is to support your message so that it's easy for the audience to understand. You want to reveal your message in the clearest way possible. Just as in the content of your actual presentation, it can sometimes be hard to streamline your design into one coherent vision. But be ruthless in your

Cluttered. Center Aligned. Enough said.

decision making. If elements do not directly contribute to the intent of the visual aid, get rid of them. If you have a multitude of images you like, pare them down to just a few essentials. Your visuals do not need to cover everything; focus on the best stuff you have. And **when in doubt, leave it out.**

Making a commitment to de-clutter your visuals means that you need to embrace the power of **white space** (also known as **negative space**). Negative space helps give your design a clean and uncluttered look. White space doesn't have to be white, and negative space is not a negative thing.

When non-designers begin to design, they normally focus on the positive space (the parts with design elements) and the need to fill up the whole page. They see white space as a land yet to conquer, so they increase their visual sizes and add more pictures, more fonts, or more flourishes to make the negative space all positive.

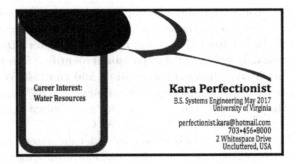

A better use of white space.

This is a huge mistake so many new designers make: they see empty space as something that must be filled in—as something that's "wasted" unless it is occupied with more visual or text elements. But it is this "negative" space that makes the positive elements of the design stand out more. It is the negative space that gives the layout breathing room and gives the reader's eyes a place to rest. It's a powerful tool for directing the reader's eye around the page and in establishing clear design.

Don't make your audience hunt for what they're looking for, or they will quickly check out. Giving your audience a handout filled to every corner with words and visuals will probably guarantee that they won't read it (it will just make them tired to even look at it). Use negative space to help your design be uncluttered and at the same time draw attention to the focal point of the page.

P Is for Proximity

The principle of proximity refers to how items are grouped and spaced on a page. The idea is to group related items together into information chunks that create one visual unit. Conversely, the principle of proximity means you should create space between unrelated items. Think of a simple visual—two people on a park bench. If they were sitting in close proximity, you would likely think that they are friends, family, or romantically involved. If they were sitting on opposite ends of the bench (a far proximity), you would likely categorize them as strangers—people who are different and unrelated to one another.

So how does this translate to presentation visuals? If you had three different points to make on a handout, and each of these points had text and a visual, you should put the corresponding images and text together. This lets the reader know that these two things belong together. Then you should surround each pairing with white space so there is a distance (and visual distinction) from the next pairing. Imagine if the images were scattered around each corner and the text was weaving back and forth throughout the middle and sides of the page. This would be very confusing. Grouping together related information helps your audience grasp key concepts and understand the relationship between the images and the words.

There are two common blunders most commonly made with respect to proximity: (1) randomly placing elements on the page or slide to fill up every bit of space; and (2) grouping elements that do not belong together. These mistakes create confusion for your audience and make the visual much harder for the audience to digest quickly. Items related to each other should be grouped close together. Grouping organizes information and reduces clutter.

KARA'S DINER

APPETIZERS
French Onion Soup - $4
Shrimp Cocktail - $5
ENTREES
Chicken Piccata - $12
Rib Eye Steak - $18
Meatloaf - $10
Pork Loin - $11
DESSERTS
Key Lime Pie - $4
Ice Cream - $3
Shortcake - $5

Poor proxemics. If everything is clumped together, relationships between items are unclear.

KARA'S DINER

APPETIZERS
French Onion Soup $4
Shrimp Cocktail $5

ENTREES
Chicken Piccata $12
Rib Eye Steak $18
Meatloaf $10
Pork Loin $11

DESSERTS
Key Lime Pie $4
Ice Cream $3
Shortcake $5

A better use of proxemics. Items are easier to digest and understand.

A Is for Alignment

Let me introduce the principle of alignment with advice from *The Non-Designers Design Book*: "Nothing should be placed on the page arbitrarily. Every item should have a visual connection with something else on the page" (Williams, 2004). Alignment gives a clean, unified appearance and conveys organization.

If you have had any experience with Microsoft Office, you probably know the three most common types of alignment: right, left, and center. **My biggest advice to you is to break your center-alignment habit.** For some reason, non-designers tend to instinctively center-align everything, both horizontally and vertically. Stuff just always ends up smack dab in the middle of the page or screen. Somewhere in life, they learned that if something was centered, then it was balanced and therefore better. In reality, center alignment is the weakest, hardest-to-read alignment, and should therefore be used very selectively.

Center aligning everything creates two significant drawbacks: first, this type of alignment is generally reserved for when you are creating a formal document like wedding announcements, certificates, etc., and may therefore look out of place in your presentation aids. Second, when you center align, you limit how you can put your visual components on the page. Most with the center-alignment habit end up with the same old design: headline at the top, picture in the middle, text at the bottom.

If you have several lines of text, center alignment becomes more difficult to read, given all those jagged edges on both the left and right sides. The more text you have, the greater the difficulty.

If your words are on the left side of the page, you should use left alignment—jagged right edges. If you put your words on the right side of a page, you should use right alignment—jagged left edges. If your words are in the dead center of the page—well, stop being so wishy-washy and pick a side. Using left or right alignment opens up space on your page and allows you more choices for where you place your images and text.

Nothing should be placed arbitrarily. Do not toss elements randomly on your page or simply try to fill space. Every element should have a visual connection with another element on the page.

R Is for Repetition

The use of repetition can create consistency, continuity, and unity in a document. It gives a cohesive feel to your visuals. The principle of repetition states that **you should repeat some elements of your design throughout the entire piece** (like using the same background and the same two fonts throughout an entire slideshow presentation). Using too many different elements in one design makes your visual look like an elementary-school collage of random magazine clippings. The excess design elements become distracting and the message gets lost. Choices are tough, but choose only one or two of each design element to give your visual a clear point of view.

Beyond the school-collage mistake, another common blunder is overdoing repeating elements to the point that they become annoying and your audience becomes confused, like bolding every other word because **they're all so important——it's just too much to grasp that everything is equally important and everything has to be bolded or UPPERCASE!** Imagine if you read that kind of visual out loud to your audience—you'd be screaming at them for the vast majority of your speaking time. Rude!

Repeat visual elements throughout the visual you are creating. Repetition develops the organization and creates a strong, unified message.

APPETIZERS
French Onion Soup........$4
Shrimp Cocktail..............$5

ENTREES
Chicken Piccata..............$12
Rib Eye Steak...................$18
Meatloaf...........................$10
Pork Loin..........................$11

DESSERTS
Key Lime Pie.....................$4
Ice Cream..........................$3
Shortcake..........................$5

An example of good alignment.

KARA'S DINER

APPETIZERS
French Onion Soup........$4
Shrimp Cocktail..............$5

ENTREES
Chicken Piccata..............$12
Rib Eye Steak...................$18
Meatloaf...........................$10
Pork Loin..........................$11

DESSERTS
Key Lime Pie.....................$4
Ice Cream..........................$3
Shortcake..........................$5

An example of good use of repetition.

C Is for Contrast

Contrast is created when two design elements are *significantly* different from one another. Contrast is all about making things stand out. When it comes to this design element, Williams (2004) says, "don't be a wimp." Don't just make things *slightly* different. Your audience will just think you made a mistake. **If two items are not exactly the same, then make them different; really different in some way (such as size, thickness, color, shape, or texture) from other elements.** Contrast on a page draws our eyes to it. That's why you are currently reading black text on a white page—the contrast makes the text easy to see.

Contrast has two purposes: one is to create an interest on the page; the other is to aid in the organization of the information. Add contrast through your typeface choices, line widths, colors, shapes, sizes, and space. Contrast attracts the attention of your viewers.

KARA'S DINER

Appetizers
French Onion Soup........$4
Shrimp Cocktail.............$5

Entrees
Chicken Piccata.............$12
Rib Eye Steak.................$18
Meatloaf.........................$10
Pork Loin.......................$11

Desserts
Key Lime Pie...................$4
Ice Cream.......................$3
Shortcake.......................$5

An example of good contrast.

KARA'S DINER

Appetizers
French Onion Soup........$4
Shrimp Cocktail.............$5

Entrees
Comes with Potatoes, Cole Slaw, or Salad
Chicken Piccata.............$12
Rib Eye Steak.................$18
Meatloaf.........................$10
Pork Loin.......................$11

Desserts
Key Lime Pie...................$4
Ice Cream.......................$3
Shortcake.......................$5

An example of even better contrast.

For contrast to be effective and still correspond to the principles of simplicity and repetition, you should only choose one or two facets of the element to change. When we want a heading to stand out in this book, we put it in **bold**. Sometimes we combine ***bold and italics***. But what you don't see is every possible treatment being applied to a bit of text to make it stand out. Why? Because that would be *C R A Z Y !*

It Takes a SPARC to Kindle a Flame

To be on your way to good design, you can't just use one or two of these basic principles. Like a puzzle, every part of SPARC goes together in some way or another. Before moving on, let me do a simple review for you here:

Simplicity
Forces you to avoid clutter and keep the focus on the intent of the visual.

Proximity
"Chunks" similar elements together to make the visual more digestible.
Alignment
Makes text easier to read and gives visuals a more polished look.
Repetition
Repeats design elements to create a cohesive feel.
Contrast
Makes singular elements stand out so the audience knows where to look first, second, third, last.

Now that you know the five basic principles of design, let's look at some other important design considerations.

Typography Speaks Volumes

Most visual channels you use will include at least *some* text. Handouts are a more appropriate place for large amounts of text, while slideshows should have very little. (In Chapter 27, you will read about just how little text should be included in a multimedia slideshow.) Nonetheless, the design choices you make with your font have an impact on your overall design—and your audience's ability to read and understand the visuals.

Typography is the design and use of typefaces as a means of communication. Non-designers frequently stress out about finding the proper typeface for a presentation, and for good reason. The right font can set the tone for your visual aids and for you. Font selection should never be an arbitrary process. Selecting the most appropriate type style is important to the overall message of your design. Think of your type as taking the place of the human voice and as having many expressive tones.

The two most important factors to consider when choosing a typeface for any visuals you design are legibility and readability. The ease with which the text and graphics can be deciphered is referred to as its *legibility*, while the ease with which something can be understood is referred to as its *readability*. In other words, *legibility* refers to one's ability to determine what the letters and pictures are supposed to be (that's a D; that's a dog); *readability* refers to one's ability to receive the intended message of the whole document (this handout wants me to adopt a dog).

Let's look more closely at both of these factors:

Legibility

In visual design, *legibility* refers to the typefaces you choose to communicate your message.

Instead of browsing your font list and looking for "something cool," instead think about the message you want to convey. The font type you choose says something about you and your message. Choose font types that are best for moving your audience to feel how you want them to feel. People have certain feelings, emotions, and associations when they see certain typefaces and fonts. Consider the fonts below as an example of how typography can communicate just by virtue of how it looks.

The above examples are just a sampling of a few typefaces and the messages they convey. These samples are meant to demonstrate how you need to take careful consideration when choosing which font you will use to get across your intended message.

For our purposes, we will break down potential typefaces into three basic types: serif, sans serif, and script. Serif fonts have flourishes or little lines on the edges of the letters; sans serif fonts (*sans* meaning *without* in French) do not. Script fonts resemble handwriting (usually cursive) or calligraphy.

All are different but valid font options, depending on the circumstances.

- **Serif typefaces** (e.g., Palatino, Cambria, Times New Roman, Century, and Garamond) are more appropriately used for long passages. Research shows that when there

ABC	ABC
serif font	sans serif font

  are several long paragraphs of words, serif fonts are easier to read than sans serif fonts. The eye tracks across the serifs of the letters to make reading easier. Serifs are viewed as more formal and traditional, and are best suited for print. This book is written using a serif typeface.
- **Sans serif typefaces** (e.g., Helvetica, Arial, Futura, Tahoma, and Verdana) are more appropriately used for shorter text, such as titles, section headings, and captions, where a limited amount of reading is required. They are viewed as informal and playful. They are best suited for digital, and they are recommended for PowerPoint slides because they tend to project better on a screen.
- **Script fonts** (e.g., Brush Script, Edwardian Script, Lucida Calligraphy, Lucida Handwriting, and Mistral) are often used in formal invitations. They are not ideal for full sentences or passages. Script fonts should be avoided when creating cover letters, résumés, or other types of professional documents. They are just too casual and informal. Because of the high potential for legibility and readability issues, script fonts should be used with caution.

Once upon a time, in a place far, far away, there was a newbie designer who really liked this font style and thought it would put the audience in a "happier" mood when listening to her presentation, so she mistakenly used it throughout all of her visuals.

Font choices become harder to make when you are creating a document, poster, brochure, or handout—all of which are likely to have more text than a slideshow presentation. Here are some simple rules for choosing the right font to ensure legibility:

- Use a common, easily recognizable, serif typeface for your body copy.
- Break up the body copy with headings and captions in sans serif.
- Use decorative type faces very sparingly.
- Use standard-looking fonts to help ensure that your design remains inside the realm of clean and professional and away from cluttered and ugly.

Readability

Readability—how well your audience can understand the message of your text—should also guide your decisions about typefaces.

Typefaces can affect readability, and will either harmonize with or distract from the overall tone of your presentation. Imagine how your audience would be confused if you were giving a serious business presentation, but your visuals used Comic Sans, Poster Bodoni, Papyrus, Chalkboard, or Curlz MT (all playful typefaces). For the font to be truly readable (and not distract the viewer), it needs to be appropriate for its audience, intent, and message.

In addition, it should help inform you where and how to place your text and graphics on the page. Follow the guidelines of SPARC to ensure that your text is easy for your audience to visually follow and quickly understand:

- **Simplicity**—Use text sparingly; avoid words for the sake of words.
- **Proximity**—Keep text near the visuals it describes. Avoid double-spacing your text in presentation visuals and handouts.
- **Alignment**—Avoid center alignment, particularly when the text is more than one line.
- **Repetition**—Use only a couple of types of fonts, and use only a few means of highlighting those fonts (bold, italics, size, color, underlining).
- **Contrast**—Make titles, headings, and important phrases stand out from the rest of the text.

Color Principles: Simple Tips for Using Color

Just as you've now chosen your fonts, you also want to pick a color scheme. Using color well can be a challenge. Start with two or three complimentary colors that work together (remember the principle of repetition). From these you might generate lighter or darker shades of the same color.

Effective use of color will impact the audience's ability to read and understand your visuals better. There is a great temptation to use too many colors, with the assumption that doing so will grab attention. But you are not Dorothy Gale just landing in Munchkin Land; you can tone it down quite a bit. With colors, consistency is the key to creating a design that holds together. Use color to make important information and data pop and the unimportant data take a backseat. Too much color can be very distracting and confuse your audience. Use color for emphasis, but don't use too many colors to do it.

The best approach is to use highly contrasting colors. If you were using color for your text, try a dark text (like blue) on a light background (like white), or the reverse—a light text on a dark background. For a pie chart, use a bold color for the most important pie piece and duller colors for the other parts. For photographs, be sure the contrast is set high enough so the image is easy to see, and make sure the image contrasts enough from the background. When you use color sparingly and intelligently in your design, it is so much easier to draw attention to important items.

Color communicates. First, it creates the mood of your design. So think what you want your design to communicate and to whom, and pick a color palette that you think expresses that mood and suits that audience. Secondly, color is often associated with specific emotional contexts. Red, for example, is considered a passionate and active color, whereas blue is considered more restrained and neutral. Selecting a dominant color that matches the intended emotional message of the presentation is a good strategy, provided that the secondary colors are harmonious and blend well. Avoid awkward color contrasts, including red text on black backgrounds or using red and green together (unless you're creating something with a Christmas theme).

Consider the color wheel shown here. Not only does the color wheel show you a lovely rainbow pie chart, but it also helps you pick out a design scheme. For a more consistent look, pick colors that are harmonious together. These are any two colors that are either directly opposite each other on the color wheel, any three colors equally spaced around the color wheel forming a triangle, or any four colors that form a rectangle (two pairs of colors opposite each other).

The choice really comes down to what you're trying to accomplish—your audience, your intent, and your message. Picking poor combinations can lead to messy and unappealing designs. With that in mind, here are some final color tips:

- For text content to be easily readable, choose contrasting colors.
- Use fewer colors. Don't make your visuals look like a circus. For an ideal impact, you can use one color on headlines/titles and another color (a complementary one) for the background.
- Use color with constraint. If you use too little color, you risk making your visuals boring. Too many colors, and you'll attract attention in too many directions.
- Make sure when you put words in color that there is significant contrast so that it can be easlily read.

Choose Images Carefully to Better Communicate Your Message

Please avoid cheesy ClipArt! ClipArt is tacky, it does not aid in audience comprehension or emotional appeals, and it will leave your audience distinctly unimpressed.

It's better to use high-quality professional images that will increase the professional appearance and visual impact of your presentation. Use stock illustrations or photos, or your own creations. A simple Google search can supply you with tons of photos and illustrations that will make it easy to find just the image you're looking for to communicate your message.

> **Websites of Copyright-Free Images:**
>
> While the brunt of the images you can find online are copyrighted (even a random blogger's photos or your friends' Instagram snapshots are not free for your use), there are some sites that offer copyright-free images free of charge. Search for these sites online:
>
> - Wikimedia Commons: http://commons.wikimedia.org/wiki/Main_Page
> - National Institute of Health: http://www.nih.gov/about/nihphotos.htm
> - World Health Organization: https://extranet.who.int/photolibrary/guest_eng.htm
> - Morgue File: www.morguefile.com
> - Unrestricted Stock: www.unrestrictedstock.com
> - Pixabay: www.pixabay.com

Just be careful of relying on stock images that *look* like stock images; don't be cliché—and, oh, how cliché some stock images can be. It takes a little bit of time and creativity, but there are resources out there that allow you to get quality images for free or at a minimal cost. Fortunately, the web is a wonderland of free resources if you know where to look. Here is a great list of sites where you can find the best free stock photos.

And if you can't find the right image online, use your cell phone (or that camera you haven't picked up in quite a while) and take your own pictures.

Choose professional imagery to support a professional presentation. (And don't forget to include the source for any images you use immediately under the image, like "From the National Institutes of Health.")

You've Got the Look

Producing your own handouts, flyers, posters, brochures, business cards, or PowerPoint slides may sometimes seem a daunting task. But, by applying the basic principles of visual design, it should be possible for you to create truly professional, legible, and readable visual aids.

Remember to avoid the pitfalls of getting fancy for the sake of fanciness (keep it simple); make use of Williams' principles of alignment, repetition, contrast, and proximity; and use appropriate typefaces and colors to gain and direct attention. Perhaps the most important thing of all to keep in mind is that it is only a good design if it is legible and readable by the audience for whom it is intended. Whatever you're creating, the basic purpose it must serve is to convey the information your audience wants or needs.

Key Takeaways

- Good design makes your visuals easier to understand and digest for your audience.
- Use the principles of simplicity, proximity, alignment, repetition, and contrast to ensure your visuals are well designed.
- White space is your friend.
- Keep your text legible and readable.
- Pick colors that complement, not detract.
- Choose images that look professional and complement your message.

Questions and Activities:

1. **Reflection Question:** Most people can recognize a poorly designed page when they see it, but they don't always know what's wrong with it. In what ways has this chapter helped you identify bad design? How do the design principles of SPARC help enhance visual communication?

2. **Learning Activity:** Take a phrase, for example, "Attitude not aptitude will determine your altitude." Copy and paste it ten times. Use ten different fonts for each copy of the phrase. Can you see how changing the font can change the meaning and feel for the phrase? Use this activity for determining what typefaces you will use that best suit the message you want to send.

3. **Learning Activity:** Can you add some SPARC? Look at the examples below to determine which elements follow the principles of SPARC and which ones don't. For rule violations, write the principle it violates and specifically how the design failed to adhere to it. Sketch out or explain how the design could be fixed to properly adhere to SPARC.

> **Summer Jazz Concert**
> Music Society Association
> New Haven, CT
> Friday, August 25, 2015 at 7 p.m.
> Shoreline Rockers
> Five-piece band
> Lead Vocalist and guitar, Keith Jones
> Special guest on keyboard, Dave Smith
> Appetizers served
> Full open bar
> Tickets $25
> No admission without a ticket
> For ticket information visit
> MusicSociety.com

KARA PERFECTIONIST

KaraPerfectionist.com • 510-501-5367 • 1234 Emily Drive • Bend, OR 06504

OBJECTIVE	To obtain a job in environmental management, consulting, or research.

EDUCATION

University of Virginia   Charlottesville, Virginia
School of Engineering and Applied Sciences
B.S. in Systems Engineering, minors in Environmental Sciences and Economics
Cumulative G.P.A. 3.34/4.0
Candidate for graduation May 2002

WORK EXPERIENCE

Little Bytes of Virginia   Charlottesville, Virginia   May 1999-present
Computer Instructor
- Teach basic computing skills to children ages three to eleven
- Prepare and develop lessons for individual and group instruction
- Maintain customer records using Excel database
- Enhance customer relations and interpersonal skills

Albemarle Planning Depart   Charlottesville, Virginia   May 2001-present
Office of Mapping and Information Resources-GIS Intern
- Update county maps using MicroStation platform
- Update and maintain housing and resident records in Access databases
- Perform queries of Access databases
- Enhance customer relations and interpersonal skills

Philips Medical Systems   Shelton, Connecticut   August 1999
Extern, Integrated Systems Department
- Assisted in the installation and debugging of software
- Observed a variety of plant operations during a volunteer program

---

4. **Presentation Preparation:** Look over the visuals you plan to use for your presentation—whether you made them yourself or not—and ensure that they follow all of the rules of good design:

- **S (Simplicity):** The visuals are simple and uncluttered.
- **P (Proximity):** Related items are grouped closely together. Unrelated items are spaced apart.
- **A (Alignment):** Multiline text is not center-aligned. Items are lined up appropriately on a page.
- **R (Repetition):** Key design elements are repeated so as to give the visual a coherent look.
- **C (Contrast):** Important parts stand out on the visual through changes in color, size, font, etc.

Credits

CHAPTER 26

The Numbers Game
Working and Presenting with Numerical Data

After studying this chapter, you should be able to:
- *Identify the benefits of using a spreadsheet.*
- *Decide which type of chart or graph to use for your data.*
- *Design an effective chart or graph to use in a presentation.*
- *Use alternative visuals beyond charts and graphs to represent numerical data.*

So often in business, presentations are "about the numbers"—how much something costs, how much profit margin exists, and what percentage of people will buy a product or endorse an idea. Even in everyday academic presentations, numbers provide a solid, logical proof that gives your audience comfort that what you are saying *must* be true.

Whether you have a natural propensity for numbers, or whether you need a calculator to add single digits, you will need the skills to compile and present numerical data. This chapter will concentrate on helping you gain some of those skills, specifically by looking at the benefits of using spreadsheets. This chapter will *not* get overly technical and provide how-to instructions on setting up spreadsheets or writing functions; the seemingly endless library of spreadsheet how-to videos on YouTube can give you a far better education on the step-by-step process than a written instruction manual can. We will instead focus here on why you should use a spreadsheet and how to turn that data into presentation-worthy visual aids.

Boxes and Columns and Formulas, Oh My!

There will be times in your presentation preparation when you will need to do your own quantitative (numerical) research. You may take a survey of your potential audience members as a part of your audience analysis. You may poll fellow students at your school to find out how many would be in favor of a new campus initiative (or how many are unhappy with the current state of affairs). You may compile the numbers needed to determine a potential selling price and profit margin for a new product.

◢	A	B	C
1			
2			
3			
4			
5			
6			
7			

A spreadsheet—easy as ABC.

In all of these instances, you would need a way to collect and analyze the results of your research. That way is a spreadsheet. I know that some of you might be having a mini freak-out in your head at the thought of spreadsheets: "I don't know anything about spreadsheets! Excel is the green X on my computer. That's all I know!" If this is you, fear not, Number Newbie. It'll be all right. Microsoft Excel (or whatever other spreadsheet program you use) is there to help you through your data analysis. It is a tool for your use, not a mountain you must treacherously climb.

So let's start with some answers to some basic questions:

- **What is a spreadsheet?** A spreadsheet is a computer program that allows you to compile, organize, and manipulate data.
- **What does a spreadsheet look like?** It resembles a grid. Each box in the grid is called a *cell*; the cells are set up in lettered columns and numbered rows, giving each cell a unique location (e.g., the cell in the first column and first row is A1; the cell in the third column and sixth row is C6).
- **What can you do with spreadsheet programs?** A lot. Besides just keeping track of numbers, the programs allow you to use formulas to manipulate cells. You can do simple arithmatic functions, like addition and subtraction, or you can apply far more complicated functions from fields like trigonometry, statistics, and engineering. If there is some information you need to glean from your research, it is likely that there is a formula to help you do it. Moreover, spreadsheet programs allow you to then turn your data into charts or graphs to make them presentation-ready.
- **Why not just use a calculator?** Unlike a calculator, a spreadsheet is dynamic, meaning the formula results will keep adjusting themselves based on new or altered data. For instance, if I had a formula that added up the total for a column of numbers in a spreadsheet, and then I changed one of the numbers, the total would automatically adjust itself. On a calculator, you would have to manually punch in all the numbers again. When working with a large amount of data, that manual calculation is unrealistic and a waste of time (and it leaves a much greater chance for error).

You may doubt that a spreadsheet is necessary for the numerical data you have to collect, but I assure you that it can help. Let me give you an example: You are preparing an informative presentation for your classmates. You are lucky enough to know the exact audience you will have for the presentation (a rare gift in the professional world), and you have access to them ahead of time. So, you decide to give your classmates quick surveys so you can determine their demographic information, their knowledge level of your topic, and how they feel about it. There are about twenty students in your class, so that would leave you with a good number of surveys to collect, compile, and analyze.

Enter the spreadsheet. You could use columns for the questions you asked and the question options, and then use rows to represent each survey you conducted. At the bottom of each column, you could total the number of responses. If you add more surveys or fix an entry error, the totals will adjust themselves. Moreover, you have a place where you can see all the survey results and start to analyze the findings.

Figure 3 represents a very simplistic way of using spreadsheets to tabulate survey results, and if you are new to the world of spreadsheets, this would be an easy setup to try. Spreadsheet programs, though, are certainly capable of doing much more than just adding. If you are familiar with Microsoft Excel or other programs, explore other formulas and functions. Learning some of the more complex formulas (like the COUNTIF formula for survey data) gives you the ability to conduct more intricate analysis, as is done in Figure 4. So, not only would you be able to tell how many sophomores there are in your audience, but your spreadsheet could tell you how many sophomore business majors with full-time jobs in your audience believe time travel will one day be possible (and there are two of them, oddly enough, in this sample).

Like any other technological tool, spreadsheet programs take practice and patience before you can feel confident using them. Most certainly you will need to seek out resources for help to master all the complexities and potential benefits that they have to offer. Be patient and keep searching for guidance. When you know how to use spreadsheet programs competently, you will have mastered an incredibly valuable tool for your academic, professional, and everyday life.

	Question #1: What year in school are you?				
	First-year	Sophomore	Junior	Senior	Super-Senior
Respondent #1		1			
Respondent #2				1	
Respondent #3			1		
Respondent #4	1				
Respondent #5		1			
Respondent #6					1
Respondent #7		1			
Respondent #8		1			
Respondent #9			1		
Respondent #10			1		
Respondent #11		1			
Respondent #12	1				
Respondent #13	1				
Respondent #14			1		
Respondent #15		1			
Respondent #16		1			
Respondent #17				1	
Respondent #18	1				
Respondent #19					1
Respondent #20			1		
TOTALS:	**4**	**7**	**5**	**2**	**2**

A simple spreadsheet of survey results that allows you to SUM up totals.

	Q1: Year	Q2: Field	Q3: Job hrs/wk	Q4: Time travel
Respondent #1	First-Year	Art/Humanities	20	Yes
Respondent #2	Junior	Art/Humanities	20	No
Respondent #3	Senior	Social/Behavioral	25	No
Respondent #4	First-Year	Business/Finance	20	No opinion
Respondent #5	Junior	Business/Finance	0	Yes
Respondent #6	Senior	Social/Behavioral	40	No
Respondent #7	Sophomore	Social/Behavioral	40	Yes
Respondent #8	Sophomore	STEM	30	No
Respondent #9	Senior	Social/Behavioral	25	No
Respondent #10	First-Year	Business/Finance	0	No opinion
Respondent #11	Senior	STEM	20	No opinion
Respondent #12	Sophomore	STEM	10	No
Respondent #13	Junior	Art/Humanities	25	Yes
Respondent #14	Junior	Social/Behavioral	20	No
Respondent #15	Junior	Social/Behavioral	20	No
Respondent #16	Sophomore	Business/Finance	40	Yes
Respondent #17	Junior	Business/Finance	40	No
Respondent #18	First-Year	Social/Behavioral	10	No
Respondent #19	Sophomore	Business/Finance	40	Yes
Respondent #20	Junior	Business/Finance	20	No
			23.25	

First-Year	4		No job	2
Sophomore	5		Part-time job	13
Junior	6		Full-time job	5
Senior	3			

Art/Humanities	3		Time travel possible	6
Business/Finance	7		Time travel impossible	11
Social/Behavioral	7		No opinion	3
STEM	3			

Business sophomores with full-time job who believe in time travel	2

The more you make an effort to learn the formulas in your spreadsheet program, the more intricate your analysis can become.

From Spreadsheet to Presentation Visual

When you learn to use a spreadsheet program effectively, you will find that you can make some really professional-looking and well-designed tables of information. But as pretty as those tables may be, they are rarely the visuals you will share with your audience.

Audiences seldom need to see the breakdown of all of your data (if they do, put it on a nice handout for them to take home and analyze later). So showing audiences the spreadsheet version of your information in the course of the presentation will constitute information overload for your audience.

Remember the design rule of **simplicity**? **You only want to give your audience what they need to understand your point—nothing more.** Showing a full table gives the audience too much to take in and too much to look at it. It might confuse them, and it certainly will pull focus from you while they try to decipher all of the table's components. In our previous example of the audience-analysis data, your audience doesn't need to see every survey response. Rather, if they needed to see any of the data, it would likely just be your totals. But don't think that copying and pasting just the table of totals is the right visual either.

In Chapter 24, you learned that numbers are best served in a visual format. You want to make your numerical data as easy for your audience to digest as possible. A table of all of the totals still makes your audience members think too much about the comparisons among the numbers. If you just gave a chart that showed the total results of how many in your audience believe that time travel would one day be possible, it might look like this:

	Time Travel Possible	Time Travel Impossible	No opinion
Total # of respondents	6	11	3
Percentage of total respondents	30%	55%	15%

Showing this on the screen to your audience, though, means that they have to read over the entire table and mentally do the work to figure out that most people believe it is impossible. I recognize that the "mental work" they have to do isn't really rocket science, but remember that every second your audience spends trying to decipher your visual aid is a second they are not able to listen fully to you. Jerry Weissman (2009) says audiences follow a consistent mental mantra: "Don't make me think." Tables make them have to think too much.

Visuals should be easy for your audience to grasp and digest. If it takes more than a few seconds on screen for the audience to understand its meaning, the visual is likely too complicated. Even takeaway visual aids on handouts and brochures that offer your audience more time to consider the data should still aim for simplicity. If the visual is too hard to grasp, your audience won't bother to try.

So how do you make numbers more visual? The most common way is to convert your data table into a series of charts or graphs.

Pies, Lines, Bars—Choosing the Right Type of Graphical Representation

Most spreadsheet programs allow you to highlight areas of your data and convert those cells into a chart or graph. Once you know what data you want graphically represented, you need to decide which chart or graph is the most logical option for that data. **Different graphing types—pie charts, bar graphs, and line graphs—are not created equal.** They are all unique visual representations used for different purposes:

Pie Charts

Uses: Representing different parts of one whole. Good for showing results of survey questions in which respondents can only choose one answer. Ideal to show relative size differences among different categories.

Characteristics: Looks like a pie. Each piece of the pie is a different category. Each piece's relative size is based on that category's percentage of the whole.

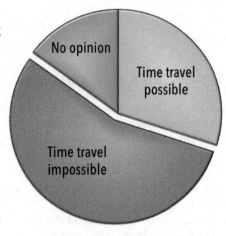

Most Believe Time Travel Not Possible

Bar Graphs

Uses: When categories are not part of a whole, when raw numbers are important, or when you need to compare multiple groups of numbers side by side.

Characteristics: Each category is represented by a bar. The length of the bar is relative to the value of the bar. Bars can be horizontal or can be columns. Use vertical columns for fewer categories; use horizontal bars for more categories.

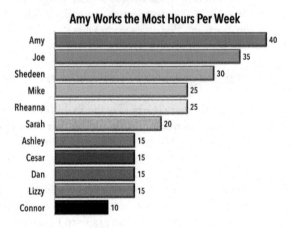

Amy Works the Most Hours Per Week

Amy	40
Joe	35
Shedeen	30
Mike	25
Rheanna	25
Sarah	20
Ashley	15
Cesar	15
Dan	15
Lizzy	15
Connor	10

Line Graphs

Uses: Shows progression of one or more categories over time.

Characteristics: Consists of data points with lines connecting those points to show patterns of increases and declines. To compare trends of different categories, use multiple lines.

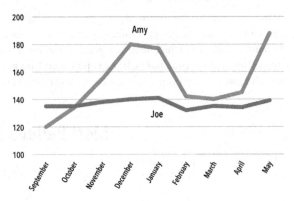

Making Your Graph Presentation-Ready

For visual aids to be effective, they need to be easy for your audience to see and easy for them to digest quickly. Unfortunately, many presenters' graphs are not designed effectively to meet those two goals.

For charts and graphs to be easy to see, you need to:

- Make sure all titles and labels are big enough to read. The ten-point default font won't be big enough.
- Use distinct colors to represent different parts. A line graph with five lines that are all a different shade of blue will be tough to distinguish through a projector screen.
- Avoid 3-D. The perspective can make it difficult for your audience to see the actual proportions, distances, or heights.

For charts and graphs to be easy to digest, you need to:

- Use a title that clearly says the main finding you want to highlight. If the graph is in your presentation, it should be there for a purpose; say what that purpose is in the heading. This lets the audience know what the claim is so they can look to the graph, assure that the claim is proven with the data, and then quickly turn their attention back to you.
- Remove the legend and put category labels directly on the pie pieces, bars, or lines. Don't make your audience look from the legend to the graph to the legend to the graph to the legend to the graph to figure out what it all means.
- Eliminate extra information. Only include the categories, labels, and details required for the chart or graph to make sense and prove your point. If you don't need the raw numbers, cut them out. If you don't need to include all the answer choices of a survey question, then lump the less important ones into an "Other" category. Don't present your audience with anything to visually consider that doesn't need their consideration.

- Use logical colors. Odd color choices can mess with your audience's heads. Don't use red for Democrat and blue for Republican, or orange for the Boston Red Sox and red for the Baltimore Orioles. Avoid red to show profit or green to show loss. Stick to the color schemes you know your audience will understand.

To consider these suggestions in practice, let's look at a problematic pie chart, and then let's consider that same data put into a better version for a presentation:

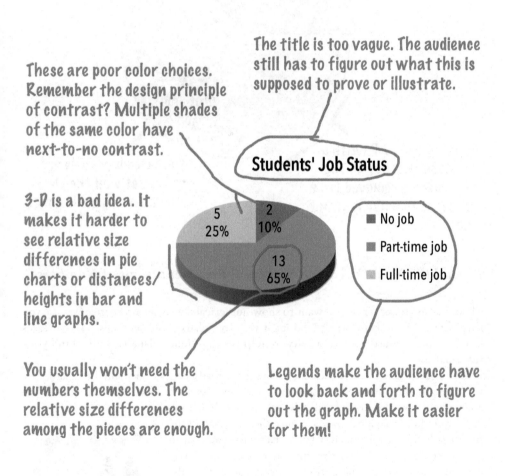

The title is too vague. The audience still has to figure out what this is supposed to prove or illustrate.

These are poor color choices. Remember the design principle of contrast? Multiple shades of the same color have next-to-no contrast.

3-D is a bad idea. It makes it harder to see relative size differences in pie charts or distances/ heights in bar and line graphs.

Students' Job Status

5
25%

2
10%

13
65%

■ No job
■ Part-time job
■ Full-time job

You usually won't need the numbers themselves. The relative size differences among the pieces are enough.

Legends make the audience have to look back and forth to figure out the graph. Make it easier for them!

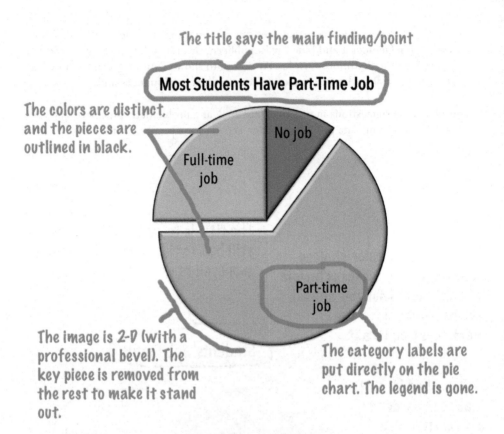

The title says the main finding/point

Most Students Have Part-Time Job

The colors are distinct, and the pieces are outlined in black.

No job

Full-time job

Part-time job

The image is 2-D (with a professional bevel). The key piece is removed from the rest to make it stand out.

The category labels are put directly on the pie chart. The legend is gone.

Beyond the X and Y Axis: Other Visual Representations of Numbers

There may be times when you want to show numerical data in an alternative way, or you have data to share that doesn't lend itself well to a chart or graph. These are the cases in which you can **use your creativity to help your audience visually understand your information.**

Let's go back to the audience analysis in the spreadsheet. If you wanted to share your fascinating finding that two of the sophomore business majors with full-time jobs in the audience believe time travel will one day be possible, a pie chart wouldn't be an ideal option. A slice that is a tenth of the pie chart will look very small, when in fact what you *want* to show is that it is pretty stunning that *two* of them are in one audience. So a non-graphical visual representation (like the one of the people figures to the right) would be better.

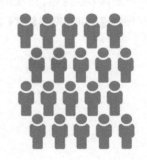

Approach your numbers with a creative eye. What type of graphic can help your audience best see the magnitude or importance of your numbers? Consider both the logical proof inherent in your quantitative data and the emotional impact its corresponding visual can have.

Numbers, Numbers, Everywhere

Numerical data make for useful presentation tools. Research findings, statistics, and prices have the potential to provide concrete proof of your claims, and they have the ability to help you get more "blue" in your presentation. Being able to provide the hard numbers will help you gain credibility with your audience, and—if the numbers are impactful enough—will help you grab and keep hold of their attention.

Even if you believe yourself to be ardently "not a numbers person," don't shy away from gathering your own research, organizing that data into a spreadsheet, and presenting those numbers to your audience. It may take time and practice to figure out the technological components required to do it, but the resulting proof will be worth the effort.

Key Takeaways

- Spreadsheets are a dynamic and organized way to record and analyze data.
- If you are new to spreadsheet programs, seek out instructional videos and help sites to give you guidance.
- Avoid tables based off your data as visual aids; instead, use charts and graphs.
- Choose among pie charts, bar graphs, and line graphs based on the data they represent.
- Follow the design rules for charts and graphs to help you keep them easy for the audience to see and easy for the audience to understand.
- Devise creative ways of representing numerical data that doesn't lend itself well to a chart or graph.

Questions and Activities:

1. **Reflection Question:** Look at the outline you have prepared for a presentation. Where in the presentation would it be appropriate to use presentation aids? Why would presentation aids help at the points you have identified?
2. **Learning Activity:** Create a Semester Assignment Spreadsheet: one single list that combines the due dates and important info from all of your classes. This is really helpful because it allows you to see which class should take top priority at any time during the semester. It is also a good idea to put the total points available for each assignment so that you can keep track of your own grades.
3. **Learning Activity:** Conduct a survey of at least twenty of your friends' or classmates' favorite ice cream flavors. Then compile the surveys into a spreadsheet,

and use functions to total each category. Then create a pie chart of your data that follows all of the aforementioned rules. If only one or two people gave a particular ice cream flavor, put that data into an "Other" category.

4. **Presentation Preparation:** Think about your next presentation. Conduct an audience analysis survey or questionnaire. Put the data into a spreadsheet and use functions to find the total number of respondents for each answer. Make charts or graphs from that data as needed for your presentation.

CHAPTER 27

Creating an Audience-Friendly Slideshow

After studying this chapter, you should be able to:
- *Understand the importance of not using text-based slides.*
- *Create an audience-focused slideshow.*
- *Organize your slideshow with the five key types of slides.*
- *Use animations and transitions to control your audience's focus.*

Right now in boardrooms, classrooms, and conference rooms across the world, the soft hum of multimedia projectors and the warm glow of images on a drop-down screen fill the air. It's a common occurrence, so common that a multimedia slideshow has seemingly become synonymous with the word "presentation." It's easy to use, it's helpful to you as the presenter, and it can bring a little or a lot of pizzazz to what you say. It's PowerPoint[1]—and it can also be the death of your presentation.

Search the Internet and you will find endless amounts of ranting on the ineffectiveness of PowerPoint and programs like it (Prezi, Keynote, etc.). Article after article bemoans the dreaded "death by PowerPoint" that plagues many meetings, lectures, and presentations (Bummiler, 2010; Cepeda, 2013; Dooley, 2012; Felder & Brent, 2005; Mahler, 2014; Narayan, 2014; Parks, 2012; "US Army," 2010; and, really, those are just a few). John Orland (2013) says slideshow presentations often cause audiences to slip into a "PowerPoint-induced coma." Even the cover of Michael Flocker's (2006) book, *Death by PowerPoint*, features a picture of a businessman icon being hanged to death by a paperclip. Yikes! Can PowerPoint really be *that* evil?

While I do think that paperclip-hanging deaths are overkill (pardon the pun), PowerPoint certainly has the potential to deaden a presentation atmosphere. Many members of the anti-PowerPoint movement would have you believe that the software itself is to blame for its constant misuse (e.g., Godin, 2003; Norvig, 2003; Witt, 2009). Swiss software engineer Matthias Poehm even started the Anti-PowerPoint Party (APPP)—an *official* political party in Switzerland aimed "at a referendum in order to seek for a prohibition of PowerPoint [or other similar programs] during presentations." (Yep, that's for real. You can look it up.) There is surely validity to the argument that PowerPoint's default designs encourage users to create bullet-laden presentations, but that doesn't make the program itself pure evil.

What is important to remember is that PowerPoint is a tool, and just like any other tool, its effectiveness rests entirely on the skill of its user. A chainsaw in my hands is

---

1 I use the term "PowerPoint" to denote any slideshow software, not just the product by Microsoft, which has become the poster child for the entire genre.

likely to be massively destructive (really, you should back *way* up), but in the hands of a skilled woodworker or tree trimmer, it has the potential to be massively *constructive* and even transformative. This is the case with PowerPoint. If you choose to slap together a last-minute slideshow overloaded with words and bullet points, then yes, your presentation will be met with deafening silence and listless listeners (or likely non-listeners). But if you take the time to follow the guidelines of AIMC and good visual design, and if you create a slideshow with purpose, then you, too, can find this tool to be massively constructive and even transformative.

So What's the Problem?

The problem with the way many people use PowerPoint is quite simply this: they are selfish. I know that seems harsh, but let me explain.

Most presenters sit down to craft a PowerPoint presentation and think, "What do I want to say?" Then, slide by slide, bullet by bullet, they transcribe that intended knowledge through text. The result is a slideshow that makes presenting incredibly easy for the presenter; it's like presentation karaoke—just read the slides to your audience and try to stay in key. Boom! Done. Knowledge transferred.

If you've thought this way before, just know that I'm wagging my finger at you right now and saying, "Tsk, tsk, tsk." Have you forgotten rule #1 of presentation preparation? **It's all about the audience.** So, switch roles for a moment. How many times have you truly enjoyed or been inspired to act by a PowerPoint covered with wordy bullet points? I'm going to guess it's about as common as snow on the equator. In those situations, you can't connect with presenters or converse with them (or even feel like you are visible to them); they're too busy staring at the screen and reading their slides word for word to notice you.

As a presenter, you need to remember this key rule: **visuals aren't for you; they are for your audience.** Consider the usefulness rules for visual aids presented in Chapter 25. For a visual to be used, it must either help the audience understand or remember your point, or it must help persuade the audience. Bullet points of information on a slide meet neither of these criteria.

Your job is to create a slideshow presentation that will have value for *your audience*, and word-dump slides don't do that. Yes, they make *your* job easier. Yes, it is comforting to know that the whole presentation is up on the screen so you won't forget anything. But your word-covered security blanket of a slide won't keep your audience interested enough to pay attention to any of it. You won't be engaging, you won't use effective eye contact, and you won't be able to carry on a conversation with your audience. You will be a slave to your slides, and when your audience's attention inevitably wanes, you will struggle to entice them to give it back with your trusty bullet points. As Orland (2013) notes, "The good news is that 90% of the problem can be solved by following one simple rule: **no bullet points.**" I know you may be afraid that following this no-bullet prescription will cause you to forget some of what you want to say, but frankly, you'd be better off forgetting to say some of your points if the audience will actually listen to the ones you do make.

Abolishing bullets completely may seem extreme to you. After all, you may think, bullet points are effective ways to deliver short bits of knowledge in organized, well-aligned lists. And, in that regard, you're right: bullet points *can* be great—in documents, in handouts, and even in presentation textbooks. But not in slideshows. Not projected on screens. Not during presentations. When presenting, *you* should be the one to impart knowledge to your audience, not your slides.

Not yet convinced that text-heavy slides are the wrong way to use PowerPoint? Then let me count the ways:

1	Slides should add *new* information to the presentation; bullet points merely repeat what you are saying aloud. Booooring.
2	Text-heavy slides put you in a catch-22. If you read the slides to the audience, that's boring and insulting. If you stay silent so they can read, things get awkward and the silence ruins your dynamic flow. If you talk *about* the slides but not read them directly, the audience reads while you talk. The problem with that? Research shows that when people are simultaneously presented with language-based information in both an auditory (your voice) and a visual channel (your word-covered slides), their comprehension rate goes down (Baddeley, 2003). In other words, your audience won't get much out of your talking *or* out of your text-filled slides.
3	Text-heavy slides hurt your credibility. How much of an expert can you possibly be if you have to read the presentation to your audience?
4	Bullet points hurt your dynamism. Read, click, pause. Read, click, pause. Read, click, pause. It's not the stuff of truly inspirational presentations.
5	Text-heavy slides stifle audience interaction and conversation. It gives the presentation a lecture feel, rather than an interactive one. Bullet points carry a sense of finality with them, like matters have already been decided. Sherry Turkle notes that a text-heavy slideshow "encourages presentation, not conversation," and that it "is designed to close down debate, rather than open it up" (qtd. in Keller, 2003). This is exactly the opposite of the conversational approach you should be trying to achieve in your presentation.
6	Bullet points make it hard for the audience to see the relationship between ideas— if they're sequential, causal, or something else (Tufte, 2003). Everything just looks like a grocery list.
7	Bullet points fundamentally change the way you present knowledge (Adams, 2007). They force you to boil down richly complex issues into "text bites." Simplifying ideas for an audience may be good, but oversimplifying them is a logical fallacy.
8	Bullets points are overdone. The moment the text comes up, the audience will get restless. They've seen this same tedious movie play out over and over and over again.
9	Bullets points are terrible communication. As Godin (2003) says, "Communication is the transfer of emotion," and bullet points just can't play on pathos.
10	Bullet points limit your eye contact. It's tough to lock eyes and really connect with audience members when you're too busy looking back at the screen to read what's next.

Does that mean that no text can appear on your slides, ever? No, of course not. There are some valid uses for words on slides: labels on graphs, headings, previews or reviews of topics, etc. But the text in those instances does not attempt to explain any of your logical arguments. **Explaining should be left to the oral channel (your voice), not to the words on your slides.**

So, if text-based slides are out, then what's in? Visuals, visuals, visuals. **Slides are meant to be *visual aids*, so doesn't it make sense that they should be *visuals* that *aid* your audience?** Let's discuss:

- **Visual** – Look back to earlier chapters in this unit for lots of visual examples. When they're done well, pictures, diagrams, charts, graphs, and videos will communicate much more to your audience than a block of text on a screen ever would.
- **Aid** – For a visual to aid, it must do at least one of two things:
  1. Help the audience understand or remember a concept.
  2. Help persuade the audience.

The key here is *the audience*. Text-based slides might help *you* remember what you want to say, but they don't help the audience comprehend or remember anything.

Later in this chapter, we will talk more specifically about how your visual-evidence slides should look, but for now let me rest my case that bullet points have no place on a proper PowerPoint slide. Hopefully you, the jury, have been convinced by my numerous arguments and are ready to condemn the text-covered slides and rule in favor of visual ones.

I want to assure you that the abandonment of bullet points will come with benefits for you. The techniques this book endorses will make it easier for you to

- keep the conversational flow with your audience;
- keep your ideas organized for both you and the audience;
- control your audience's attention; and
- set the right emotional tone for your presentation.

Be brave as we enter into a new world of better slideshows. This approach will probably seem difficult at first, but with practice, you will find it to be much easier for both you and your audience.

Organizing Your Ideas and Visuals with Slides

You've learned from my anti-text rant that your slides shouldn't tell you what to say, but they can do one thing for your memory: they can tell you when to say it. A good slideshow will mimic the organization of your oral presentation. That is, the slideshow should include slides that present the main focus of the presentation, preview your points, transition between points, offer evidence, and review your points at the end.

The reason for including organizational slides in your presentation is not to benefit you; that's just a happy by-product. Organized slides help your audience follow the logic of your ideas. If you remember back to Chapter 9: Speaking in Outlines, there are a lot of components in a well-organized presentation, and sometimes your audience doesn't always pick up on them. Despite your best efforts at previewing, transitioning, listing, summarizing, and reviewing, your audience may still feel jumbled within your outline from time to time. Your slides can help make sure they stay on track.

Slides to Include

A title slide – This slide should be up as soon as possible. While you prepare yourself or wait for your audience to file in and get ready, the title slide is what will catch their eye and hopefully excite them for what's to come.

The title slide should include a title for your presentation (try to make it catchy and appealing), your name, and the date. If you were presenting professionally, you might also include your company name, company logo, your job title, and/or your contact email. Keep in mind that, as your first slide, the title

Figure 1 Title slide for a presentation on how to deal with presentation nervousness.

slide should also set the tone for the entire presentation. Choose an image or graphic that will intrigue your audience—make them think, laugh, emotionally connect, or question. Think of the title slide as your visual attention-getter.

A preview slide – At a paper-and-pen type of meeting, participants get a written agenda of what will be covered. In a multimedia presentation, your audience should get a projected equivalent of your agenda on the screen: your preview slide. Unsurprisingly, this slide should accompany your verbal preview and include the main points you want to cover.

If you can use an icon or image to represent each main point, then do so. If not, use very short phrases to represent each topic your presentation will cover.

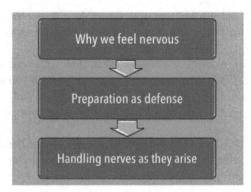

Figure 2 A preview slide that lists all three main points the presentation will cover, each point appearing one at a time.

You should not include any explanation of the points; **the preview slide should merely list them out as the ideas that will be discussed later in the presentation.** If you do use text to write out the main points that will be covered, the no-bullets rule still applies. Find a more interesting way to represent your preview that shows the relationship between your main ideas (e.g., SmartArt in PowerPoint, using relevant graphics, using visual metaphors).

Transition slides – Chapter 9 can remind you how important transitions are for an audience to keep track of where the presentation is heading. **Transition slides are visual cues for both you (to remind you to actually say the transition) and your audience (so they can literally see the transition from one point to the next).**

Transition slides can be effective with simplicity. Duplicate your preview slide, and merely highlight, underline, bold, or enlarge the topic you are about to cover. Thus the audience can see what you've

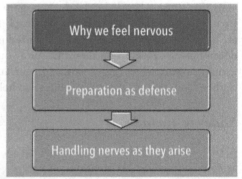

Figure 3 Transition slide—a modified version of the preview slide.

already discussed, what you'll cover now, and what's coming up on deck.

Evidence slides – These are the heart of the slideshow presentation—the slides that give visual evidence for the points you make aloud. If you have no evidence slides to show, you should not show a slideshow at all. As already discussed ad nauseam, these slides should *not* include bullet points or text to explain or reiterate what you are saying. **Evidence slides should provide visual support for what you are presenting aloud.** If you're talking numbers to your audience, show them a graph. If you're explaining a location, show them a map. If you're discussing how a machine works, show them a diagram. If you're using a metaphor to explain a concept, show a visual to accompany that metaphor. If you're telling someone's story, show her picture. If you're explaining the physics of a curve ball, show a silent, slow-motion video of the ball curving.

Consider the examples shown to the right. These highly simplistic diagrams illustrate the presenter's explanation of the biological aspects of nervousness. Your normal self is cool and calm (the blue figure). When you are put into a presenting situation, your body gets a rush of adrenaline (the lightning bolts in the yellow body). This slight nervousness is a good thing—it helps to keep you energized and ready to tackle your presentation with enthusiasm. The problems with nervousness really start when the nerves are too strong and your body has an excess of adrenaline (the red body). Then you start to sweat, your hands start to shake, your throat closes up, and your body physically reacts to the nerves.

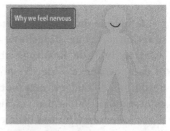

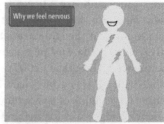

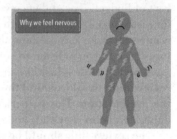

The visuals you use on your evidence slides should follow all of the rules for good design already discussed earlier in this unit. If you can't remember those rules, be sure to brush up before creating these slides. Slides that are too busy or have designs that counteract the intended message will negatively impact your slideshow's effectiveness.

A Quick Guide for Visuals on Evidence Slides

Visual Type	Best Uses	Quick Tips
Photographs	Emotional impact	Use high-resolution, easy-to-see images. Make sure you cite its source if photograph is not your intellectual property. Put one picture per slide; collages violate the rule of simplicity.
Diagrams	Show parts of a whole / Simplify photographs / Logical impact	Only include labels to parts you will discuss. Use color to point out relevant areas. Keep diagram simple and easy to understand.
Charts/ Graphs	Demonstrate numerical data / Logical impact	Only include necessary data. Use distinct colors. Remove legends and put label directly on chart/graph pieces.
Videos	Show actions you can't demonstrate yourself	Keep videos with audio very short (less than ten percent of presenting time). Use high-definition videos. Embed videos into slide (avoid links). Use videos that show action, not just talking.

To help maintain the organizational function of your slideshow, you may want to include headings at the top of each evidence slide. A simple topic heading like "Budget" may not be sufficient, though. While that certainly might jog *your* memory, it does little to nothing for your audience. Instead, succinct sentence-like headlines that say the main point of the slide are more effective, memorable, and persuasive for the audience (Alley et al, 2007). So, if the slide's image was a pie chart indicating that a large chunk of an academic depart-

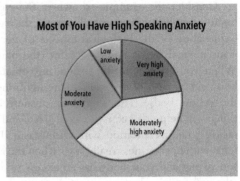

An example of a sentence-style headline for an evidence slide.

ment's budget was for making copies, a good headline might be "Duplicating Is Large Part of Budget." The audience will read the headline quickly and then look to the chart for visual proof. Within a matter of seconds, they will have understood the point you wanted to make and see how the visual supports that point. Then they can turn their focus back to you to listen to your explanation and suggestions for the next steps.

A review slide – Just like the review you should say aloud in your conclusion, **your review slide should remind the audience of the main points you covered throughout the presentation.** This is, perhaps, the easiest of all your slides to construct. Simply duplicate the preview slide and drag it to the end of the slideshow. Done.

The review slide should be the last slide of your presentation. It's particularly helpful to leave up as you enter into your question-and-answer session so your audience can be reminded of what you had covered and to use in your post-Q&A wrap-up. Keeping up the review slide will also prevent you from simply shutting down the PowerPoint during Q&A—a rookie presentation mistake. If someone has a question on a particular topic discussed earlier, you can easily go back to the relevant slide as reference instead of having to awkwardly reboot the computer or file. If you think the slide is distracting and you'd rather have a blank screen until after Q&A is over, simply insert a blank, black slide in your presentation, or hit the letter B to black out the screen.

Slides to Leave out of Your Slideshow	
Begone! You have no place here.	
Works Cited or Reference slide	Who's fast enough to look up all of your sources in the five seconds you leave up your references slide? Nobody, that's who. Reference lists are for paper, not for projector screens.
Slide that says, "Questions???"	Will the PowerPoint *answer* the questions, too? Maybe you should just ask for questions yourself.
Slide that says, "Thank you!"	You can thank your audience aloud and in person with a handshake and a smile.
Slide that says, "The End"	"The End" carries too much finality with it. You need your relationship with your audience and the ideas you shared to keep going. Declaring "The End" is just bad vibes.

If you've used all five of the slide types—title, preview, transition, evidence, and review—with success, you will have a coherent and organized slideshow that will be easy for your audience to follow. It may seem tedious to create the slides beyond the ones you're using for your visual evidence, but I assure you the trade-off in the clarity to your audience (and to you) is worth the effort.

Not long ago, I was asked to give an hour-long presentation to university staff on the topic of managing email, for which I had a PowerPoint presentation that followed these guidelines. Afterward, I got compliments on various aspects of the presentation, but the coordinator of the event was most impressed by my organization: "It was just so clear. One point just built on another." And even if *your* audience doesn't marvel at your slideshow outline, their increased comprehension will be reward enough.

The Appearing and Disappearing Act: Using Animations and Slide Transitions

PowerPoint can do some crazy stuff. Text can spin in, visuals can appear or disappear in sudden flashes of light, and images can even travel around the screen endlessly on their own unique motion paths. The inclusion of such nausea-inducing visuals in a professional software program is really mind-boggling. So, let me make this point clear now: just because you can do something in PowerPoint, it most certainly does not mean that you *should*.

Since it's likely some of you have never used either slide transitions or animations, let us first differentiate between the two. A *slide transition* is the way one full slide changes to the next (e.g., dissolve, fade, push, flip). An *animation* is the entrance, emphasis, or exit of a particular part of a slide (text box, picture, piece of SmartArt, etc.).

Some of the PowerPoint haters argue that animations and slide transitions are always problematic. Seth Godin (2003) goes so far as to proclaim in his article on how to avoid "Really Bad PowerPoint" that no slide transitions are ever appropriate. His prescription, though, may be an oversimplified reaction to those presenters who use on-screen movement merely to liven up an otherwise-dull presentation. Other presentation experts have differing opinions. Jerry Weissman (2009) equates a lack of slide transitions to a "crash cut" between slides, which he says is jarring for audience members. In his view, slide transitions are needed to guide the audience more gently from one slide to the next.

There is no definitively correct resolution to this debate, but the motto we'll follow is this: slide transitions and animations have the potential to be distracting, but when used cautiously and purposefully, they can complement the message your slideshow is trying to send. Let's explore each type of movement separately: first slide transitions and then animations.

Slide Transitions

How you choose to move from slide to slide is at your discretion. Like every other design element of your visuals, the slide transitions you choose should echo the feel you are hoping to achieve. If you were going for a more solemn feel, a slow fade might be appropriate. If you want a little more pep, perhaps you could make the screen wipe from one slide to the next instead (Weissman notes that wiping from the left is the most natural direction for your audience's eyes to follow, since it mimics the way we read from left to right).

Whichever movement you choose, be sure that you keep it purposeful and subtle. Overly artistic slide transitions that send one slide bouncing, twirling, swirling, or shattering into the next take too long for what should be a simple slide change. Moreover, too much flash leads to *visual noise* that distracts your audience from the heart of your message, much in the same way auditory noise would. These over-exaggerated slide transitions are particularly problematic in Prezi, a popular online slideshow program that is known for its unique movements from one idea to the next. While many hail Prezi as being more dynamic than PowerPoint, its spin and zoom feature to move from point to point not only pulls focus from the presentation message, but it also might induce nausea for some of your queasier audience members. Keep your transitions low-key—short and simple. In most cases, a simple cut, fade, dissolve, or wipe will suffice.

Once you've chosen the slide transition that works best for your slideshow, apply it to all of your slides. Consistency is key. If every slide comes in with a new movement, the slideshow will seem disjointed and chaotic. Varying or overpowering slide transitions will also call too much attention to themselves, and if your audience is busy playing the mental guessing game of "How Will the Next Slide Appear?," then they've lost focus on the actual point of the presentation.

Animations

Animations may seem like an afterthought to you when creating a slideshow—like a little extra flourish you throw in if you have time—but the animations function is actually one of the more powerful tools you have at your disposal to control your audience's visual focus. Because animations allow you to make certain elements of a slide appear, highlight, or disappear on the click of a button, you can decide what your audience looks at when.

Imagine you are showing your preview slide. If you put the whole slide up as is, the audience will inevitably read all of it before you've had the chance to explain each point (sorry, they can't help it). In this instance, we say that the visual channel (what your audience is looking at) doesn't match the verbal (what you are saying). This is particularly problematic because when the visual and verbal channels don't match, your audience's comprehension decreases (Baddeley, 2003). If, however, you animate each main point so it appears as you mention it, your audience will be forced to follow along: "Hopefully I can convince you to invest in my product. We will discuss (click) what the U-Board is, (click) its target audience, (click) its manufacturing, and (click) its profitability." With each click comes the corresponding main point, thus keeping the audience on track the whole time.

Animations have uses beyond just controlling the audience's attention. Animations can also create a forceful visual impact. Years ago I had my presentations class engage in a mock competitive presentation that asked them to pitch potential businesses to move into an empty building space on campus. Three of the four teams in class pitched restaurants. The one remaining team that advocated for an on-campus bank had to therefore make the case that our campus didn't need any more places to eat. Their initial slideshow showed one slide after another of the current restaurants or eating spots on campus. While the information was accurate and the images didn't break any particular design rules, the slides lacked impact. I suggested that they use animation to their advantage. What resulted was a slide for each building that housed food locations. The slide featured a picture of the building's exterior. As the presenters listed and briefly described each food location in that building, the logo for that restaurant/eatery appeared on the screen. By the end of each list, the audience saw an image of that building cluttered with restaurant logos, an impactful visual that more forcefully proclaimed the message: "We have enough food on campus. It's time for a new type of business."

Like transitions, animations have the potential to get weird. While you may find rare cases to use motion paths and other oddball options—like boomeranging, flipping, or dropping elements on or off screen—chances are, you won't. Thus, as with transitions, the animations you choose should be purposeful and consistent.

See What Movement Can Do for You

If you are a newbie to animations and transitions, take the time to play with the options available to you. PowerPoint and other presentation programs allow you to change the effect, direction, order, and timing of your animations to make sure that you keep control of the audience's focus. If you learn to use these tools well, you can increase the visual impact of your slideshows.

Just remember two key points: (1) too much flash will overshadow your message; and (2) spending too much time fancying up your PowerPoint, instead of planning your message or practicing your presentation, will hurt your end product dearly. Explore and create, but keep it in moderation.

Make Your Slideshow SPARC

For your slideshow to be taken seriously, it needs to look professional. As you design your multimedia slides, don't forget the rules of designing with SPARC that you learned in Chapter 25:

- **Simplicity:** Keep your slides simple and uncluttered. There should only be one idea, picture, graph diagram, or other visual per slide. Too many images on one screen make it difficult to keep your audience focused on the visual elements you are currently discussing.
- **Proximity:** Keep similar objects close together and dissimilar objects far apart. Put labels next to the images or graph elements they represent. Represent preview and review slides in ways that show the relationship among ideas, rather than lists of points that all appear to be equally similar.
- **Alignment:** Keep items neatly aligned on the slide so the design looks professional, rather than haphazard. Don't presume that every slide must have its main elements in the dead center of the page. Play with alignment to create more interesting design.
- **Repetition:** Use the same color schemes and fonts throughout the entire slideshow. Using different design elements on every slide calls too much attention to those elements and pulls focus from the presentation's overall message.

- **Contrast:** Use contrasting colors on charts, graphs, diagrams, photographs, and other visuals so the audience can see them clearly. Use markedly different colors for background and foreground elements, including very dark text on a very light background, or vice versa. The level of contrast you see on your computer screen almost always gets washed out to some degree when projected onto a screen. Use very high contrast to avoid those potential projecting problems.

An Effective Slide Show: It Can Be Done

As mentioned throughout this chapter, PowerPoint is a tool that has great potential to support your verbal message in an impactful and effectual way. If you thought yourself to be a PowerPoint expert and this chapter systematically destroyed that self-image, I hope you now see how to regain the title.

Avoid text-filled slides, use visuals, include slides that organize your presentation, and use transitions and animations to your advantage. This prescription will help you create a slideshow that will not only increase your audience's understanding of what you are trying to say, but will also likely impress them. Crafting a well-organized slideshow also helps you organize and order your ideas, and the time you dedicate to creating a slideshow that works will increase your comfort level with the material. You want to project yourself as a confident, well-prepared, and organized presenter; let your slideshow support that image.

Key Takeaways

- Keep slides visually based, and avoid any and all bullet points.
- Organize your ideas by including title, preview, transition, and review slides with your evidence slides.
- Eliminate unneeded slides that fail to help or persuade your audience.
- Use short and subtle transitions to move from one slide to the next.
- Use animation to control your audience's focus while you speak.

Questions and Activities

1. **Reflection Question:** Reflect on the argument that slideshow presentations should avoid text and bullet points. Do you agree with the points made in the

chapter? How well (or not well) have your previous slideshows exemplified this no-bullet rule? How effective were those presentations for your audience?

2. **Reflection Question:** Think of the last slideshow presentation you did. Did you have any organizational slides included (title slide, preview slide, transition slides, review slide)? How do you think adding organizational slides will affect your organization within the presentation? How will it affect audience understanding?

3. **Learning Activity:** Consider the terrible, text-based slide below. Turn this slide into a full, visual slideshow presentation that follows the guidelines from this chapter. Be sure to include all the required organizational slides, and create evidence slides to illustrate the points made in text below. Each numbered item should be one main point for the presentation. Create as many slides as you need to adequately prove/illustrate all the points in a coherent and organized slideshow.

Things College Students Waste Money On

1. Books
   - Renting vs. buying can save $5,760 over four years.
2. Credit Cards
   - Average college student graduates with $4,100 in credit-card debt.
   - Use debit cards or cash instead to avoid spending money you don't have.
3. Automobiles
   - If you are a resident student, sell your car or don't bring it to school.
   - Set up rideshare to hitch rides home when needed.
   - Students that bike, walk, or use local transportation save about $20,000 over four years of college.

---

4. **Presentation Preparation:** Create the slideshow for your next presentation. Start by making a skeleton slideshow with just the organizational slides (title, preview, transitions, review). Then add in evidence slides as you find stellar visual exemplars of the points you want to make. Ensure that the visuals you include follow the rules mentioned earlier in this unit. Also, be sure that all of your slides adhere to the rules for good visual design outlined in Chapter 25.

Credits

CHAPTER 28

Point Here, Look There
Presenting with Visuals

After studying this chapter, you should be able to:
- *Know where to stand when presenting on-screen visuals.*
- *Interact effectively with visuals on a screen.*
- *Avoid slide dependency.*
- *Develop and implement strategies for dealing with technological failures.*
- *Effectively incorporate low-tech visuals into your presentation.*

Your visual aids have been prepared: they are effective, they are audience-focused, they are ideally designed, and they are stunning. In short, they are perfect. Well—maybe your visual aids are really just "pretty good." But perfect or pretty, **they won't have much impact if you don't know how to present them to your audience.** Jannette Collins (2004) notes that, "No matter how great the visual aids are, if a presenter does a poor job communicating with the audience, the presentation will suffer" (p. 1186).

For many, how to present with a visual seems like an afterthought. Many students I know work on their PowerPoint presentations and handouts right up until the last moment, which leaves them no time to practice with them and ensure they use them effectively. And **that lack of preparation does show to the audience.** If you are looking at slides on the screen or handouts in your hand like this is the first time you've ever seen them, it will make onlookers question your credibility. Audiences want presenters who know what they're talking about, and if you're looking at your visual like you're waiting for it to tell you what to say, you will hardly win any votes of confidence.

Because PowerPoint and similar slideshow programs are the most regularly abused by presenters, we will start with those. Then we will move onto lower-tech options, like handouts, objects/props, and whiteboards.

Don't Go into the Light: Where to Stand with a Projector Screen

The first step of presenting effectively with a projector screen is to figure out where to stand in relation to it. Before I tell you the ideal positions, let me first explain two awkward—and yet remarkably common—standing spots that you should avoid:

Do not go into the bright, white light, Ashley!

Awkward Position #1: In front of the projector screen

Standing in front of the screen means the projector's light will be shining directly into your eyes. This is a problem for a number of reasons:

- It prevents you from making genuine eye contact. All you'll see is a bright, white light, and movies should have taught you by now that you should *not* go into that light.
- It hurts your eyes. Your eyes were not built to stare straight into a high beam of light; don't put them through that kind of abuse.
- You will likely start squinting. Has anyone ever taken a picture of you while you squinted into the sun? My guess is that it wasn't your most attractive moment. Now imagine showing that face for a prolonged period of time to your audience. Yikes.
- It puts a weird strip of light over your face. Your face (or just the top of it) is illuminated, and your body is not. If there is some visual on the screen large enough to reach the bottom, then that will be stretched out over your face as well. From the audience's perspective, your head cutting into a pie chart looks bizarre.

Avoid creating awkward shadows that block your visuals.

- You create shadow puppets. Well, actually they're not puppets (those would be more entertaining). You just create a huge shadow behind your head that prevents your audience from seeing a sizeable chunk of your visual aid.

Awkward Position #2: The other side of the room

I can understand the impulse to want to get out of the projector's spotlight, but standing on the other side of the room when showing a visual is the wrong solution. If you're on the left side of the room, and you put a visual on a screen on the right side of the room, you put your audience in a visual dilemma. As you discuss the visual, where should they look—at you, the person talking to them, or at the screen, the thing you're talking about? Don't stand so far away that your audience has to keep flitting

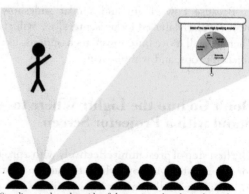

Standing on the other side of the room makes the audience have to choose between looking at the screen or looking at you. They can't keep both in their line of sight.

their eyes back and forth from you to the screen like they are in an uncomfortable game of visual ping pong.

The Ideal Positions

Here's the simple prescription: **When you first introduce a new slide and are directly discussing its contents, you need to stand *next* to the screen.** It doesn't matter which side of it you stand on, so long as there is enough room for you. This will allow you stay close to the visual so your audience can see both of you at once, and it will give you the ability to interact with the screen without standing awkwardly in front of it.

Once you are done directly engaging with the screen, walk away. So often I see presenters get stuck in one spot next to the screen for the full duration of their presentation. Don't let the lessons of **Chapter 15: Look at Me! I'm Presenting!** fall by the wayside just because you add visual aids to the mix. You still need to move, work the room, and demonstrate your confidence by not getting rooted into one spot. Then, when it's time to click over to the next slide, make your way back toward the screen to interact with the new visual aid.

Face Forward, Point Back: How to Interact with Visuals on a Screen

Remember from the previous chapter how using animations in a PowerPoint slide can help to control the audience's focus? Well, you can further help the audience key in on the most important parts of your visual aid by directly interacting with the image.

Visuals should never be difficult for your audience to digest or overwhelming for them to decipher; if they are, your audience will just give up. Hopefully you have followed the KISS design principle and kept your visuals simple. Still, you should make digesting an image as easy as possible for your audience (really, they're lazy; they like the help). **When discussing specific parts of an image, chart, graph, diagram, or other visual, you should literally point out the important parts to your listeners.**

What should you use to point? The easiest, cheapest, and most readily available tool is—cue dramatic drum roll—your first finger; that's why they call it the "pointer" finger. Students often ask me if they can use a laser pointer instead, and you may be wondering the same. I'm not sure what the appeal is (maybe it makes you feel like a PowerPoint Jedi or something), but that little red dot is often difficult for your audience to see right away, unless you move in tiny, rapid circles on the screen so everyone can find it. That might be a fun game to play with your cat, but it's annoying for your professional audience. Make everyone's life easier and just opt to go laser-free.

The biggest danger in interacting with your visuals is the potential for a long break in eye contact with your audience. Nervous presenters love to stare at their projector screens, even when there are no words on them to read. It's like teenagers with bad "reality" TV: they know they should look away, but for some reason they just keep getting sucked in.

When you talk to a screen rather than to your audience, the break in eye contact hurts the conversational feel of your presentation and projects a lack of credibility and confidence. You will likewise lose the ability to gauge your audience's reactions and comprehension of your points if you're too busy looking away from them. Moreover, talking to a screen muffles the projection of your voice, often making it harder for your audience to hear you.

Clearly, **you need to interact with visuals without facing the screen to do it.** Here is the way to achieve this:

- Plant your feet perpendicular to the screen so that they are facing the audience directly.
- Quickly glance back at the screen to get your finger on the part of the visual you want to point out to your audience, but *don't move your feet.* Keeping your feet pointed away from the screen will force you to twist backward to look at the image. Since it's not a particularly comfortable movement, you won't be keen on holding it for too long.
- Once your finger is in position, turn back to look at your lovely listeners while you talk.
- Repeat as needed—but preferably not a lot.

Keep in mind that the more you practice with your slides, the more comfortable you will feel when focusing on the audience instead of the screen. In team presentations, it's never hard to pick out the members who didn't help construct the PowerPoint slides; they are the ones staring at the screen like deer caught in headlights. Avoid that awkwardness; get to know your slides and practice presenting with them.

Slides Are Not Cue Cards: Avoiding Slide Dependency

Even the best wordless slideshows can end up sucking the life out of a presenter. Something about the light of the projector seems to deadpan otherwise-enthusiastic talkers. Instead of feeling free to tell their stories and let the visuals serve as their illustrations, they feel stuck to the slides—that they can only talk about what is on them and *nothing more.*

If you click to a new slide and then have to pause to look at it so you can remember what to say, you are suffering from a common disorder known as *slide-dependency.* That is, you are using your slides as crutches to get through your presentation, perhaps as compensation for your lack of knowledge or (more commonly) for your lack of practice.

Slide-dependency is a problem for two main reasons:

1. Slide-dependency hurts the audience's perception of your credibility. The awkward pause—sometimes followed by a telling "Oh, okay" or "Right"—after you change the slide hardly paints a portrait of confidence and expertise.
2. Slide-dependency really becomes a case of slide-primacy. The slides become the backbone of the presentation. If it's not on the slides or part of the explanation of the slides, it doesn't get said. All the brilliant message planning you do is abandoned when the presentation just plods forward one slide at a time. The idea of conversational flow is lost when you just "stick to the cards."

Presenters who are confident in their ideas and are comfortable with their visuals can talk through the transitions of their slides or preview the slides to come *before* **they appear. You should not need to look back to the screen and pause for a second or**

two to remember what this new slide means before you can continue your presentation. In those cases, your audience will rightfully question your credibility and your preparation.

Remember that slides are visual *aids*, not the stars of the show. If your slideshow and all its many backups inexplicably imploded right before your presentation began, you should still be able to deliver a competent and effective presentation. **If you need your slides to help you make it through the presentation, what you really need is more practice.** You cannot effectively interact with your audience and make your points in a compelling way if you are relying too heavily on your slides.

Technology Is a Fickle Friend: Strategies for Dealing with Technological Difficulties

Sometimes technology doesn't feel like a friend at all—maybe more like a "frenemy." After all the time you spend creating your slideshow, animations don't do what you thought they would, videos don't play, color combinations don't look right, fonts change, and consequently you feel the overwhelming urge to scream obscenities at the computer. Unfortunately, that is *really* uncomfortable for your audience to have to witness.

Any help guide on technology will fail to account for every issue you might encounter, so before I start rattling off tips, let me start with the most important one: stay calm. Getting visibly agitated over tech issues (relatively "small stuff" to sweat in the grand scheme of things) makes you look unprofessional. The most competent communicators are masters of adaptation. **Deal with tech issues as best you can, and adapt your presentation to the circumstances you cannot fix.**

So, with your breathing regulated and your heartbeat at a nice, steady pace, let's look at some more specific suggestions surrounding technology in your presentation:

- Practice with your slides to work out the kinks. Run the slideshow in presenter mode as you practice giving your presentation, and ensure that all your animations and transitions are correct.
- Practice on the computer you will use for the presentation. Sometimes in the file transfer from one computer to the next, videos cease working, sounds don't play, and fonts default to other typefaces that ruin your formatting. Test your slideshow ahead of time to identify and fix those issues before you get in front of your audience.
- Keep all the files relevant to your slideshow (the images, videos, sound files, and the slideshow itself) in one folder on your computer or USB key. This will make it easier for you to ensure that all the linked files stay linked. Even if a link still fails you mid-presentation, you will at least be able to pull up the individual file for your audience quickly and easily.
- Practice hooking the presentation computer up to the projector. If you are using your own laptop for the presentation, make sure you have all the necessary connections to get the image to the screen. Cables for Macs are different than cables for PCs, and even the connections available for each computer type are inconsistent. Avoid last-moment tech dramas and figure out the connector cables beforehand.

- Use universal fonts. When moving from a PC to a Mac, or vice versa, fonts often get screwy. If you use a Mac-only font (even in a PC-friendly program like Microsoft PowerPoint) and then put that slideshow on a PC, the font will be changed to a default typeface that will likely mess with your formatting and design. To avoid this issue, use fonts that are available on both platforms.
- Have multiple backups of your slideshow on multiple platforms. If you only send it to yourself through email, the Wi-Fi might be down. If you only put the file on a USB, the USB could be lost or incompatible with the presentation computer. If you only put it on a CD-R, the computer may be without a DVD drive. In other words, if you only put your slideshow file in one place, there is a greater chance for trouble.
- Have a low-tech backup for really big presentations. If the PowerPoint is essential, come prepared with printouts. You need not print one slide per page (that's a waste of paper), but an overview of your slideshow that spans one or two sheets of paper (six to eight slides per page) is at least a decent reference point if the real version fails.

Clickers and Humans

If you have a presentational clicker—the wireless handheld remote that allows you to change slides with the click of a button—moving from one slide to the next is easy. Like anything else, though, clickers can break, get lost, lose battery power, or just fail to work on specific computers (which happens to me with frustrating regularity). Whether or not you have a clicker, you should have a human plan; that is, you need to decide how you would change the slides with people rather than remotes.

You have two options: change the slides yourself, or enlist the help of someone else to be your Official Slide Changer. Let's consider both options:

	Pros	Cons
You change slides	You know when you want slides to change; no chance for miscues.	You have to keep walking back and forth from screen to computer to make every animated piece of every slide to appear. Otherwise you end up talking about the slide from a distance (a presenting no-no).
Someone else changes slides	You are free to work the room and focus on the audience without having to pace back and forth from the computer to the screen.	Greater chance for miscommunication about when slides should change.

It may feel safer to just change the slides yourself, but if you can lessen the chance for miscues with your Official Slide Changer, you will reap more benefits by having someone else do it. Quite simply, you need to work out a system ahead of time with the person advancing your slides. As Ron Hoff (1997) notes, "If you're expecting a stranger to recognize your cues…you're expecting a degree of mind reading that probably doesn't exist" (p. 46). This doesn't need to involve hours of practice—just a quick conversation to agree on the signal that means, "go to the next slide."

While a verbal signal would certainly be the least mistakable, barking out, "Next slide!" cuts into the flow of your presentation and makes you look too diva-like. Nonverbal cues are the least distracting, so long as they are not exaggerated—like a finger-gun shot at your slide changer (even worse with a wink and clicking sound effect). Not sure what to do? Try a simple head nod and smile. If you do this while making *direct eye contact with the person running the slides*, the message will be clear.

And should a miscue happen, just politely say, "Oh, Sam, I want to add something. Do you mind going back one slide?" That's far more palatable for the audience to hear than, "Uggghh, Sam! I wasn't done!" or "Whoa! Whoa! WHOA! Go back!" Slide changers will be happy to help if you'll be happy to let them.

Going Old-School: Presenting with Low-Tech Visuals

While multimedia slideshows are certainly the norm for modern-day presentations, low-tech visuals have not lost their benefits or appeal. We will talk about three types in particular: leave-behinds, objects, and writeable surfaces.

Leave-Behinds

The next chapter will go into depth about how to create an effective leave-behind or handout, so I will focus here only on how to use it once you have it. The biggest mistake that many presenters make with handouts is that they don't talk about them. Because they're not on screen, projected in bright lights for all to see, they just pass them out silently or leave them on the audience members' chairs or desks as though they just magically appeared there through divine presentation intervention. Even though leave-behinds are intended to be documents participants can take home *after* the presentation is over, that doesn't mean they lose their function as a visual *aid* to the presentation itself. If it is given out as part of your presentation, it must be related to your content somehow. Make that connection clear to the audience.

Here is the ideal use of a leave-behind: you reference the handout within the presentation itself to let the audience know that it's coming and what it is about, but you don't physically pass it out until the end. Explaining what the leave-behind contains tells the audience what they are getting and what tangible value it has to them. Passing it out at the end of the presentation avoids the problem of your entire audience reading a piece of paper while you are talking. You can neither command their full attention nor engage them with eye contact when they are too busy reading what you just gave them.

The only exception to this rule is if your handout is part of a workshop activity. If you have an exercise you want the audience to complete and it requires a handout, you may pass that handout to them when it is relevant. I strongly encourage you to pass out only what they need at that time; save the rest of your leave-behinds for after the presentation is over.

Objects

Sometimes in a presentation, your audience will benefit most from a physical prop. If you were doing a product pitch, for instance, it would make sense to bring a physical mock-up or model. Objects are ideal when you want the audience to see how something works or let them use their senses (beyond sight and hearing) to experience it.

So, let's say you want to let your audience feel a fabric you plan to use for your new product—a backpack pillow to help you go from class to nap on those days you are stuck on campus and can't get to your actual bed. If your audience is small, you could bring several swatches of the fabric and let the clients touch them as you explain the material. If your audience is large or you only had one piece of fabric with you, then you could call an audience member or two to come up, touch it, and give a brief testimonial about it: "Ooooh. That's soft!"

What you should *not* then do is pass that swatch of fabric around. Passing any object or prop around the room for audience members to inspect is a bad idea. Listeners can't focus on what you're saying if they're playing with something in their hands. The people next in line to receive the prop aren't listening to you either; they're too busy paying attention to the person with the item to make sure they don't miss their cue to take it. If you want everyone to have the opportunity to touch, smell, or taste your prop, then let them know after your demonstration that anyone else who wants a turn can come up when the presentation is over.

Hide your prop until you are ready to use it, so listeners don't stare at it, wondering, "Ooh, what's that?" Then, when you are done, put it away so you can move your audience's focus on to your next point.

Writeable Surfaces

Great presentations have elements of both audience input and spontaneity, and pre-planned, high-tech visuals don't reflect either. If you have your audience brainstorm ideas, you should write them down so everyone can see them. If someone is stuck on a concept, and you can sketch out a visual to help him better comprehend your point, you should do it. Visuals are helpful tools for audience understanding, even if they are created on the spot. That is why, when presenting, you should always bring your greatest low-tech tool: a marker or a piece of chalk.

Most conference rooms and classrooms are equipped with either a whiteboard or chalkboard, but some are not. If you have access to a document camera, you can simply put a piece of paper on its surface and write down your ideas as they project onto the screen. Or perhaps your room contains a flip chart or easel you can use.

Regardless of the actual writeable surface you choose, take care to write largely and clearly enough for everyone to read your words. If you have terrible handwriting or spelling, enlist someone from the audience to write for you while you lead the conversation. Moreover, don't write too much or rely too heavily on board writing; your audience will not want to feel like they're in the midst of an academic lecture and they ought to be taking notes.

And Now, Disappear!

When a visual aid is no longer needed—that is, when you have moved onto a new main point not related to the point of the visual—the image should disappear. **Your verbal content (what you say) should always correspond to your visual content (what you show).** When it does not, the result is jarring and confusing for your audience, and you lose control over the audience's focus.

In a slideshow, this means that you must be timely when changing slides to make sure that what's on the screen relates to what is being said. If you had points for which you had no visuals, or if someone asks an off-topic question you need to answer, you should make the screen blank until you again have relevant visuals to show (in PowerPoint, you can hit the letter B, or your projector's control panel may have a "Display Mute" option).

With low-tech visuals, this means you need to physically remove the stimulus. In our fabric example, you should keep the fabric hidden until you are directly discussing the materials. Then, when that topic is over, you can move the fabric out of reach and sight of the audience.

Controlling when audiences see your visuals helps them understand both the point of the visual and the content of what you are saying orally. Moreover, it helps to keep your listeners focused on the topic at hand. An audience member shouldn't still be staring longingly at your fabric swatch thinking, "I wanna touch it" when you're now talking about profits. They should be thinking about money and lots of it, but they need your help to stay focused.

Do You See What I See?

Most presentations you do will involve some form of visual aids. Audiences rarely take note of when speakers present well with their visuals, but they most certainly notice when they don't. To let both your verbal ideas and your visual aids reach their fullest persuasive potential, you need to include visual aids as an integral component of your practice sessions. You have learned how visual aids can be an effective tool. Well, like any other tool, you must practice using them wisely to realize their true potential.

Key Takeaways

- Stand next to the screen to show a visual; then move around the room again.
- Point to relevant areas on the visual without losing eye contact with the audience.
- Eliminate slide dependency by keeping your audience and message primary, rather than your slideshow.
- Prepare for technological failures so you have backup plans in place.
- Avoid giving your audience tangible visuals that will pull focus from you while you present.
- Make your visual content match your verbal content by controlling when visuals appear and disappear.

Questions and Activities:

1. **Reflection Question:** Reflect on your own past use of visual aids in presentations. Which of the presenting mistakes from this chapter did you make with your visuals? What was the result of those errors? Which suggestions from this chapter do you need to work the most on improving for the next presentation you give with visual aids?

2. **Learning Activity:** Engage in a rousing game of Slideshow Karaoke! If you're doing this as a class, each of you should create a slideshow presentation on any topic you like. Then in class, you will each present someone else's slideshow without having been prepped beforehand on what it is on. If you are doing this as an individual, go to SlideShare.net, and search for a slideshow topic that interests you. Then, without previewing the slides, present the slideshow for an audience. Notice how slide-dependent you become when you don't make the slides yourself and you are unfamiliar with the content that is supposed to accompany each slide.

3. **Presentation Preparation:** Once you have your slideshow for your next presentation completed, practice presenting with it—a lot. Ensure that you are comfortable enough with the slides that you can effectively avoid slide dependency.

Credits

CHAPTER 29

Leave an Impression with Your Handout

By M. Sandra DiFrancesco

After studying this chapter, you should be able to:
- *Identify how, why, and when it's appropriate to use handouts.*
- *Apply design principles to develop effective handouts.*
- *Understand the real value of handouts and how they can enhance your presentations.*
- *Identify the advantages and disadvantages of different types of handouts.*
- *Understand the benefits for both the audience and the presenter.*

Suppose you're listening to a college official talk about how to apply for a particular scholarship on your campus. Wouldn't it be helpful if you had a handout of the steps to follow, or the actual form that you need to complete? Maybe you're participating in a workshop focusing on how to create better cover letters and résumés. Wouldn't it be helpful if you had a sample of a really effective résumé so you could refer to it later on? You might even find yourself listening to a sales pitch on a new product. Wouldn't it be helpful if you had a handout with a list of the specs and benefits of the new product?

A presentation without handouts you give to your audience is like a peanut butter sandwich without jelly, or worse, an early department meeting without bagels and coffee.

Many presenters treat handouts like an afterthought and justify their action with, "They'll just get trashed." That scenario is more often true than not. Many handouts do get trashed, but it's mostly because they aren't useful for your audience. Your handouts are hastily prepared and are apt to be as effective as last week's newspaper. Big mistake! Plan your handouts as you plan your presentation.

Great Materials Make Your Audience Remember Your Message

The bad news for anyone delivering a presentation is that, despite spending countless hours preparing for what might take a mere five, thirty, or sixty minutes to deliver, and despite the careful choice of content to include in your presentation, most of it will go in one ear and out the other.

Presentations are fleeting. When the lovely melodic tones of your voice are done reverberating in the ears of your audience, they will have only their memories to serve as their guide for all that you discussed. There's a cure for this. Give them a handout.

Good handouts help your audience to recall and apply the details that tend to ebb away with time. It is how your audience will remember you and the presentation you gave. When you meet with a client, you should leave them with something memorable, something that serves as a point of reference and reminds them of what you have to offer.

Since handouts are an important part of the total experience for the audience, your handouts should be as carefully planned as your presentation.

The problem is that most people focus on preparing what happens *during* the presentation and only give a last-minute thought to what happens *afterwards*. If you want your presentation to achieve its goals, make sure your handouts are as effective as you are.

Why Use Handouts?

What is a handout? A handout is a page(s) that contains text or images, or both, related to a presentation that helps extend your message beyond the presentation room. Handouts have a wide variety of uses and benefits, including the following:

1. To provide more details you don't have time to cover. A handout saves you the trouble of trying to portray time-consuming detail on a chalkboard, whiteboard, or PowerPoint to illustrate what you are discussing
2. To illustrate specific key points of your presentation.
3. To provide statistical data (preferably done visually) or other information that supports your key points.
4. To present information that is too complex to effectively present in another way.
5. To provide material beyond the presentation.
6. To provide additional resources beyond those contained in the presentation.
7. To serve as worksheets for your audience.
8. To obtain the feedback you need to determine whether the audience understood your message or to help you do a better job with your next presentation.

Presentation Handouts: Yes or No, What Kind, and When?

There is no one answer that fits all situations. But the key to an answer is that, if it isn't of value to your audience, you need to rethink the intent and use of your handout.

It's clear to me that you shouldn't provide just a print-out of the slides. This is lazy and ineffective. Often, these get tossed in the recycle bin immediately, and rightfully so. Why would the audience need to keep them? An exception might be a handout (print out as six to eight black-and-white slides per page) with lots of space for people to take notes next to each slide. Then they can write down what you're saying. But this is really only appropriate for a longer presentation

Rule of Thumb: Distribute Handouts at the End

You need to make it clear that **the handout is meant to be taken away**. Let your audience know early on that you've prepared a handout and that you will be distributing it at the end of your presentation.

Unless you have been asked to prepare a presentation deck (a large packet of reports or other documents that you will review with your audience), it is best *not* to pass out handouts during your presentation. Giving your audience something to look down at and read is giving them a reason to stop paying attention to you. They may even be impolite enough to use them as fans or paper airplanes. If there is some picture or other element on the handout that you really want them to see during the presentation, add that visual to your PowerPoint. Then you can say, "At the end of the presentation, I will give you a handout that better explains some of the product specifications, but for now, I want to focus on these three areas."

Then distribute the handout at the end of the presentation as a takeaway document for your audience.

Don't Forget WIIFM!

To create a handout that will leave a *positive* lasting impression, there are several tips to keep in mind:

1. **It's still all about the audience.** It is imperative that you focus on your audience rather than yourself. For example, if you are doing a presentation to investors to ask them to make an investment in a product you are developing, you might create a handout with a chart that demonstrates the benefits of your product over those of your competitors. On the other hand, a handout that tells your personal story and how you came up with the idea for your product would not serve your intent.

   This isn't about you; it's about providing the audience with the information they need to make the decision you want. Who is your audience and what do they value? What visuals, text, and formatting will "speak" to them? And, in terms of content, what's in it for them?

2. **Let your presentation's intent be your guide.** Like every other facet of your presentation, your handout should support your overall intent. So, if you want your audience to buy a product, a good handout might include product information and ordering instructions. If you want your audience to consider investing in a new product, a recap of the product's specifications and benefits to investors might be the best choice. And, in all handouts, leaving your contact information will help to keep the communication lines open between you and your audience after the presentation has ended.

3. **Make it unique.** Many programs, from Microsoft Word to more sophisticated design software, include a wide variety of templates for brochures and other types of handouts. While the templates certainly would make your design job easier, the problem with this shortcut is that those in the business world—and your professors—have seen these template handouts hundreds of times and will not be impressed by their styling. A word to the wise: you should avoid using these templates like you should avoid friending your boss on Facebook.

Some Kinds of Handouts to Consider

Handouts are another part of the channel and another type of visual aid. Use them in a way that works best for your audience. Select the appropriate type of handout for the planned learning outcome and prepare them effectively.

I've seen a lot of presenters in classrooms and conference rooms give out unnecessary materials that do, in fact, get thrown in the trash. Why? Because little thought was given to why the audience needs this handout and what is it that you want them to do with it. Ask yourself, "What information will people really want to take away from my presentation?" What will be really useful for them—your audience?

You can enhance and complement your presentation by distributing pictures, examples, resources, brochures, articles, charts, summaries, or other supplements.

- **References Sheet:** Make sure you annotate these. Let your audience know where they can find out more: books, websites, blogs etc.
- **Summary Sheets:** Summarize the key effects — for example, how new health care legislation will affect small business owners. Include the names and contact information of state agencies.
- **Product Information/Sales Sheet:** You're ready to sell your new toy or game to retail stores. You provide critical information needed to compel retailers to try the product. *Unique selling proposition: What is it? Who is it for? What makes it special? Product details are needed to make the sale.*
- **Bio Sheet/Team Bio Sheet:** A great vehicle for quickly communicating who you are and what you do, and in establishing your expertise and credibility. In most cases, should be one paragraph long and cover all the need-to-knows for your audience. End your bio with your contact details. Product is *you*. Make sure it sells you and/ or your team.
- **Informational Handouts:** Benefits or advantages of your proposal, product, service. Could just include key information such as complex diagrams, maps, formulae, quotations, and references.
- **Examples:** For example, for a career-workshop presentation, you might provide the audience with an example of an effective résumé format, a list of the most frequently asked interview questions, or visuals of appropriate professional attire.
- **Brochures and Flyers:** Reinforces the points you made and should cause your audience to have further interest in your business, product, and service. Your audience can take this home and read it again when they're making a buying decision.
- **Worksheets:** This is using handouts as the equivalent of "activities" or "self-assessment questions" that can be used during a presentation or for reflection after a presentation.

Good Handouts Stay Out of the Trash

Make sure it looks good. Outdated or scruffy handouts and third-generation, barely legible photocopies are an insult to your audience. Poorly designed and poorly presented handouts can undermine your presentation.

When people pick up your handout, they should be impressed—by the way it looks, the way it feels, the way it's organized, and ultimately by the way it complements your presentation. No handout can save a bad presentation, but a well-executed handout can make the difference between a good presentation and a great one.

Graphic design and page layout are fields of study in and of themselves, but just because you may not be an expert in these areas does not mean that you can't create a visually appealing handout. Here are few tips to help you create a handout that aids the audience's understanding and is visually appealing:

1. **Focus on the goal.** While it's important that your handout say something of value, it does not need to say *everything*. If you have multiple items you want your audience to remember, perhaps you should make multiple handouts. Each handout you make should be focused on *one specific goal*. Perhaps you want to better explain some of the consumer research you had conducted. That means that other items, like your product's specifications, do not belong on that same handout. If you need a spec sheet,

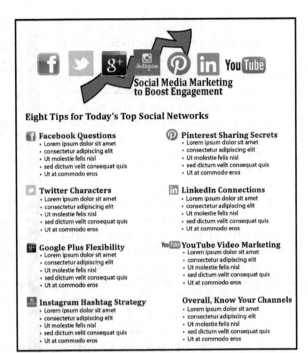

Handout for a presentation on social media.

   create a spec sheet, separate from your research handout.

2. **Be concise.** If you hand your audience a handout with large blocks of text in an itty-bitty font so you can fit it all in, it is likely they will suddenly feel quite sleepy and lose the will to read. Cut down the number of words you use to keep the text brief and to the point—just don't cut out so much text that the handout no longer says *anything* of value.

3. **Use purposeful graphics.** A page of just text—even if that text is concise—is hardly a handout; it's more like a paper. Pictures draw the eye to the page and can often say more in less space than your text can (you know the old saying: "a picture is worth a thousand words"). Don't, however, just throw in graphics for the sake of throwing in graphics. The graphics you choose to include should follow the same rules as your other visual aids: for a graphic to be included, it needs either to (1) aid in the audience's comprehension and/or memory; or (2) aid in persuasion. If that cute little Clip Art cartoon you're considering doesn't meet either of those two rules, leave it out.

4. **Use white space.** Have you ever heard the phrase "Less is more"? This is what graphic designers call the principle of *economy*. Graphic design is about controlling the audience's eye. A page chock-full of text, graphics, and colors is overwhelming at first glance; the eye doesn't know where to look first or how to process all of the stimuli it sees. Keep your page simple and use strategic white space so the page is easier to scan and digest.

5. **Use purposeful color palettes.** If you have Microsoft Office and want to change the colors on a picture or other elements, you may notice the program offers

up "color schemes," in which you have a limited color palette from which to choose. This is done on purpose. Color can be highly beneficial to your design, but using too many widely varying colors is distracting. If you stick to a color scheme and choose shades within that palette, your design will look much more purposeful and pleasing to the eye.

6. **Proofread.** Spelling and grammatical mistakes anywhere in your presentation are unprofessional and speak poorly of your preparation and diligence, but on a handout, those kinds of errors are perhaps even more egregious. A handout is your audience's way of remembering the information you presented to them. If your content targeted the audience well, they might keep this piece of paper for a long time and, perhaps, show it to multiple people in their travels. A glaring error will continue to stare your audience in the face each time they reference the page to recall you and your ideas. Don't let foolish typos and grammatical errors continue to cloud your good work long after the presentation is over.

7. **Avoid copyright infringement and cite sources.** As the chapter on research stated, copyright infringement is a big deal. Yes, the wonderful wizard of Google makes it easy to find a plethora of images that can capture the feel and content of your presentation's points—but you don't have the right to use the vast majority of them. For an image to be fair game, it needs to be designated as copyright-free. When an image does not carry copyright, you are able to distribute it on your handout to others without infringing on the original artist's right to intellectual property. Overall, remember to include the proper source citations for any material in handouts that is not your original material.

Bookmark handout promoting campus organization.

Presentation Handouts that Wow

You never notice the design when it's good, but when it's bad it catches your immediate attention, hurts your eyes, and even makes you shudder! For a more detailed explanation, go back and review the chapter on guidelines for designing effective visuals that will make your audience remember your message. As you work on designing your handouts, use the following tips to ensure they are purposeful and professional:

- Unity is of the utmost importance in your printed materials. They should be consistent with your other visuals and the message and tone of your presentation. Color, font, and tone must all support the message you are conveying.
- Avoid long, dense handouts. Try to keep handouts as concise as possible. Make them look attractive: leave spaces, etc.
- Not everything should be center-aligned. It is boring and doesn't draw the eye to anything particular on the page.
- No more clip art! Take your own photos; you can make your images more relevant and meaningful that way.
- Edit those photos; every photo in your handout need not be square!
- Limit the number of fonts. In general, use no more than two to three different typefaces per visual, and use them consistently with all visuals.
- How you lay out the text counts, too. Every choice you make will send a message. If you choose to put color behind the text, right alignment or left alignment will change the look, feel, and emphasis. Focus on readability. Don't use all caps. It's the equivalent of shouting and is difficult to read.
- Visuals have weight. Your eye will be drawn to certain items; use that to guide your audience members' eyes to where they should focus.
- Less is more. Less is better. One or two well-chosen graphics will usually do a better job than having many graphics that divide your audience's focus.
- Double check your work—typos, grammatical errors, correct names, phone numbers, e-mails. Nothing will hinder your credibility more than a handout full of typos and grammatical errors.
- Margins: A narrow 0.5-inch margin maximizes page space while leaving plenty of edge room for printers and copiers.

Most importantly, don't rush through your handout construction. Even without being a professional graphic designer, you can look at the work you have created and decide whether or not it "looks right." If something seems off, keep moving elements, changing sizes, switching colors, etc. until it is more visually appealing. Your handout is your lasting impression. Make it a positive one.

Key Takeaways

- Every presentation aid should be created with careful attention to content and appearance.
- Handouts give your audience a document that supports your performance and adds value to your key messages.
- Your handouts reflect you. How they look gives a non-verbal message about you, your team, your company, and your presentation. Good handouts identify an organized, competent individual.
- Apply basic principles of visual design for your handouts to have a sharp, professional look. It will enhance the perception people have of you.

Questions and Activities:

1. **Reflection Question:** Consider the last handout you made (or if you haven't made one before, consider one you find at school or on your car windshield). What was effective about it? Not effective? Thinking of the guidelines listed in this chapter, what would you change to increase this handout's appeal?
2. **Learning Activity:** Find a flyer on campus or on a public bulletin board that looks poorly designed. Take a picture of it or, if there are multiple copies, take it with you. Recreate the handout so that it is more effective and visually stimulating, using the guidelines from this chapter.
3. **Presentation Preparation:** Create a handout to support your next presentation. Follow all of the guidelines above and in Unit 4, and be sure that the handout helps you meet your presentation's intent.

Credits

1. Leave an Impression with Your Handout Copyright © 2015 by M. Sandra DiFrancesco. Reprinted with permission.
2. Handout for a Presentation on Social Media Copyright © 2015 by M. Sandra DiFrancesco. Reprinted with permission.
3. Bookmark Handout Promoting Campus Organization Copyright © 2015 by M. Sandra DiFrancesco. Reprinted with permission.

Unit 5

Planning and Presenting in Groups

On the first day of class, I inform my students that many of the presentations they will do throughout the course will involve teamwork. Some students look unfazed by this announcement, but every semester, I see eye rolls and scowls of disappointment from others. If only I could show them *then* what I know will happen *later*.

In most cases, when I disband their teams after each project, students raise protests: "Can't we just stay in our teams? We work so well together!" And, if I give students the option to pick their own teams later in the semester, they often go back to their original groupings. The simple truth is that *most teams find more success together than they would have found as individuals.*

One person brings *one* specific set of skills and *one* perspective to a project or problem. Multiple people bring a much wider array of skills and expertise, as well as varied suggestions for how best to tackle the issues at hand. Yes, these varying viewpoints have the potential to cause some friction within your group, but learning how to handle conflicts in a positive way will allow you to reap far more benefits than hindrances from your collaboration.

This is why so much of what you will encounter in the professional world will involve teamwork. Creative teams brainstorm together, sales teams sell together, editing teams collaborate on publications together, and even accountants handle large clients together. Therefore, being able to "play well with others" is an important skill for the job market.

In the 2012 Job Outlook survey from the National Association of Colleges and Employers (NACE), employers voted that the most important candidate qualities are the "ability to work in a team structure" and the "ability to verbally communicate with persons inside and outside the organization." Learning to prepare and present presentations in team units will help you hone both of these skills.

Before you read about the specifics involved in effective collaboration and team presentations, let me first give you this warning: *team presentations should be team efforts, from start to finish.* So often, I see groups that come up with the basic ideas of their plan together and then delegate individual parts to individual members without sufficient check-ins on their progress. What results is a mess—a piecemealed, mish-mashed, overlapping, and sometimes even contradictory mess.

For a team presentation to work and to capture all of the benefits of true collaboration, you have to work with your group through every step of the process. Yes, there can be some delegation. If Jill is far superior at PowerPoint than you are, then let Jill reign as your team's Chief Slide Creator. If Jaden is a meticulous researcher, then congratulations, Jaden: you are now the Head of Research and Logic Development. Jack is uber-organized and great at time management? Elect him to be your Official Schedule Supervisor.

But none of these individual roles will work well together if there isn't *consistent communication* among all team members. Jill may design killer slides, Jaden may find killer research, and Jack may establish a killer calendar, but if they haven't planned these elements together, all these killer parts will kill the presentation. You should all have some input into each other's tasks. For teams to work, you have to communicate—a lot.

If you've been placed into a presentation team, get to know your group mates. Talk to them. Laugh with them. Learn to love them, because, to design and present a stellar presentation with them, you'll need to spend lots of quality time together.

CHAPTER 30

United We Stand
The First Steps to a Productive and Harmonious Team

By Bonnie Farley-Lucas, Meg Sargent, and David John Petroski

After studying this chapter, you should be able to:
- *Articulate the advantages of working in a group.*
- *Follow the steps to get to know your team in your first meeting.*
- *Understand how to develop a positive working relationship with your group.*
- *Identify your responsibilities as an individual member of a group.*

Regardless of your particular field, you will be working as part of a group, team, crew, department, committee, task force, or some other collaborative relationship within your professional career. *Forbes* and other workplace-related sources consistently rank effective group collaboration, decision making, and problem solving among the most important workplace skills in the 21st century. As many successful professionals would attest, the ability to contribute positively to a team-based environment increases career options, earning potential, job satisfaction, self-esteem, and overall quality of life. Therefore, **along with oral-presentation skills, developing strong group communication skills should be at the top of your professional-skills development list.**

Groups can provide several advantages over working alone. First, groups provide different perspectives and the strengths associated with diversity. Group members all have different experiences, knowledge, abilities, and relevant contacts, all of which can be brought in as part of the solution to group tasks. Second, diversity of opinions allows the group to look at problems and tasks from a variety of angles, hopefully leading to alternative solutions or paths to achieving goals beyond what an individual could produce. Third, groups allow for higher levels of creativity than individuals because of their ability to rapidly generate new ideas. There is even some evidence that groups tend to learn and retain new information better than individuals (Young & Henquinet, 2000). Finally, groups also provide more socialization so group members can learn more about themselves and others. Group tasks and interactions help members learn new roles, skills, and knowledge, and allow for practicing

Look how happy they all are to be working together. That can be you, too!

interaction and leadership skills. Group members can also benefit from social support and informal mentoring.

Unfortunately, for some students, working as part of a group conjures up negative emotions. Some students may have worked on a group project where they perceived inequity in how the workload was divided among members. When some individuals underperform, other group members feel taken advantage of as they take on extra work to meet group objectives. For some particularly diverse groups, collaboration and consensus building can be difficult. Other people wary of group work may be concerned about the extra time needed for meetings, coordinating tasks, and rehearsing presentations. While some groups certainly have their fair share of issues to work through, most get along well and benefit from their collaboration. Therefore, the "Group from Hell" stereotypes are often based on negative perceptions more often than they are on actual negative experiences with group work.

While the groups you will be part of as a student are temporary, the results can have a lasting impact on each member. You will have a chance to practice interaction skills, you will get a "group grade" that reflects the quality of the group's efforts, and you will learn from each other. Following are some practical suggestions for making group work more productive and more enjoyable. With these guidelines, you can hopefully avoid your team turning into the "Group from Hell."

Doesn't pay attention. Misses most meetings. Has no opinions. Believes she's always right.

Very few people end up with a Group from Hell, like the one above, but take precautions to get your group off to a productive and cooperative start.

Your First Meeting: Get to Know Your Group

One of the greatest predictors of a group's success is the makeup of its individual members. Not only is it important for your team to work well on tasks together, but it also is crucial that you all have a positive rapport. This will make your time together more productive and enjoyable. Furthermore, teams with good rapport among themselves will have an easier time creating a good rapport with their audience. The following are some practical ways to get to know your group better in your first meetings together:

- **Find areas of common ground.** Groups tend to experience some initial tension when members feel they are among strangers. You can reduce some of that tension by figuring out what you all have in common. Talk about courses you have all taken, work or volunteer experiences, hobbies or interests—even television shows you all enjoy. Finding a common point of interest can be the first building block in creating rapport together.

- **Create a list of strengths and weaknesses.** Talking about strengths and weaknesses identifies where individuals can contribute most, as well as identifying areas that the group will need to focus more attention on if members do not have the needed skills. Discuss the roles you are each comfortable playing in your group, based on your skill sets.
- **Devote some time to talk about work preferences.** Do you procrastinate, or do you prefer to get things done well in advance? Do you work best late at night or early in the morning? Do you prefer writing things out on paper first or jumping straight to the computer? Are you a Mac person or Windows person? Clarifying these issues early on can save a lot of hassles.
- **Share your schedules.** Creating a group schedule before you start planning is helpful in heading off potential problems. Know when you each have "open time." Some group members may be more flexible than others, but it's critical to know where negotiation of time is possible. The busier you are, the more important it is for you to plan ahead.
- **Share contact information.** Whether by e-mail, text, group message, phone, Facebook, a wiki, or some other form, clarifying preferred modes of communication up front aids group functioning. You should also share multiple channels for contacting each other. That way, in case something unexpected happens, you have options for connecting. Make sure you plan how to best exchange work with each other, as well. What happens if you spend hours preparing a PowerPoint presentation and try sending it to your teammates by e-mail, but the file is too big? Thinking these types of issues through in advance can prevent a lot of panicky moments.

Working Together: The First Steps in a Positive Working Relationship

In order for a group to be effective, there must be a shared sense of purpose, commitment, and group identity. Group membership is a social obligation. Your group members will rely on you to do your part, so aim to respect them and expect them to respect you. Following are some ideas for fostering a shared responsibility for the group:

- **Develop a group identity.** Groups thrive when they establish an identity or a "brand," communicating to members and outsiders that they are part of a unique system. Group members can create a shared name, logo, or slogan to foster a sense of togetherness and solidarity.
- **Build a team structure.** Decide how your group will work best together.

Canadian geese each learn their role in the group to help create a cohesive whole. Do the same with your team.

Consider the strengths and roles each group member has. How can you each play to your strengths effectively without stepping on other members' toes or leaving major gaps in the workload? For instance, if three people want to be responsible for taking the lead in the Q&A session, how can you negotiate that issue so those three are not constantly jockeying for power? On the reverse, if no one is comfortable taking questions, how will you respond as a group to audience concerns?

- **Create group ground rules**. Talk about how you each prefer to communicate and work. Discussing both expected behaviors (civility, effort, and collaboration) and those that will not be tolerated (lateness, absences, attacking, slacking) helps clarify how group members want to interact and how they might deal with negative actions. Write down the ground rules, and be sure they are visible whenever the group meets.
- **Identify team goals.** Clearly identifying goals makes it easier to maintain a shared sense of purpose and commitment. If everyone participates in clarifying the group's goals, there's likely to be more personal investment in a quality outcome. Have an honest conversation about what you are trying to accomplish. What is your purpose? Write the goals down to create a clear record of what you're trying to do.

How to Be a Good Individual Group Member

Few people believe themselves to be the "problem" in a group, but if you are in a dysfunctional team, it is likely someone is pointing a finger at you for at least part of the blame. Groups are systems, which means that every part of it influences the whole. If one member slacks, the whole team suffers: they have to do more work and they are likely bitter because of it. If one member is overly contentious, other members might become more withdrawn to avoid constant conflict. And, on the reverse, if some members don't voice their opinions in group meetings, other members might get louder and more argumentative to goad them into talking. The simple lesson is this: **what you do affects the behavior of those on your team.** If you don't like the way your group is working, you need to avoid the blame game and first ask what *you* can do to improve the situation.

As previously mentioned, your group should discuss your collective code of conduct for how individual members are supposed to act and interact. Nonetheless, here are a few universal guidelines for you to follow whenever you are a part of a team:

- **Speak up.** Silent, agreeable members may not cause major disruptions in a group, but they are not particularly helpful either. To be of use to your group, you need to share your ideas and expertise.
- **Maintain civility.** When you do speak up, it is unlikely that your group mates will adore every idea you offer. Remember that the goal of a group is to be collaborative and choose the best ideas for the group as a whole. If you take comments personally, you will be more likely to be rude, disengage from the group, or make others uncomfortable with your grumbling dissatisfaction. Keep conversations civil and work to put the team's best interests before your own ego.
- **Meet others halfway.** Sometimes communication is such a difficult task to do well because everyone has different communication styles. You may be a happy-

go-lucky, collaborative person who thrives on easy consensus, but another in your group may prefer more debate and critiquing to ensure your group's work is as good as it can be. Neither of you are wrong; there is room for both styles. Point out the difference in how you communicate and come to an agreement on how to make decisions as a group (e.g., you can debate an issue for a set amount of time; then you all vote, majority wins, and you move on).

- **Do your work well.** Teammates rarely complain about group members who give a strong effort to do the work assigned to them on time and to a high standard. Slacking, failing to meet deadlines, or doing low-quality work are fast ways to lose the good graces of your group mates.
- **Communicate issues.** Problems may arise in your own life that could prevent you from being a fully participating member. While you don't need to share intimate details of your personal life with your group, you do owe them the courtesy of letting them know that you are having complications. Be honest about what you can finish, and in what time frame, so your group has time to make and enact a Plan B.
- **Don't isolate others.** Some group members can be difficult to work with. Some are even more than difficult. Turning that person into a group scapegoat, however, is not the right answer. The marginalized person will have no motivation to improve his or her behavior if s/he no longer feels a part of the group, and the group will spend a lot of its energy on negativity. Your lack of collaboration and cohesion will make your tasks

Somehow Amy has been isolated from the group. Her team needs to find ways to include her in their conversations and decisions—and Sarah's "stink eye" is not helping.

difficult and will likely show to your audience (and if you don't even like each other, why would your audience want to give you a chance?). Talk openly with the isolated group member and review your agreed means of communication. Perhaps the way the group is working simply does not work for that one person. Find a common solution so you can all move forward together.

From "I" to "We"

Good groups work well because individual team members put the group's best interests before their own individual egos. To be an effective group member takes a lot of honest self-reflection. Consider what is working well in your group and what is not, and make honest efforts to adjust your own communication and working styles to accommodate the team.

The ideal group will be collaborative—individual members will share differing ideas, and the group as a whole will make critical decisions about which ideas are best for the project, rather than group members simply promoting their own suggestions for the glory of having the team's approval. Aim to work effectively as a collective unit, but ensure that you are doing your own part to make that happen. In many ways, working in a group is a larger responsibility than taking on a project alone: more people are counting on you, and you don't want to be the one "bad apple" that spoils the basket. Your group's success depends on your contributions and your hard work. Give a genuine effort to your group, and see how productive and fun it can be to work with others.

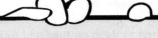

Key Takeaways

- Working in a group has many advantages, and a strong group is likely to outperform an individual person working alone.
- Work to build a positive rapport in your first group meetings by getting to know each other.
- Establish a group identity, structure, ground rules, and goals to keep all members in sync.
- Groups are systems; what you do affects the way the rest of the group functions.
- Ensure that you are acting as a fully participating and responsible member of your group.

Questions and Activities

1. **Reflection Question:** Reflect on the last project you worked on with a group at work, for school, in sports, or somewhere else. What made the group successful together? What do you wish was different about the group, if anything?
2. **Reflection Question:** Reflect on the group you are currently in. What aspects of your collaboration are going well? What needs to be improved? Lay out a clear and specific plan for how you will attempt to resolve those issues soon.
3. **Learning Activity:** Create a chart to visually track the work each group member has put into the project. Discuss the results as a team.
4. **Presentation Preparation:** In your first group meetings, answer the following questions as a team:
   - What are three similarities that you all share, beyond similarities relating to school (like the fact that you are all students, are all the same year in school, or are all the same major)?
   - What is the greatest strength each group member brings to the team? Strengths should be relevant to the type of work the group will need to accomplish.

- What is the greatest weakness each group member brings to the team? Weaknesses should be relevant to the type of the work the group will need to accomplish.
- How will your group work best together?
- When can you all meet together? Set up several potential meeting times just in case you need them.
- How should you all best contact each other? Be sure to exchange several ways to contact each person, and discuss potential technologies you can use to talk and work as a group.

5. **Presentation Preparation:** As a group, create a list of team rules. These should not only span rules for behavior (coming to meetings, getting work done well and on time, etc.), but also the ways in which you plan to work and communicate together (e.g., no phone calls before 9:00 a.m.; problems with specific group mates must be told to that person to avoid talking behind others' backs; in the event of a disagreement about a group decision, the group will vote).

Credits

1. United We Stand: The First Steps to a Productive and Harmonious Team Copyright © 2014 by Bonnie Farley-Lucas, David John Petroski, and Meg Sargent. Reprinted with permission.
2. Collaboration Copyright © 2014 by Isabel Chenoweth / Southern Connecticut State University. Reprinted with permission.
3. Group from Hell Copyright © 2014 by Audrey Mora. Reprinted with permission.
4. Canadian Geese: C. C. Trowbridge / Copyright in the Public Domain.
5. Isolated from Group Copyright © 2014 by Isabel Chenoweth / Southern Connecticut State University. Reprinted with permission.

CHAPTER 31

Making the Most of Your Team's Time

With contributions from Bonnie Farley-Lucas

After studying this chapter, you should be able to:
- *Explain the importance of a specific schedule and group plan.*
- *Choose an appropriate role for yourself within your group.*
- *Develop a schedule for getting group tasks accomplished.*
- *Run an effective group meeting.*
- *Select the programs that will work best for your team's virtual meetings, communication, and collaboration.*

Let me tell you the sad story of a team I had in my presentations course not so long ago. The groups were chosen randomly (the students selected cards), and by bad luck one of the resulting teams consisted of members who all had one unfortunate habit in common: they were all self-proclaimed procrastinators. From the beginning, I stressed the importance of developing a solid team schedule, but the group never did so, and very quickly they began to fall behind. While other groups were fine-tuning their arguments and PowerPoint slides, this group was still trying to decide on an initial idea. When they arrived for their trial run with me (an ungraded practice session that I watch and critique), they warned me that, "This will be the worst presentation you've ever seen." On that promise, they did not fail to deliver.

They had a week after that practice session to work on refining their presentation before they would present the final, graded version. Though they all made a renewed effort to get their acts together, the final project still fell far shorter than where it should have been, which was particularly disappointing because their overall idea was actually quite strong. In the end, their inability to manage their time was their fatal flaw.

This is precisely the presentation train wreck I want your group to avoid. If you are in a group for a project or presentation, it is likely that the task set before you is large and complicated. You won't be lucky enough that all the little pieces will somehow get magically done in a timely manner without you having to plan who will do what and when. Individual members have different—and often busy—schedules. To make sure they can save time to participate fully in the group, you need to use your team's time as wisely as possible. This is what this chapter will show you how to do.

Know Your Role

As mentioned in the previous chapter, it is helpful for each individual member to have a defined role in the group. This is not only helpful to avoid conflict within the team, but defined roles also help to make sure that work gets done. Groups work best when individual members can take on roles that play to their strengths, but this does not mean that they can never work outside of those roles. As was exemplified in my sad team example above, sometimes group members need to "step up" to other roles for the good of the team.

Every group should have a **coordinator.** A coordinator is the person some might call the *leader,* but the term *coordinator* is far more representative of what that person should actually do. It is not the coordinator's job to delegate tasks or boss people around; rather, it is his/her job to help manage the overall project. **Coordinators help develop schedules and ensure that the group stays on task.** They are the official schedule keepers of their groups, checking in with individual members to ensure that they are capable of carrying out their tasks on time.

Your group's coordinator should be chosen by the group as a whole; it should not be a self-appointed role. Because the coordinator is the one who will be in contact with everyone the most and will be the one in the best position to make decisions about whether or not the group needs to meet again or practice more, s/he should be someone the group respects. If not, the coordinator will have an exceedingly difficult time managing the team's progress.

The Power of a Plan: Making an Effective Schedule

Executing a group project takes coordination and planning, and doing that well requires a schedule. Often groups—and individuals—don't realize just how complicated a task is until they sit down to plan out how to get it all done in time. Avoid last-minute scrambling by developing a clear and well-thought-out schedule.

The first step is to figure out all of the tasks that need to be completed and all of the steps involved in each task. So, for instance, a list of tasks and steps for a product pitch might look something like the box on the next page.

The second step is to determine a basic schedule of when tasks should be completed. Work backwards from the due date to figure out how much time should be devoted to each major agenda item. For example, if you have three weeks before your presentation, you may decide that the last week will be just for practicing and tweaking visual aids. That means that all the other tasks need to be done before Week Three. You can then continue to work backwards to develop the rest of your schedule. For now, just decide on deadlines for the major tasks. You can get to the deadlines for each specific step a bit later.

Once you have the basic task schedule established, decide which of the tasks and steps should be done as a group and what can be designated to individual members (or even to duos). For instance, everyone in the group should decide on the presentation intent together, but one person can handle calling clients for audience-analysis information. Consider everyone's individual strengths and weaknesses as you decide as a group who would be best suited for each step. If there are tasks or steps that no one is particularly good at, then resolve to do those together.

Be sure that you divide responsibilities evenly. Not only should you look to make sure that the workload is similar for all group members, but you should also ensure that no one is too overloaded for just one part of the planning process. For instance, Amy may be good at technology, but if her only individual tasks are the PowerPoint and handout, she will have very little to contribute for the first two weeks of the project, and then will suddenly find herself overwhelmed for the last one.

After you have assigned the group and individual tasks, you are ready for the fourth step: deciding on specific deadlines. The reason you should wait to do this until after the tasks have been assigned is because the specific deadlines you establish should work with individuals' schedules. For instance, if Amy is going to handle compiling and designing the PowerPoint presentation, your group will need to establish a deadline for everyone to get their slide requests to her so she can get the slideshow done on time. You could arbitrarily pick a date (the Friday of Week Two), but if Amy works all weekend, that time might not allow her to do her part before the task deadline. She might prefer Thursday at noon to give her a more realistic working time frame.

How you want to write out your schedule is up to you. I have seen some groups use a photocopied

- Audience Analysis
  - Research client company
  - Call clients for info
  - Make list of company's core values
- Presentation Intent
- Research
  - Research competing products
  - Research our potential customer base
    - Write survey
    - Distribute survey
    - Tabulate survey results
  - Research our manufacturing costs
- Message
  - Identify our main arguments
  - Organize points and sub-points
  - Assign speaking parts
- PowerPoint
  - Build basic structure
  - Add in evidence slides
  - Design slides and add animations
  - Proofread
- Handout
  - Determine content
  - Write copy
  - Add visuals
  - Proofread
- Practice
  - Video
  - Review video and revise
  - Full trial run

A sample list of tasks and steps for a product pitch. Tasks follow the solid circles; steps follow the open circles.

calendar page with deadlines written out on each day in coded colors (one color for each group member, and another color for the team as a whole). I have seen other groups use a chronological list of all of the tasks and steps with their due dates next to them. Others have drawn more complicated tables that visualize the overall schedule. Find a system that you can all understand easily.

Once your schedule is completed, ensure that everyone has a copy of it to follow (electronic copies are often more effective, since they can't be "misplaced" the same way paper ones can be). The coordinator should be responsible for ensuring that the group sticks to the plan. If the group cannot complete its tasks on time, the coordinator should alert the group so they can adjust the schedule as needed. The coordinator should then make sure that all group members are aware of the schedule change and have made the corrections to their copy.

Stick to the Plan: Holding Effective Meetings

Finding common meeting times is often the hardest task of working in a group. School and work schedules differ, commutes differ, and time preferences (early birds vs. night owls) differ. While many tasks in your project may not require face-to-face meetings of the entire team, some will. It is particularly important to meet in person for your initial meetings (when you develop rapport and decide on the presentation intent and basic plan ideas) and for your practice sessions (they're not effective trial runs if you're not all there).

Whether you meet in person or online (to be discussed later in this chapter), common meeting times are rare. Treasure those moments together. No, I don't mean by holding hands and singing *Kumbayah* around a campfire; I mean by using **agendas** and **meeting minutes** to make the most of your time together. (If you preferred the campfire version, try bringing s'mores to the meeting. Fun and delicious!)

An agenda is a simple list of what you want to accomplish at a meeting. Since the coordinator is the person in charge of keeping the tasks on track, s/he might be best suited for formulating the agenda, but everyone should be invited to contribute. If Amy realizes she needs more information from everyone to be able to do the PowerPoint slides, she should be able to request that this issue be added to the meeting list. For larger meetings, it is customary to have a formal agenda printed and set at each participant's seat. For your presentation group, it is sufficient enough for the coordinator to send out an email telling everyone what's planned.

Once you've set an agenda, you need to stick to it. Sure, other issues may arise that you have to deal with during your time together, but your meeting goal should be to get through your to-do list. Having clear goals for your time together will help your team stay on task. The coordinator should use this agenda to run the meeting, moving everyone through each bullet point like a to-do list.

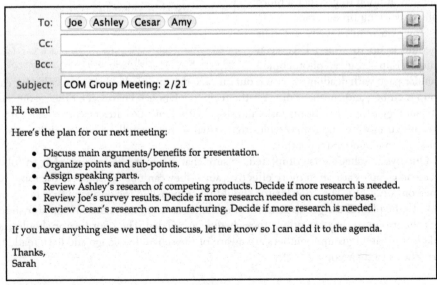

To: Joe Ashley Cesar Amy

Cc:

Bcc:

Subject: COM Group Meeting: 2/21

Hi, team!

Here's the plan for our next meeting:

- Discuss main arguments/benefits for presentation.
- Organize points and sub-points.
- Assign speaking parts.
- Review Ashley's research of competing products. Decide if more research is needed.
- Review Joe's survey results. Decide if more research needed on customer base.
- Review Cesar's research on manufacturing. Decide if more research is needed.

If you have anything else we need to discuss, let me know so I can add it to the agenda.

Thanks,
Sarah

A simple emailed agenda from Sarah to her group mates.

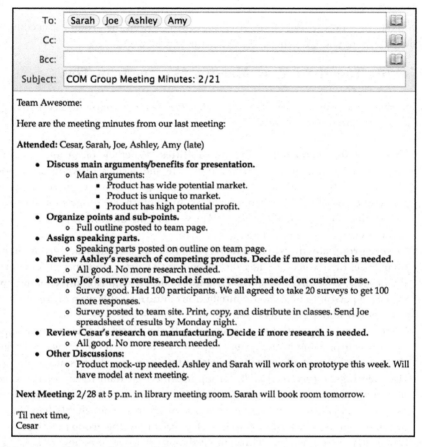

To:	Sarah Joe Ashley Amy	
Cc:		
Bcc:		
Subject:	COM Group Meeting Minutes: 2/21	

Team Awesome:

Here are the meeting minutes from our last meeting:

Attended: Cesar, Sarah, Joe, Ashley, Amy (late)

- **Discuss main arguments/benefits for presentation.**
  - Main arguments:
    - Product has wide potential market.
    - Product is unique to market.
    - Product has high potential profit.
- **Organize points and sub-points.**
  - Full outline posted to team page.
- **Assign speaking parts.**
  - Speaking parts posted on outline on team page.
- **Review Ashley's research of competing products. Decide if more research is needed.**
  - All good. No more research needed.
- **Review Joe's survey results. Decide if more research needed on customer base.**
  - Survey good. Had 100 participants. We all agreed to take 20 surveys to get 100 more responses.
  - Survey posted to team site. Print, copy, and distribute in classes. Send Joe spreadsheet of results by Monday night.
- **Review Cesar's research on manufacturing. Decide if more research is needed.**
  - All good. No more research needed.
- **Other Discussions:**
  - Product mock-up needed. Ashley and Sarah will work on prototype this week. Will have model at next meeting.

Next Meeting: 2/28 at 5 p.m. in library meeting room. Sarah will book room tomorrow.

'Til next time,
Cesar

Simple meeting minutes from Cesar to his group mates.

As you accomplish the tasks listed on the agenda, it is helpful to designate someone to keep track of the decisions made. This record of the team's ideas, discussions, and accomplishments are called **meeting minutes.**

Successful meeting minutes follow the structure of the agenda and recount the decisions made. They also track where and when the meeting was held, who attended the meeting, any other discussions the group had, and what the next steps for the group are. Minutes are helpful reminders as to what happened in the meeting for those who attended, but they are even more helpful in the event that a group member could not make it for all or part of the meeting. That absentee member can look over the minutes to see what happened without having to expect other group members to fill him/her in.

Meeting minutes may seem like a tedious chore to do, but for your purposes, they do not need to be elaborate. You can send them out to your group via email, or, if you have a team Web page or wiki, you can post them there. They do not need to be done by the coordinator; in fact, it's often easier if someone else handles the note taking. The team scribe can simply open a laptop, pull up the agenda, and then just type in decisions as they are made. When the meeting is over, the scribe can fill in any necessary details, and then upload or send the file. Done! A clear record of what the group has accomplished and decided, and where it is headed next, with very little effort.

Let's Stay Together: More Meeting Management Tips

Beyond sharing a clear agenda, there are other tips you can follow to keep your group meetings productive:

- **Share meeting-management responsibilities**. Whether on-ground or online, meetings need timekeepers to monitor time and scribes to write up important meeting points. These roles should rotate among members to increase participation and ownership of the group process. In addition, everyone should be invited to contribute to each meeting's agenda to ensure the meeting is productive and all tasks can continue on as planned.
- **Be sure group meetings are inclusive**. Conflict can escalate when group members do not feel their voices are heard or if one or two group members take control of the process. One effective approach is to use the "Round Robin Technique," which asks each person to give their contributions in turn so all have a say on each of the main points under consideration.
- **Start each meeting with progress updates.** It's important that everyone is apprised of what is happening in the group and with its tasks. Start meetings by reviewing the current "state of affairs" before getting into your specific business.
- **Use meetings to give feedback**. Group members all want to succeed and receive honest feedback on their contributions to the project. Regardless of effort, all group members deserve an honest appraisal of how their efforts have impacted group outcomes. The best time to offer feedback is during group meetings and presentation practice sessions. Throughout the process, group members need to note each other's specific contributions to the overall process and outcomes. Group members should also plan for follow-up and evaluation after the presentation.
- **Vow to maintain civility**. Maintaining civility requires using assertive communication that respects one's own rights without infringing on the rights of others. Civility carries the responsibility of respecting other's values as valid and equal to one's own and listening for both content understanding and emotional understanding (empathy). Civility also requires taking responsibility for one's own perspective (using "I believe/I feel" statements) and responding respectfully to others without using generalizations or offensive language. When group mates can remember not to take group decisions personally and can learn to set their own egos aside, civility becomes much more attainable.
- **End each meeting with an open floor.** Before you disband your group members from the meeting, allow individuals to raise concerns, ask questions, air grievances, or share successes. All group members want to have their voices heard; be sure that you save time to hear them.

A Group Place in Cyberspace

Meeting in person is not always possible. If one or more group members can't make a meeting time, decide if technology can help bridge the distance. Below are a number of online tools some of our students have found helpful. Some are synchronous (you all meet at the same time) and some are not (you check into and post on a site). You may find a variety of these programs will work to your group's benefit:

- **Google Hangout** – Allows up to ten people to video chat at once for free. Can be used as an app on your smartphone or through a plugin to Google Chrome. Browser-based version supports screen sharing so you can show your group what you've been working on. All users must have a Google account.
- **Skype** – Allows up to ten people to video chat at once for free. Requires download to your computer, or can be accessed through Xbox One. As of the time of this book's publication, group chatting was not supported through the Skype phone app.
- **Group Me** – A particularly popular option with my students that allows for private group text messaging. The app is free and available on most smartphone and tablet platforms. Program is easy to use, as it mimics normal texting.
- **WeChat** – Another app for group chatting and texting that also allows for voice, video, and photo messages. The walkie-talkie feature can be used with up to forty members.
- **Google Docs** – Another Google-based program that allow groups to write papers together. Multiple users can write, edit, and comment on the same document online. The interface resembles most word-processing programs. An additional benefit: documents automatically save as you work, so computer crashes won't result in lost work.
- **Weebly** – A web-hosting service with an easy website building interface. The site can serve as a central location to upload files, images, and slideshow presentations, and can link to videos and music.
- **WhenIsGood** – A simple online tool that has only one function: help your group to find the best time to meet. One person sets a list of possible meeting times and sends a link to the other group members. They indicate whether they can meet or not. It keeps a running tally of what times work best.
- **Dropbox** – A helpful tool that can be used on computers, tablets, and smartphones, and that allows for file sharing. Upload pictures, documents, and other files so all group members can see and edit them.

There are many more available group apps, software, and programs to help your group meet and accomplish tasks together when you can't physically be together. Explore all your options and choose the programs that work best for your team and the work you need to do together.

The More We Get Together, the Happier We'll Be

For group projects to work, groups need to find ways to utilize their time effectively. A solid schedule and a commitment to meeting as a group will do wonders for your end product: your presentation. As much as professionals may bemoan the endless barrage of meetings they are forced to sit through, you can ensure that *your* meetings will be a productive use of your group time by planning in advance what issues your meeting will cover.

In my own viewing experience, the teams that present the best are often the teams that have had the highest number of productive meetings together. Don't presume that the project will somehow work out on its own. You need to make a plan and then follow through to find group-project success.

Key Takeaways

- Groups need to schedule their time wisely to make the most of their limited time together.
- Choose a coordinator to help keep the group's schedule on track.
- Develop a group schedule that incorporates all the tasks and steps needed to complete the project.
- Create agendas to keep the group on task, and write meeting minutes to serve as the record for the meeting.
- Explore and choose online tools that will help your team communicate with each other.

Questions and Activities:

1. **Reflection Question:** Think of the last time you worked in a group. How well did your team manage its time? How organized was the project? What was the result? What did your team do well in its time management that you think could work again, and what would you like to do differently now with your new group?
2. **Learning Activity:** Create a simplified agenda for your next group meeting (even if it is just for a few minutes during class). Then, after the meeting, modify the agenda to include the meeting minutes.
3. **Learning Activity:** As a group, agree to test out one (or more) of the online collaboration tools listed earlier in this chapter. Report to the class about how effective or ineffective the tool was. Discuss the strengths and weaknesses of the tool you tested. Does it seem like this would make coordination and group work easier or harder? Would you recommend this tool to other groups?
4. **Presentation Preparation:** Develop a group schedule for the tasks you need to complete leading up to your group's presentation. Include due dates for each specific task, and indicate who on the team will be responsible for getting it done. Ensure that all group members have a copy of or access to that schedule.

CHAPTER 32

When Trouble Arises
Handling Team Conflicts

By Bonnie Farley-Lucas and Meg Sargent

After studying this chapter, you should be able to:
- *Explain the reasons for group conflicts.*
- *Identify the five approaches to dealing with conflict and when each one is appropriate.*
- *Follow a problem-solving approach to deal with conflict.*

While the strategies offered in the previous chapters on planning and establishing a solid group structure will help reduce the potential for conflict, they won't eliminate problems completely. At times, groups face situations where unresolved differences turn into interpersonal conflicts. Interpersonal conflict occurs when

- two or more people have an interdependent relationship (they rely on each other for something);
- they perceive that they have incompatible goals or differing means of achieving their goals;
- the issue has the potential to harm the relationship; and
- there is a sense of urgency for resolving the issue (Cahn & Abigail, 2014).

During the course of a group presentation or project, common interpersonal conflicts stem from group members' perceptions about unfair and uneven participation in the project, lack of attention to the quality of the presentation, lack of respect for others' contributions, lateness or absence from group meetings, lack of professionalism, rudeness or incivility, and misinformation.

People tend to have preferred ways for approaching interpersonal conflict, but since each conflict is unique to the relationship and situation involved, several options should be considered. There are at least five general approaches for managing conflict, and each brings different outcomes:

Collaboration

The optimum choice is to pay equal attention to the needs of all group members and to work together for the best possible presentation. Collaboration requires civility, mutual respect, openness to different ideas, and a sense of professionalism. Group members working in collaboration report the highest levels of satisfaction with the process and with their outcomes. This is the ideal learning and working environment.

Compromise

Compromise usually entails giving up something in order to get something else. For example, you may have to settle for a group meeting time that is less than convenient for you, but you do this in exchange for taking control of designing the visual aids. Or, you may have to take on a part of the presentation that you find more difficult or less enjoyable than others in exchange for better group harmony and a better group outcome. In the interest of moving your group forward, these compromises are often necessary.

Accommodation

Sometimes it may be necessary to suspend one's own needs and give in to the wishes of others for the sake of the group's success. If one person has a great idea, special skills or resources, or a better way of approaching the presentation, it may be best to give in and accommodate occasionally. For temporary group arrangements with limited time frames, accommodation may actually help move your group forward, so you all can focus on your work.

Force

At times, group members may attempt to impose their will on others for their own benefit without thinking of others' needs. **Most group members resent being forced and may resist the attempts.** However, when deadlines are fast approaching and stress levels get higher, force is commonly employed. Some examples are making one group member do much more work than the others or assuming that one member will buy the majority of the resources needed for a project. Group members working in conditions where force is used report the lowest levels of satisfaction with the process and with the outcomes.

Avoidance

At times, it may be best to avoid a confrontation if it can be more effectively handled at a different time or place. If the degree of anger or stress is too uncomfortable or if people feel threatened, waiting or moving to a safer place where the conflict can be dealt with more effectively might be best. Some conflicts may not seem worth ever spending energy on, but **neither the quality of the group's work nor the relationships among group members will improve if no actions are taken to resolve the issue.** Avoidance is best used as a temporary solution, not a permanent one.

If You Have to Address a Group Conflict, Try a Problem-Solving Approach

At times, interpersonal conflict in groups must be managed directly. It may feel a bit uncomfortable to confront these issues head-on, but conflict does not need to be a destructive element within group work. The groups that learn to reflect on their own faulty interactions and find ways to improve upon them together are more likely to be successful than those that constantly seek to avoid their problems and let their frustrations build silently. On the other hand, **engaging in a problem-solving process helps interactions go more smoothly, because doing so sets expectations for how participants should proceed.**

When interpersonal conflict is defined as a problem or issue that needs to be resolved, it makes the problem less personal and easier for the group to discuss and manage. The worst approach is for group members to "gang up" on a particular group member. This leads to defensiveness, and ultimately damages both relationships and group outcomes. Once a problematic situation or pattern of behaviors is determined, the group should gather together to work through the problem and collectively work toward a resolution.

The following are the key steps that groups can work through when using a problem-solving process for interpersonal conflict:

- **Identify the problem and root causes.** What behaviors or actions are problematic?
- **Identify the ideal state or behaviors and the criteria.** What do we want?
- **Generate options.** Brainstorm as many possible options that will resolve the issue. Consider how each group member might change or act to help resolve the conflict.
- **Test options.** Talk through the costs and benefits and the ease of using each option. What are reasonable and realistic expectations and behavioral changes?
- **Implement the best option(s).** Put the best option into practice. Make the change.
- **Review the situation.** See what changes have been made and how it impacted group processes and outcomes. Check on group progress.
- **Provide feedback to group members.** This is particularly useful for those who are working on changing their behaviors. What are they doing differently, and what is the specific positive or negative impact on the group and its outcomes?
- **If there are unresolved issues, or if new issues have been raised, repeat the problem-solving process until the group is satisfied with its process and its outcomes.**

When All Else Fails . . .

When all else fails, or if the group situation feels unbearably out of control, communicate with your instructor. Let your instructor know as many specifics about what you have tried and what is occurring. Be honest about your role in the group. The time to have this discussion is prior to the presentation, as it is often too late to make positive change once the group presentation is complete. Since the emphasis is on learning, chances are great that your instructor will have some effective means for addressing the group conflict.

The "Group from Hell" does not actually materialize very often. In the vast majority of cases, group work can be very satisfying and can lead to better outcomes than individual effort. However, they do require a bit more effort and flexibility. Clear goals, responsibilities, collaboration, and civility will help make the group project a positive experience.

Key Takeaways

- Conflict is a normal part of group interactions, and addressing it effectively can help your group grow stronger.
- When faced with group conflict, try a collaborative approach first.
- When necessary, use other approaches to conflict—compromise, accommodation, force, and avoidance—so long as they are an effective solution to the problem.
- Treat group conflicts as problems to be solved, not as personal wars to wage.
- Problem-solving as a team can help the group can move forward as a productive and cohesive unit.

Questions and Activities:

1. **Reflection Question:** Think of the last time you've been in a group that has had conflict—whether it was major or minor. Describe the conflict. Which of the five approaches above did your group (or just you) take toward this issue? Did that approach resolve the conflict in a way that suited everyone? Explain what could have been done better (if anything) to improve the outcome of the issue.

2. **Learning Activity:** Write down a brief explanation of a conflict you have had or have witnessed in a prior group. Use fake names to protect the innocent (and the not so innocent). Do not discuss the ways in which the group tried to resolve the issue; only discuss the problems themselves. In class, exchange your group-conflict story with someone else. Analyze the story you are given and review each of the five approaches to conflict—collaboration, compromise, accommodation, force, and avoidance. For each of the five approaches to conflict, write at least one example of an action the group could take that would fit that approach. When you have done this for all five, decide which of the approaches would make the best problem-solving strategy (you may use more than one if needed).

3. **Presentation Preparation:** Identify conflicts your current group has had thus far. As a group, vote on the conflict you think is the most pressing. Then follow the problem-solving steps listed above together to try to find a mutually agreeable resolution to your issue.

Credits

CHAPTER 33

Dear Aimee C
More Troubles from Team Land

With contributions from Meg Sargent

After studying this chapter, you should be able to:
- *Respond effectively to social loafers.*
- *Identify and combat groupthink.*
- *Explain the importance of effective consequences for ground rules.*
- *Handle group members who consistently interrupt others.*
- *Establish a no-phone rule for group meetings.*
- *Devise strategies for dealing with an overly difficult group member.*

Despite all that can go right with teams, some issues can certainly go wrong. Let's look at some of these potential situations and their solutions with some student letters to Aimee C.

Dear Aimee C...

The Slacker Syndrome

DEAR AIMEE C.: Our group has been assigned a final project that is worth forty percent of our final grade, and for the most part we've been working well together. Recently, however, it seems one of our team members has just "checked out." He's missed two of the last three meetings, and when he *does* show up, it's usually late—and with an attitude! Even worse, he's missed important deadlines for assignments. Short of running to the instructor and "telling" on him, is there anything we can do?
  FRUSTRATED FOURSOME

DEAR FRUSTRATED: What you're describing is the number one reason people do not like working in a group: slackers. Termed "social loafers," these individuals are those who tend to exert less effort on a task when working in a group than they would if they were working individually (Karua & Hart, 1998). And, gone unchecked, even a single social loafer can have a significant negative impact on the entire team. It's time for the team coordinator, designated members, or your group as a whole to confront this member. Here's what I suggest:

- Begin by asking this member about his or her current lethargic attitude, seeking input for its cause.
- Indicate specific behaviors that are troublesome, using descriptive, nonjudgmental language.
- Reaffirm the importance of this person's contribution to the group effort.
- Solicit his/her suggestions for how the group can improve and encourage more constructive participation.

Ultimately, use this as a problem-solving opportunity in which a cooperative and collaborative team environment can be reestablished. Only if all else truly fails should you sidestep the loafer and reconfigure tasks to ensure a successful project completion.

Afraid to Rock the Boat

DEAR AIMEE C.: My group and I are getting along fine—we're getting along great, actually, and that may be the problem. I think we're all so happy that we've gone without any major conflicts, we're afraid to criticize anyone or anything. No one questions any ideas, even the really, really bad ones. How do we offer opinions without hurting feelings?

  CAT GOT MY TONGUE

DEAR CAT: It sounds like you are having the problem of being so cohesive that you have developed "groupthink." Coined by Irving Janis (1972), *groupthink* means that your group members feel such a pressure to conform that they abandon the critical thinking and questioning needed to generate quality ideas.

Try assigning the role of devil's advocate to one or more of your group members at each meeting. This person's job is to attempt to poke holes in the group's plan. All group members should applaud and appreciate the devil's advocate's contributions. No one should take the critiques personally.

If group members are still having trouble critically examining the group's work, invite critical outsiders to hear your ideas and offer their opinions. Listen carefully to the critiques you get and agree to make the necessary adjustments to accommodate those comments.

Rule Breaker

DEAR AIMEE C.: Our group has been having a serious issue with one of our group mates. We have established group ground rules, but he is just not adhering to them. We've confronted him about this and tried a problem-solving approach, but his behavior hasn't changed. How do we make him follow the rules we *all* agreed on?
  FEELING LIKE A PARENT

DEAR FEELING: When you establish group rules and norms, you would like to think that individual members will follow them to stay in the group's favor. But, as you well know, that's not always the case. If your code of conduct isn't resulting in the behavior the group wants, then you need to establish consequences for breaking the rules. Sit the whole group down, reiterate how much you need everyone's input and help, an then draw up the consequences together.

Ultimately, the punishments associated with each group "crime" will be up to your group, but I would caution you to choose consequences that make sense. For instance, if I didn't complete a group task on time (a violation of a group rule), the consequence should not be to do the Chicken Dance in front of my group. If I'm not a shy person, that's not a punishment—and frankly, a short Chicken Dance is much faster and easier than just doing my part of the project. Devise logical consequences to go with your rules so there is an increased incentive for everyone to stay on task.

Quiet in Front

DEAR AIMEE C.: I have one group member who is driving me bonkers. Every time someone talks, he always feels the need to interrupt and give his own opinion. Sometimes I think he interrupts because he's just excited about his own ideas, but other times he is just downright rude, shooting down ideas before we can even finish our thoughts. How can we get him to shut up?
  MISSING MY QUIET TIME

DEAR MISSING: Remember that having a devil's advocate and a little conflict in a group can be a good thing; that's how groups get to the best and most vetted ideas. But, if this member's behavior is hurting feelings and deteriorating the team's cohesion, then it is time to correct the issue.

Revisit your rules and consequences and ensure that *not interrupting* is clearly listed as a group norm. If your overzealous group member still struggles to stay quiet until it is his turn, try the old hack of the speaking stick. Really, you can use anything—a stick, a ball, a notebook, an origami swan—it really doesn't matter. But the rule is this: only the person holding that object can speak. If your hands are empty, your mouth needs to be shut. If someone has something to say, they can reach for the stick, but they cannot grab it without permission. This means that the person holding it doesn't have to give up their speaking turn until they are finished. I know this seems a little crazy and elementary, but you only need to use this method during key discussions so everyone's opinions are heard. And, after a while, your group members will get the hang of listening more carefully to what everyone has to say, and you can just leave the stick on the ground.

Lost in the Phone Zone

DEAR AIMEE C.: Our group is usually pretty good in how we work together, but what really grinds my gears is that, mid-meeting, several of my group mates will start playing on their phones. They apparently cannot handle even the slightest bit of silence. If we all take ten seconds to brainstorm quietly or think about an idea, they've given up after five and have started trolling through Instagram photos. I can't tell them not to bring their phones to meetings; that's just not realistic. What do I do?
SMARTPHONES MAKING US DUMBER

DEAR SMARTPHONES: If the lure of the phone (or tablet) is just too great for people to resist, create a no-phone rule. Have everyone put their phones, screens down, in the middle of the table while you meet. If someone's phone rings or vibrates, its owner will still be able to hear it and respond as needed. Otherwise, though, the phones are untouchable during the course of the meeting. It's a simple but effective step in breaking the invisible chains we often feel to our phones.

Crossing the Line

DEAR AIMEE C.: I have one group member who is really just too much. She is rude, she calls people names, and she is aggressive in how she talks to us. Truthfully, we feel bullied by her, but no matter how we respond, she is not easing up at all. Fighting back seems to rev her up even more, but staying quiet seems to frustrate her, which only makes her meaner and louder. We're afraid to even approach the issue at this point to try the problem-solving method. What do we do?
SAD AND CONFUSED

DEAR SAD: Have you directly addressed this issue with your group mate? Don't just hope that she'll figure out how you feel on her own; that's not likely to happen at this point. She may not realize just how hurtful her actions have been to the group; that contentious and aggressive communication style may just be how she normally converses with others.

This is not to say that you don't have the right to be upset about being on the receiving end of her taunting, because you most certainly do. But if you approach her under the presumption that her actions have been malicious and mean-spirited, she will probably get very defensive, very fast. In her mind, it is likely that *your* communication methods are also faulty. Instead, if you sit down as a group and discuss—in a non-confrontational way—which communication styles you *all* prefer, then you might be able to find a suitable middle ground. Rework your group ground rules following these new communication norms.

If this tactic doesn't work—or if the bullying has become so bad that group members are actually uncomfortable being together—it is time to alert someone in power (your instructor in the classroom, or a supervisor in work situations). Take yourselves out of the line of fire, and let someone with more authority deal with the issue.

Key Takeaways

- Confront team members directly—but non-confrontationally—to deal with most group issues.
- Adjust rules, create consequences, and follow them to keep group members in line.
- When issues are too difficult for the group to deal with on its own, consult the advice or request the intervention of your instructor or boss.

Questions and Activities:

1. **Reflection Question:** Have you ever been in, or witnessed, any of these unfortunate group conflicts? What strategies were used to resolve the issue? How effective were those strategies? What other strategies would have been equally or more effective?

2. **Learning Activity:** Consider the following issue, and then devise a strategy for dealing with it:

    Jane is a member of a four-person group. She is by far the best writer and the fastest typist on the team. As a result, she is often in charge of taking meeting minutes and typing up documents the group needs. She therefore brings her laptop to every group meeting so she can fulfill those roles. Well, it seems Jane is also easily distracted, and she often has social media pages and text messages open on her screen while the group talks. Jane effectively handles all of her typing duties while "multitasking" on social media, but she rarely engages with the group's decision-making process beyond taking notes. The group wants her to participate more, but doesn't know what to do. They have tried telling her their concerns, but she got defensive, arguing that she does everything she is supposed to do well. They cannot enforce a no-laptop rule, because she needs it to do her tasks in the meetings. The group also recognizes that she is the best choice to continue to do these typing tasks. Devise several strategies the group could use to resolve this issue with Jane.

3. **Presentation Preparation:** Reflect on your group's ground rules for behavior and the issues raised in this chapter. Do your group rules account for these types of situations? Amend your rules as needed to help protect your group from difficult conflicts.

Credit

CHAPTER 34

We're All in This Together
Presenting as a Team

With contributions from Meg Sargent

After studying this chapter, you should be able to:
- *Identify the benefits of presenting in a team.*
- *Identify the best ways to conduct a team presentation.*
- *Demonstrate cohesion and dynamism in your next team presentation.*

When teams are tasked with difficult projects—ones that need to be researched, planned, and tested—they often spend so much time focusing on their overall ideas that they leave little time to develop an effective presentation. The "easy way out" of assigning different parts to different people and hoping it all comes together nicely in the end will likely result in a piecemealed mess. The audience will have difficulty seeing the strength of your team's fantastic, well-tested ideas if your presentation leaves your listeners baffled, bored, or annoyed.

There are great benefits to be had from presenting with others. Just as in all team-work, individual members get to play to their strengths and have others cover for their weaknesses. For instance, if you are a "blue" presenter, you can focus on presenting the team's data and research; your more dynamic "red" teammates can take care of the attention-grabbing introduction and conclusion. If you are a nervous presenter and are petrified that you will forget massive parts of the presentation, you will have several teammates behind you who can help to cover the ideas you missed. While team presentations may take some more coordination than individual ones do, I have found that most of my students prefer the team experience. But, **for your team presentation to work well, you have to learn to present like a team.**

Presenting with a Team, as a Team: It's One Presentation

Successful presentation teams look seamless and collaborative, as though they planned every step of the process together. They smoothly transition from one person to the next, they reference each other's points, and they smile at one other as though they are glad to be in each other's company. To achieve this ideal team cohesion in your presentation, you must do the following:

Demonstrate Uniformity

Your team presentation should look as though the team created each element to-gether. The presentation content should all fit coherently into an overall organizational structure. PowerPoint slides should have one consistent theme and appearance. You should all use similar terminology. Even your attire should be somewhat consistent. You don't all need to wear blue (although you can, if you want), but one teammate shouldn't be in khakis when the rest of you are in suits. When these elements are inconsistent from presenter to presenter, the audience may start to lose faith in the credibility of your team.

Choose an Ideal Speaking Order

Team presentations are collaborative efforts; therefore, your presentation style should also be collaborative. Boring teams stand in a straight, horizontal line facing their audience, and then, one at a time, members step out to say their parts. Your presentation should not resemble a military roll call, nor should it feel as though you are each giving your own mini presentation one after another.

Instead, break up the presentation to allow each person to explain the areas of the plan that they are most comfortable explaining, whether that means they end up taking just one long turn to say their bit (no longer than six minutes) or they have the speaking floor five separate times. Your most enthusiastic presenters should begin and end your presentation. Your numbers guru should explain your data. Your quick thinker should handle Q&A. Perhaps there are even parts when two or three of you will have the floor at once: "While I explain how our product functions, Taylor and Carissa will demonstrate how it works." Show your collaboration and the strengths of your teammates by dividing your speaking time logically, not necessarily just into separate, subsequent parts.

Give Friendly Introductions

It seems trivial, but how you introduce your team makes an important impression to the audience. If the opening presenter fails to mention who any of the lovely people standing beside or behind her are, it sends the message that she deems them less important (as if those little peons even had names!). If the opening presenter *does* introduce them but trips over pronunciations (which happens far more frequently than it should), it gives the impression that they just met for the first time out in the hallway a few moments ago. If, however, the opening presenter introduces the first and last name of each person as that person smiles and gives a small wave, the message to the audience is, "Hi! You're so important we brought out a whole team of our best people. We're *all* here to help you."

Pass Clearly from One Presenter to the Next

I have many times seen the silent presenter switch-off go awry. One presenter delivers his part and then when he's done, he just stands silently for a second before sitting down. The audience is left to wonder, "Is this thing over? I thought we were just getting started." Finally the next presenter gives a little startle as she realizes, "Oh! It's my turn!" So, she quickly jumps up to break the silence. Yikes. These aren't religious readings. Your audience doesn't need such a lengthy silent pause for inward reflection in between each speaker.

Instead, picture a successful presenter transition as a pair of runners passing the baton in a relay race. The transition is smooth because both parties reach toward each other to be sure the baton isn't dropped. Pretend the presentation is the baton; long, awkward pauses between presenters are the equivalent of dropping the baton. Let your audience know where the presentation is going next and who is taking it there: "Now that I have discussed the financial benefits of investing in our product, let me turn this over to Nick, who will talk to you about our concepts for future product accessories." As you step back or sit down, Nick would step toward the audience and begin his part by accepting the pass: "Thanks. As [your name here] just said, I am going to share with you some of the innovative ideas we have designed for future product accessories." **Transitions hold the group together, and they are far less jarring for the audience.** Practice doing them effectively so there are no dropped batons in your presentation.

Practice Your Choreography

I usually don't laugh at my students' presentation mishaps (really, I don't!), but the funniest errors I see are when teams don't know how to coordinate their movements. They walk around each other like they are in the midst of a half-hearted do-si-do, or they stroll around their seated teammates like they're the odd ones out in a game of awkwardly quiet musical chairs. I've even seen teammates just bump full force into each other (and not in celebratory chest bumps, but in oh-wow-I-didn't-even-see-you-there kind of bumps).

Plan your room setup and movements ahead of time. Are you sitting or standing? Where is the presenter's space (remember to leave enough room for the presenter to walk around)? Where does everyone else go when they are not talking? Who will help with the demonstrations, hold the visuals, or pass out the handouts? Where will you stand or sit for Q&A?

Don't just presume these elements will fall into place naturally. Do full run-throughs of your presentation with the room setup you want to use (whether you have access to the actual presentation room or not) so you can practice the movements and get out the awkward bumps, trips, and missteps when your audience is not there to witness them.

Use Internal Linkages

Presentations expert Jerry Weissman (2009) describes **internal linkages** as "statements that tie together the various parts of your presentation" (p. 169). Although Weissman focuses on presentations done by individuals, this concept most certainly applies to team presentations.

It's as simple as this: **to help your team seem more cohesive, include statements that reference back or look forward to what the other presenters have said or will say.** Consider these examples:

- "Kendall alluded to the convenience of this product earlier. Now, let me show what it is that makes it so convenient for the everyday user."
- "The handle is made of a durable plastic, so it won't snap off under a lot of weight. Jackson will talk to you in a bit about how the material we use will make the

product more cost-effective, but for now, let me show you just how sturdy this stuff really is.

The technique is subtle, but it communicates quite clearly that you are a team that planned and practiced together.

Have Backup Plans

Wouldn't it be wonderful if all of your best-laid plans *never* went awry? Unfortunately, that's not life, and that may not be your presentation either. Technology may fail, audiences may be largely absent or disengaged, or—worst of all—one of your teammates might have to bail on presentation day. Gasp! Unfortunately, you can't cancel a presentation just because one person was too sick to come (even if s/he was the only one with a copy of your slideshow, your handouts, or your product). You have to be able to adjust as a team and still get the information across to your audience.

You all need to know the content of the entire presentation—not just what has been designated as "your part"—and you all should have access to the visuals. Even if you are the only teammate to show up for the presentation that day, you should be ready to take over and "get 'er done." Audiences don't want to reschedule because your teammates are sick, are having car troubles, or are simply too lazy to roll out of bed. Devise your backup plans so you won't be thrown into panic mode for every minor (or major) hiccup on presentation day.

Pay Attention When Your Teammates Are Presenting

Big presentations can be stressful (and if you're in a team, it's probably a big presentation). When your speaking part is over, it might be tempting to retreat off to the back or side of the "stage area" and mentally zone out to recover. You must, however, remember that as long as your audience can see you, you are still "on stage," even if you are no longer the one talking.

Ashley with disengaged teammates. Not a comforting visual for the audience.

When your teammate is presenting, be aware of your own nonverbal communication to avoid sending unintended messages to your audience. When one member is presenting, and the other members are whispering, fidgeting, yawning, crossing their arms, looking at their notes, rolling their eyes, or showing disinterest, it doesn't look good for the team. The audience may

Ashley now with attentive and engaged teammates. Much better!

perceive that the team doesn't get along, and that members don't value each other's contributions or even perhaps the team's ideas as a whole. If you want your audience to look forward to building a working relationship with you, your team has to look like they are capable of having positive interactions.

Instead of spacing out, look at your presenting teammate and smile. Then look to the audience to gauge their understanding and acceptance of your team's message. If you notice confused faces or skeptical smirks, you can signal to the presenter that s/he ought to take some questions from the audience. Use your "off time" productively; don't spend it staring off into space, doodling, or leaning lazily against the wall.

Tackle the Q&A Session Together

Teams who present well together sometimes fall apart in Q&A. Teammates disagree on answers and tack onto each other's responses, multiple people try to chime in on one question, or there is an awkward silence when no one on the team wants to attempt a response to a tough question. All of these situations serve to hurt your team's credibility with your audience. Avoid these types of discordance by following these two steps:

1. **Plan your answers out ahead of time.** Brainstorm the meanest, most difficult questions you are likely to receive, and—as a team—plan out your answers together. This way, no matter who gets asked, you'll all be able to give the "official party line" without any tack-ons or interruptions from other group members.
2. **Elect a "funnel person" to handle the final Q&A.** Have this person step forward and ask for questions so it's clear to the audience that they are supposed to direct their inquiries to him or her. Then, the funnel person can direct the question to the appropriate authority on the team for the answer: "Yolanda is our financial guru, so I'm going to let her answer this one for you. Yolanda?" If a question doesn't seem to belong to any one person on the team, the funnel person can answer the question him/herself.

Plan Together, Present Together

A team presentation that is done well can provide a rich description and delivery of your ideas to your audience. Moreover, demonstrating cohesion within your team gives the audience the perception that your entire company or organization stands behind your words and claims. Think of it: if someone you loved were really sick, would you want her to have one specialist or a *team* of doctors to choose the best treatment options? Do you want one carpenter to build an entire house from foundation to roofing, or do you want a *team* of experts each to contribute his/her skills? Give your audience that same reassurance that they have a *team of professionals* working hard on their behalf; show them your unity of purpose and your ability to work together cohesively.

Let your presentation demonstrate the collaboration of strengths, skills, and ideas that have helped you plan your project up to this point. Don't neglect the importance of the presentation itself. All your brilliant ideas and stellar research won't mean much if your team can't communicate them effectively to an audience. Plan together, practice together, and improve together.

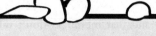

Key Takeaways

- Team presentations allow individual members to play to their strengths and get much-needed help from their teammates.
- Show cohesion through your presentation's uniform look, your team's introductions and passes, internal linkages, and team members' appropriate nonverbal behaviors.
- Avoid mishaps by practicing your team's movement around the room, preparing backups for bad situations, and planning your team approach to the question-and-answer session.

Questions and Activities:

1. **Reflection Question:** Think of the last time you presented with others. How smoothly did the presentation go? Did you practice together? If you have a limited amount of time to practice with your full team for your upcoming presentation, on which areas would you spend the most time? Why?

2. **Learning Activity:** Choose a movie that everyone on your team knows fairly well. Then, as a team, retell the plot line while you video record your performance. Practice physically moving around the room, as a team and as individuals, the way you would for a real presentation. Practice passing from one person to the next. Practice using internal linkages. Practice looking interested in what the presenter has to say when you are not speaking. Watch the video as a team to reflect on what looked smooth and what looked awkward.

3. **Presentation Preparation:** As a team, decide on your backup plans. Where will you store visuals so everyone has access? Who will be each person's understudy if s/he can't make it to presentation day? Who is the understudy's understudy?

4. **Presentation Preparation:** As a team, brainstorm the questions you are most likely to get on your presentation. Then, come up with the official team answer for each. Practice asking different team members the same questions to be sure that everyone's answers are similar (they don't need to be word-for-word the same, but they should make the same basic points).

Credits

Final Thoughts

Applying Presentation Lessons to the Professional World

Years ago, I and several other members of the Communication Department at Southern Connecticut State University came up with this crazy idea to write our own textbook for our course Fundamentals of Professional Presentations. We had searched high and low for a book that helped teach the lessons we wanted our students to learn—a book that better prepared students of today for the professional world they would enter tomorrow. We needed a book that avoided a focus on public-speaking techniques like how to write a script or how to use notes to get through a speech. The books we found that aligned with our *presentations* approach were meant for professionals already in the field, not for students preparing to enter it. We just couldn't find a modern, student-oriented book on learning the art of script- and note-free presenting—so we wrote it ourselves.

This book is the manifestation of the communication- and conversation-based approach we teach at SCSU. Within this text, you have read the strategies we give our students and the secrets we have learned over the years. We have shared them with you with the intent of helping you learn to present more effectively and confidently, just as these methods have done over the past several decades for our students.

This book has guided you through each stage of becoming a more effective professional presenter, from preparation to execution. We have given you advice on how to become the perfect *purple* shade between *red* and *blue*, how to plan your presentation with AIMC, and how to keep your presentation like a conversation.

We See Your True Colors Shining Through

Early in the book, we introduced the concept of presenter colors—energetic and emotional presenters are *red*, intellectual and credible presenters are *blue*, and those without much impact are *gray*. Throughout this book and your presenting experiences, we hope you have engaged in enough self-reflection to determine where you fall in the color spectrum. If your colors are still a little washed out by some gray, don't get discouraged: improving your presenting skills is a lifelong process. Keep reflecting, keep adjusting, and keep practicing.

An improvement in your presenting style does not mean that you need to abandon who you are. We want you to "do you"—but just keep trying to improve that "you" that you "do." With honest reflection and a commitment toward improvement, you will breathe a bit more *purple* into each new presentation you deliver, while still retaining the essence of what made you a promising presenter in the first place.

And hopefully you will love whatever job you find after you graduate, because, if you do, you'll find it much easier to inject enthusiasm (redness) and expertise (blueness) into any presentation you might have to give. You will be become that dynamic and knowledgeable presenter you have wanted to be.

Our Four Favorite Letters: AIMC

Throughout this book, you have learned the four-step presentation preparation process of AIMC (say it with me now!): Audience, Intent, Message, Channel. This has provided an important framework as you have moved through the process of learning to devise and execute an effective presentation.

But beyond giving you the "big picture" of how all the varying components of a presentation fit together, AIMC can also be a guideline for every individual component of your presentation. Not sure what to do in a handout? Well, who is your *audience*? What is the *intent* of the handout? What *message* do you want it to send? Which visuals or graphic design style would be the best *channel*? If you want to include a story in your presentation, identify your *audience*, the moral of the story (its *intent*), what details you want to include (its *message*), and in what tone of voice you want to tell it (the *channel*).

AIMC stresses preparedness. It's easy to get up and talk about whatever for ten, fifteen, or even twenty minutes (unless you're painfully shy). But to give an *effective* presentation takes a lot more work, and once you move into the working world—where the stakes are much higher than just assignment grades—you will find that extra work worth the effort.

The AIMC process arms you with the critical questions you need to ask in order to make sure your arguments are hitting home for your audience, whether you are intending to inform or persuade them. We recognize that you will not become *perfect* presenters by following all the guidelines in this book, but who is perfect, really? Hopefully, though, we have taught you to think about what you are doing and why you are doing it. So many presentations fail because the presenters didn't critically examine the approach they were taking while preparing and delivering the presentations. We want your efforts to be better guided.

Love Your Audience

Throughout this book, we have told you that the audience comes first, that the presentation is all about the audience, and that your entire approach from choosing your topic to choosing your channel should focus on your audience's wants and needs. We hope by now we have made it abundantly clear that this audience-centered approach is crucial to your success. Many presenters get caught up in the details of the topic and what *they* want to say, and they lose sight of the audience and what those integral people need to gain. The emphasis should be on the listener, not on the presenter.

This is perhaps the most critical lesson of AIMC: that your audience must come first. Your job as a presenter is to demonstrate to your listeners that this presentation is *for them*. They are the most important people in the room, and nothing you say or do should make them doubt that you understand that. This audience focus should be ongoing: while it is the first step of the planning process, it is a perspective that must never be lost at any point in your preparation or delivery of the presentation. Audiences can be fickle, and every audience is different; it is your job to continually evaluate how you can best communicate your message and your organization's message to them.

Good Conversation, Good Presentation

The conversational approach to presenting is one of the greatest departures of our book from the approaches of other presenting and public-speaking textbooks. Academia often privileges the more traditional methods of writing, reading, and memorizing—techniques that reduce oral communication to papers that are merely recited aloud.

The approach of this book may be unique in the academic world, but it is common-place in the practical business world you will soon enter. In the professional world, true speeches are rare—but presentations are everywhere. And the best presenters don't write scripts, use notes, or attempt to memorize information—they know their stuff, they plan which stuff to share, they organize it well, and then they talk about it with their audience. They rely on the art of intelligent and well-informed conversation to engage their audience and meet their presentational intent. They are the people in the working world whom others see as confident, charismatic, and leadership material. Hopefully you are on your way to being that type of *purple* person.

Marching Forward and Presenting Beyond the Ivory Tower

From this book, we hope you have developed good presentation habits to replace what-ever bad ones you may have had before. Use these lessons as your guiding checklist moving forward:

- Analyze your audience, first and foremost.
- Identify a clear intent at which your presentation is aimed.
- Research your topic well to give yourself credibility on the issue.
- Develop strong, audience-centered arguments.
- Organize your claims in a clear structure, and support those claims with reputable evidence.
- Use language and approaches appropriate for your audience.
- Avoid scripts, notes, memorization, and other common crutches.
- Deliver your presentation in a conversational style, not in a lecture style.
- Involve, engage, and respond to your audience while presenting.
- Present yourself verbally and nonverbally to show your confidence and trustwor-thiness.
- Practice your presentation to increase your comfort level and familiarity with the material.
- Design useful visual aids with impact.
- Use visual aids as message support rather than as presenter support.
- Work in teams collaboratively to reap the benefits groups can offer.
- Deal with group conflict appropriately to reduce or eliminate barriers to your team's success.

If you have embraced the lessons this book has to offer, you have not only gained the necessary know-how to help you prepare and deliver effective presentations in a class-room setting, but you have also prepared yourself for life beyond school. Job interviews, employee training, sales pitches, departmental meetings, information sessions—all of these are possible scenarios in your future that may require you to present, whether or not presenting is an official part of your job description. The strategies and techniques you have learned in this book can and should be applied to any and all presentations in your career.

The approach in this book has been one from a communication perspective. At the heart of the lessons for a *purple* presentation style, AIMC, and a conversational approach is our true underlying goal: to help you become a better communicator. Communication competency is a skill that will aid you in every facet of your professional (and personal) life. Good communication is the stuff of leaders, managers, and Employees of the Year. Keep diligently improving your presentation skills, and watch your job-market stock rise.

If you keep the lessons of AIMC in mind, and if you never forget the old mantra to make your presentation feel like a conversation, you should find the task of preparing and delivering a presentation less overwhelming. You'll know where to start, how to plan, and how to focus on your audience as participants in your conversation—not as silent, critical judges that you should picture naked.

So go forth with your newfound presenting knowledge. Prepare, practice, and deliver presentations that are impactful for your professional audiences. Follow the guidelines we have provided in this book, and go forward having the kinds of presentation conversations worth having.

Contributors

M. Sandra DiFrancesco, Editor and Contributing Author — Sandy is an Assistant Professor of Communication at Southern Connecticut State University, with an MA in Communication from Purdue University. Sandy has the distinction of being one of the pioneers of the AIMC approach toward presenting, and she was the longtime coordinator for the Professional Presentations course. Her presenting techniques have played a large role in shaping the SCSU approach toward practical presentation skills.

Dr. David John Petroski, Editor and Contributing Author — Dave holds an MCIS (Master's in Communication and Information Studies) and a PhD in Communication, Information, and Library Studies from Rutgers University. With more than fifteen years of consulting experience in advertising production and design, four years of consulting in Web design, and experience as the chair of the Semiotics and Communication Division of the National Communication Association and as the chair of the Southern Connecticut State University's Communication Department, Dave has prepared and delivered a wide variety of professional presentations.

Dr. Ho-Young (Anthony) Ahn, Contributing Author — After serving as an Assistant Professor of Communication at Southern Connecticut State University, Anthony found his way to warmer winters as a faculty member at Pepperdine University. With a notable background in research and a career in marketing, Anthony has expertise in both conference presentations and the art of persuasion.

Mike Bay, Contributing Author — Mike is an Associate Professor of Communication at Southern Connecticut State University. While Mike's specialties include media production, photography, and editing, he has brought his conference and work experiences to the teaching of the Professional Presentations course at SCSU.

Dr. Bonnie Farley-Lucas, Contributing Author — Dr. Bonnie Farley-Lucas is a Professor of Communication at Southern Connecticut State University. With more than fifteen years of experience as an organizational development consultant and trainer, Bonnie has gained extensive expertise as a presenter.

Stephanie Kelly, Contributing Author — Stephanie is an Assistant Professor in the School of Business and Economics at North Carolina Agricultural and Technical State University. She additionally serves as the Director of the Business Communication Center.

Dyan Robinson, Contributing Author – Dyan has been a part of the Southern Connecticut State University community as an alumna, a staff member, and an instructor. She has taught numerous courses in the field of Interpersonal and Relational Communication at SCSU, in addition to the Professional Presentations course.

Dr. Linda Sampson, Contributing Author – Linda is an Associate Professor of Communication at Southern Connecticut State University. As the primary instructor of the Communication Research Methods course at SCSU, Linda has shared her research knowledge with countless students.

Dr. Meg Sargent, Contributing Author – Meg is an Associate Professor of Communication at Southern Connecticut State University. She teaches a number of courses that involve presentations in the fields of organizational and interpersonal communication, including a course on training and development.

Dr. Frank Tavares, Contributing Author – Frank, a Professor of Communication at Southern Connecticut State University, is a longtime instructor of the Professional Presentations course. Outside of SCSU, Frank has had a long career in broadcast management, media production, advertising, marketing, and voiceover work, most notably as the familiar voice of National Public Radio's funding credits.

Dr. Joseph Alan Ullian, Contributing Author – Jos is a Professor of Communication at Southern Connecticut State University. While his primary background and professional experience is in video production, Jos has been a frequent instructor for the Professional Presentations course and an advocate for presentation skills in his courses' curricula.

Audrey Mora, Cartoonist – Audrey is a student at Southern Connecticut State University majoring in Communication with a concentration in Advertising and Promotions.

Isabel Chenoweth, Photographer – Isabel is an award-winning photographer specializing in portraits and events. She currently serves as the official university photographer for Southern Connecticut State University.

Rheanna Behuniak, Connor Etter, Cesar Garcia, Zakiya Hamm, Elizabeth Hess, Michael Howard, Ashley Indrisek, Dan Jennings, Amy King, Sarah Lauture, Shedeen Neil, Mike Rabiej, Joe Rhivbs, and **Ashley Steigler**, Models – All of our lovely and photogenic models are students in or alumni of the Communication Department at Southern Connecticut State University.

References

Adams, C. (2007, February 20). PowerPoint, habits of mind, and classroom culture. *Journal of Curriculum Studies, 38*(4), 389–411.

Addington, D. W. (1971). The effect of vocal variations on ratings of source credibility. *Speech Monographs, 38*(3), 242.

Alley, M., Schreiber, M., Ramsdell, K., & Muffo, J. (May 2006). How the design of headlines in presentation slides affect retention. *Technical Communication, 53*(2), 225–234.

Argyle, M., & Dean, J. (1965). Eye contact, distance and affiliation. *Sociometry, 28,* 289–304.

Aristotle. (2004). *Rhetoric* (W. R. Roberts, Trans.). New York: Dover. (First published in 1910).

Baddeley, A. (2003). Working memory: Looking back and looking forward. *Nature Reviews: Neuroscience, 4,* 829–839.

Barks, E. (2012). Does anybody have any questions for my answers? The 411 on Q&A. *Barks Communications.* Retrieved from http://www.barkscomm.com/wp-content/uploads/2013/11/Barks-position-paper-QA.pdf.

Beebe, S. A. (1974). *Eye contact: A nonverbal determinant of speaker credibility.* Speech Teacher, 23, 21–25.

Boud, D., Keogh, R., & Walker, D. (1985). *Reflection: Turning experience into learning.* London: Kogan Page.

Breslaw, A. (2013, September 16). The 9 most humiliating beauty pageant gaffes ever. *Cosmopolitan.* Retrieved from http://www.cosmopolitan.com/entertainment/celebs/news/a4788/pageant-gaffes-2014/

Bumiller, E. (2010, April 26). We have met the enemy and he is PowerPoint. *The New York Times.* Retrieved from http://www.nytimes.com/2010/04/27/world/27powerpoint.html.

Burgoon, J. K. (1978). Attributes of the newscaster's voice as predictors of his credibility. *Journalism Quarterly, 55,* 276–281.

Burke, K. P., Conway, Sr., R., & DiFrancesco, S. (2000). *AIMC: A communication tool for life.* New York: McGraw-Hill.

Burke, K. (1969). *A rhetoric of motives.* Berkeley: University of California Press.

Butler, J. A. (1992). Use of teaching methods within the lecture format. *Medical Teacher, 14,* 11–25.

Cahn, D. D., & Adams, R. A. (2014). *Managing conflict through communication* (5th ed.). Boston: Pearson.

Cepeda, E. J. (2013, July 29). Educational death by PowerPoint. *Albuquerque Journal*. Washington Post Writer's Group. Retrieved from http://www.abqjournal. com/226989/opinion/educational-death-by-powerpoint.html.

Collins, J. (July–August 2004). Giving a PowerPoint presentation: The art of communicating effectively. *RadioGraphics, 24*(4), 1185–1192.

Covey, S. R. (1989). *The 7 habits of highly effective people: Powerful lessons in personal change*. New York: Simon and Schuster.

Craig, J. D., & Savage, S. J. (2014, September). Instructor attire and student performance: Evidence from an undergraduate industrial organization experiment. *International Review of Economics Education, 17*, 55–65.

Denning, S. (2011) *The springboard: How storytelling ignites action in knowledge-era organizations*. New York: Routledge.

Dewey, J. (1991). *How we think*. Buffalo, NY: Prometheus Books (Originally published: Lexington, MA: D.C. Heath, 1910).

DiSanza, J. R., & Legge, N. J. *Business and professional communication: Plans, processes, and performance (5th ed.)*. Boston: Allyn & Bacon.

Droney, J. M., & Brooks, C. I. (1993). Attributions of self-esteem as a function of duration of eye contact. *The Journal of Social Psychology, 133*(5), 715–722.

Eisenberg, A., & Smith, R., Jr. (1971). *Nonverbal communication*. Indianapolis: Bobbs-Merril Co.

Ekman, P., Davidson, R. J., & Friesen, W. V. (1990). The Duchenne smile: Emotional expression and brain physiology II. *Journal of Personality and Social Psychology, 58*(2), 342–353.

Felder, R. M. & Brent, R. (2005). Death by PowerPoint. *Chemical Engineering Education, 39* (1), 28–29. Retrieved from http://www4.ncsu.edu/unity/lockers/users/f/felder/public/Columns/PowerPoint.pdf.

Fisher, M., Shay, L., & Goodwin, J. (1929). When you're smiling [Recorded by Louis Armstrong and His Orchestra]. On *Some of These Days* [phonograph record]. New York: OKeh.

Gallo, C. (2009). *The presentation secrets of Steve Jobs: How to be insanely great in front of any audience*. New York, NY: McGraw-Hill.

German, K. M., Gronbeck, P. E., Ehninger, D., & Monroe, A. H. (2012). *Principles of public speaking* (18th ed.) Boston: Pearson Education.

Godin, S. (2003). Really bad PowerPoint (and how to avoid it). *Seth Godin*. From http://www.sethgodin.com/freeprize/reallybad-1.pdf.

Gordy, B., Perren, F., Mizell, A., & Richards, D. (1970). ABC [Recorded by The Jackson 5]. On *ABC* [Vinyl record]. Los Angeles: Motown.

Goudreau, J. (2011, January 12). Deepak Chopra on enlightened leadership. *Forbes*. Retrieved from http://www.forbes.com/sites/jennagoudreau/2011/01/12/deepak-chopra-on-enlightened-leadership-happiness-meaning-work-employee-engagement-president-barack-obama/2/

Goudreau, J. (2012). Is your body language costing you a promotion? *Forbes.com*, 50.

Greer, M. (2010). *The Project Management Minimalist: Just Enough to Rock Your Projects!* http://michaelgreer.biz/?page_id=636.

Hammerstein, O. (1965). Do-re-mi [Recorded by J. Andrews]. On *The sound of music (an original soundtrack recording)* [LP, Album]. New York: RCA Victor.

Haskell, J. (2013, March 19). Supreme Court lets verdict stand in recording industry case against downloader. *ABC News*. Retrieved from http://abcnews.go.com/US/supreme-court-lets-verdict-stand-recording-industry-case/story?id=18765909#. Udm32m2wchw.

Heitmeyer, J. R., & Goldsmith, E. B. (1990). Attire, an influence on perceptions of counselors' characteristics. *Perceptual and Motor Skills, 70*, 923–929.

Hoff, R. (1992). *I can see you naked*. Kansas City: Andrews and McMeel.

Hoff, R. (1997). *Do not go naked into your next presentation: Nifty little nuggets to quiet the nerves and please the crowd*. Kansas City: Andrews and McNeel.

Howlett, N., Pine, K., Orakçıoğlu, I., & Fletcher, B. (2013). The influence of clothing on first impressions: Rapid and positive responses to minor changes in male attire. *Journal of Fashion Marketing and Management: An International Journal, 17*(1), 38–48.

Howlett, N., Pine, K. J., Cahill, N., Orakçıoğlu, I., & Fletcher, B. (2015, February). Unbuttoned: The interaction between provocativeness of female work attire and occupational status. *Sex Roles, 72*(3–4), 105–116.

Institute of Management & Administration, "News Briefs," *HRfocus 9* (June 2008).

Janis, Irving L. (1972). *Victims of Groupthink*. New York: Houghton Mifflin.

Karau, S. J., & Hart, J. W. (1998). Group cohesiveness and social loafing: Effects of a social interaction manipulation on individual motivation within groups. *Group Dynamics, 2*, 185–91.

Keller, J. (2003, January 22). Is PowerPoint the devil? *Chicago Tribune*. Retrieved from http://faculty.winthrop.edu/kosterj/WRIT465/management/juliakeller1.htm.

Kerr, B. A., & Dell, D. M. (1976, November). Perceived interviewer expertness and attractiveness: Effects of interviewer behavior and attire and interview setting. *Journal of Counseling Psychology, 23*(6), 553–556.

Kwon, Y., & Johnson-Hillery, J. (1998). College students' perceptions of occupational attributes based on formality of business attire. *Perceptual and Motor Skills, 87*, 987–994.

Lind, E. A., Erickson, B. E., Conley, J., O'Barr, W. M. (1978, December). Social attributes and conversation style in trial testimony. *Journal of Personality and Social Pyschology, 36*(12), 1558–1567.

Lindley, R.H. (1966). *Recording as a function of chunking and meaningfulness*. Psychonomic Science, 6, 393–394.

Mahler, L. (2014, August 20). How social media and PowerPoint kill communication. *The Australian Financial Review*. Retrieved from http://www.afr.com/p/national/work_space/how_social_media_and_powerpoint_CyVN213cwNvRyiqMC6DJmJ.

Meriam Library (2010). Evaluating information—Applying the CRAAP test. *California State University, Chico*. Retrieved from http://www.csuchico.edu/lins/handouts/eval_websites.pdf.

Mitchell, O. (2014). How to survive watching yourself on video. http://www.speaking-aboutpresenting.com/nervousness/survive-watch-video/

Moon, J. A. (1999). *A handbook of reflective and experiental learning*. London: Routledge.

Moran, R. T., Harris, P. R., & Moran, S. V. (2007) *Managing cultural differences: Global leadership strategies for the 21st century*. New York: Butterworth-Heinemann.

Moriarty, E. (2011, February 6). Did the Internet kill privacy? *CBS News*. Retrieved from http://www.cbsnews.com/news/did-the-internet-kill-privacy.

Murray, H. G. (1991). Effective teaching behaviors in the college classroom. In J. Smart (Ed.) *Higher education: Handbook of theory and research* (7th ed.). New York: Agathon, 135–172.

Narayan, S. (2014, May 13). Death by PowerPoint also marks the demise of storytelling. *The National.* Abu Dhabi Media. Retrieved from http://www.thenational.ae/thenationalconversation/comment/death-by-powerpoint-also-marks-the-demise-of-storytelling.

National Association of Colleges and Employers. (2011, October 26). Job outlook: The candidate skills/qualities employers want. *Spotlight for career service professionals.* Retrieved from http://www.naceweb.org/s10262011/candidate_skills_employer_qualities.

Norvig, P. (2003, August 2). PowerPoint: Shot with its own bullets. *The Lancet, 362*(9381), 343–344.

O'Keefe, D. J. (2002). *Persuasion: Theory and research.* Thousand Oaks, CA: Sage.

Ong, W. (1988). *Orality and Literacy: The Technologizing of the Word.* New York: Routledge.

Orland, J. (2013, November 13). Improve your PowerPoint design with one simple rule. *Faculty Focus.* Retrieved from http://www.facultyfocus.com/articles/teaching-with-technology-articles/improve-your-powerpoint-design-with-one-simple-rule.

Pappas, P. (2010). *A Taxonomy of Reflection: Critical Thinking for Students, Teachers, and Principals.* http://www.peterpappas.com/2010/01/taxonomy-reflection-critical-thinking-students-teachers-principals-.html

Paridympictures. (2010, November 2). *The Slobstopper.* Retrieved from http://www.youtube.com/watch?v=AZsiOTVLKGI.

Parks, B. (2012, August 30). Death to PowerPoint! *Bloomberg Business.* Retrieved from http://www.bloomberg.com/bw/articles/2012-08-30/death-to-powerpoint.

Peluchette, J. V., & Karl, K. (2007). The impact of workplace attire on employee self-perceptions. *Human Resource Development Quarterly, 18*(3), 345–360.

Peterson, R. (2014). Presentations rehearsal...fact or fiction? *Presentation Coaching Institute.* Retrieved from http://www.passociates.com/presentation_rehearsal_techniques.shtml.

Pike, R. W. (1994). *Creative Training Techniques Handbook: Tips, Tactics, and How-To's for Delivering Effective Training.* Amherst, MA: HRD Press.

Redding, O. (1965). Respect [Recorded by Aretha Franklin]. On *I Never Loved a Man the Way I Love You* [Record]. New York: Atlantic Records Studio (February 14, 1967).

Sharma, M. (2009). How important are soft skills from the recruiter's perspective. *ICFAI Journal of Soft Skills, 3*(2), 19–28.

Shockley-Zalabak, P., Staley, C., & Morley, D. (1988). The female professional: Perceived communication proficiencies as predictors of organizational advancement. *Human Relations, 41*(7), 553–567.

Sullivan, L. (2008). *Hey, Whipple, Squeeze This: A Guide to Creating Great Advertising*, 3rd Edition. Hoboken, NJ: John Wiley & Sons, Inc.

Tavares, F. (2012). Syllabus for "COM 430: Communication Strategies in the Corporation."

Tessler, R., & Sushelsky, L. (1978, December). Effects of eye contact and social status on the perception of a job applicant in an interviewing situation. *Journal of Vocational Behavior, 13*(3), 338–347.

The Anti-PowerPoint Party (2011). The cause. *The Anti-PowerPoint Party.* Retrieved from http://www.anti-powerpoint-party.com/the-cause.

The Ellen Show. (2012, September 17). *Clint Eastwood on criticism, gay marriage, and his daughter's boyfriend.* Retrieved from http://www.youtube.com/watch?v=7mIC8Nw7LqI.

The New York Times. (2012, August 31). *Clint Eastwood's RNC speech—elections 2012.* Retrieved from https://www.youtube.com/watch?v=v4KZMjUPIhY.

ThePajamaJeans. (2011, March 4). *Pajama Jeans—official commercial.* Retrieved from https://www.youtube.com/watch?v=rcfF0vPiOaM&feature=c4-overview&playnext=1&list=TLz39FA96AdMk

Tufte, E. R. (2003). *The cognitive style of PowerPoint.* Cheshire, CT: Graphics Press.

US Army creates world's worst PowerPoint slide. (2010, April 30). *National Business Review.* Retrieved from http://www.nbr.co.nz/article/us-army-creates-world-s-worst-powerpoint-slide-122255.

Weiner, D. (2005). *Reality check: What your mind knows but isn't telling you.* Amherst, New York: Prometheus Books.

Weissman, J. (2009). *Presenting to win: The art of telling your story (updated and expanded edition).* Upper Saddle River, NJ: FT Press.

Wheatley, M. (2005). *Finding our way: Leadership for an uncertain time.* San Francisco: Berrett-Koehler Publishers.

Williams, R. (1994). *The Non-Designer's Design Book: Design and Typographic Principles for the Visual Novice.* Berkeley, CA: Peachpit Press.

Witt, C. (2009). *Real leaders don't do PowerPoint.* New York: Crown Business.

Young, C. B. & Henquinet, J. A. (2000). A conceptual framework for designing group projects. *Journal of Education for Business, 76,* 56–60.

CPSIA information can be obtained
at www.ICGtesting.com
Printed in the USA
LVOW05s0830230816
501395LV00004B/11/P